Praise for *Undoing Border Imperialism*

Harsha Walia has played a central role in building some of North America's most innovative, diverse, and effective new movements. That this brilliant organizer and theorist has found time to share her wisdom in this book is a tremendous gift to us all.

—Naomi Klein, author of *The Shock Doctrine*

Border imperialism is an apt conceptualization for capturing the politics of massive displacement due to capitalist neoglobalization. Within the wealthy countries, Canada's No One Is Illegal is one of the most effective organizations of migrants and allies. Walia is an outstanding organizer who has done a lot of thinking and can write—not a common combination. Besides being brilliantly conceived and presented, this book is the first extended work on immigration that refuses to make First Nations sovereignty invisible.

—Roxanne Dunbar-Ortiz, author of *Indians of the Americas* and *Blood on the Border*

Harsha Walia's *Undoing Border Imperialism* demonstrates that geography has certainly not ended, nor has the urge for people to stretch out our arms across borders to create our communities. One of the most rewarding things about this book is its capaciousness—astute insights that emerge out of careful organizing linked to the voices of a generation of strugglers, trying to find their own analysis to build their own movements to make this world our own. This is both a manual and a memoir, a guide to the world and a guide to the organizer's heart.

—Vijay Prashad, author of *The Darker Nations: A People's History of the Third World*

This book belongs in every wannabe revolutionary's war backpack. I addictively jumped all over its contents: a radical mixtape of ancestral wisdoms to present-day-grounded organizers theorizing about their own experiences. A must for me is Walia's decision to infuse this volume's fight against border imperialism, white supremacy, and empire with the vulnerability of her own personal narrative. This book is a breath of fresh air and offers an urgently needed movement-based praxis. *Undoing Border Imperialism* is too hot to be sitting on bookshelves; it will help make the revolution.

—Ashanti Alston, Black Panther elder and former political prisoner

UNDOING
BORDER IMPERIALISM

Undoing Border Imperialism by Harsha Walia

ISBN: 978 1 84935 134 8 | Ebook: 978 1 84935 135 5
Library of Congress Number: 2013930244

Cover Design and Interior: Josh MacPhee/Antumbradesign.org
Illustrations: Melanie Cervantes/DignidadRebelde.com

Printed in the USA on recycled, acid-free paper.

AK Press, 674-A 23rd Street, Oakland, CA 94612
www.akpress.org | akpress@akpress.org | 510.208.1700

AK Press UK, P.O. Box 12766, Edinburgh EH8 9YE
www.akuk.com | ak@akedin.demon.co.uk | 0131.555.5165

Institute for Anarchist Studies, P.O. Box 15586, Washington, DC 20003
www.anarchist-studies.org | info@anarchiststudies.org

At least 50 percent of the net sales from each title in the Anarchist
Interventions series are donated to the IAS, thanks to the generosity

UNDOING
BORDER IMPERIALISM

Harsha Walia

Foreword by Andrea Smith

AK Press / Institute for Anarchist Studies | 2013

Anarchist Interventions:
An IAS/AK Press Book Series

Radical ideas can open up spaces for radical actions, by illuminating hierarchical power relations and drawing out possibilities for liberatory social transformations. The Anarchist Interventions series—a collaborative project between the Institute for Anarchist Studies (IAS) and AK Press—strives to contribute to the development of relevant, vital anarchist theory and analysis by intervening in contemporary discussions. Works in this series look at twenty-first-century social conditions—including social structures and oppression, their historical trajectories, and new forms of domination, to name a few—as well as reveal opportunities for different tomorrows premised on horizontal, egalitarian forms of self-organization.

Given that anarchism has become the dominant tendency within revolutionary milieus and movements today, it is crucial that anarchists explore current phenomena, strategies, and visions in a much more rigorous, serious manner. Each title in this series, then, features present-day anarchist voices, with the aim, over time, of publishing a variety of perspectives. The series' multifaceted goals are to cultivate anarchist thought so as to better inform anarchist practice, encourage a culture of public intellectuals and constructive debate within anarchism, introduce new generations to anarchism, and offer insights into today's world and potentialities for a freer society.

Contents

Foreword

Harsha Walia demonstrates the importance of rearticulating the immigrant rights movement as a struggle against settler colonialism. Within the United States, the immigrant rights movement is gaining traction. These movements, however, often do not question the settler-colonial logics that make "immigration" an issue to begin with.

For instance, many activists in the United States have organized around the Dream Act, which provides pathways to citizenship for those who attend college or join the military. Immigrant rights thus become articulated at the expense of those who are the victims of US imperialist wars abroad. In addition, while increasingly more people, even conservatives, have started to support easier pathways to citizenship, they do so by simultaneously calling for increased border enforcement. This increased border enforcement then negatively impacts Indigenous nations that straddle the border, such as the T'ohono O'odham nation, which has become essentially a US militarized zone.

What remain unquestioned are the capitalist and colonial logics that make immigration an issue in the first place. To begin with, for immigration to be a problem, people must live in a propertied relationship to land. That is, land is a commodity that can be owned and controlled by one group of people. Yet as many Indigenous scholars and activists including Leanne Simpson, Glen Coulthard, Mishuana Goeman, Patricia Monture Angus, and others have pointed out, we all have a responsibility to care for the land that cares for us. Land does not belong to "us"; we belong to the land. A proprietary understanding of land is what settler colonialists used as the excuse to invade Indigenous nations. Because Indigenous peoples did not individually own the land, they were thought to not be properly developing the land, and hence land could become commodified by settlers.

Second, let us consider even the term *immigrant*. This term presumes that people must naturally be bound to one place, and if they travel, then they are where they do not belong. Again, many Indigenous scholars and activists have criticized this assumption. Renya Ramirez and Myla Vicenti Carpio have argued that the concept of "urban Natives" presumes that Indigenous peoples never traveled before colonization; that Indigenous peoples must be in a fixed location. If they go somewhere else, they have left their place of authenticity and are on a one-way road to assimilation.

Indigenous activists have been organizing in Arizona against SB 1070—which further criminalizes undocumented peoples—by questioning the "immigrant" paradigm. On May 21, 2010, Indigenous activists occupied the Border Patrol headquarters at Davis-Monthan Airforce Base in Tucson to protest SB 1070. Among their demands were the following:

> On this day people who are indigenous to Arizona join with migrants who are indigenous to other parts of the Western Hemisphere in demanding a return to traditional indigenous value of freedom of movement for all people. Prior to the colonization by European nations (spaniards, english, french) and the establishment of the european settler state known as the United States and the artificial borders it and other european inspired nation states have imposed; indigenous people migrated, traveled and traded with each other without regard to artificial black lines drawn on maps. U.S. immigration policies dehumanize and criminalize people simply because of which side of these artificial lines they were born on. White settlers whose ancestors have only been here at most for a few hundred years have imposed these policies of terror and death on "immigrants" whose ancestors have lived in this hemisphere for tens of thousands of years, for time immemorial.
>
> In addition, the migration that the U.S. government is attempting to stop is driven more than anything else by the economic policies of the U.S. Free trade agreements such as NAFTA have severely reduced the ability of Mexicans and others

from the global south to sustain themselves by permitting corporations to extract huge amounts of wealth and resources from these countries into the U.S. This has led to millions of people risking the terror and death that so many face to cross into the U.S. looking for ways to better support their families. Thousands of women, men, children and elders have died crossing just in the last decade. If the U.S. really wants to reduce migration it should end its policies of exploitation and wealth extraction targeted at the global south and instead pursue policies of economic, environmental and social justice for all human beings on the planet, thus reducing the drive to immigrate.

The protesters are demanding:

—An end to border militarization

—The immediate repeal of SB1070 and 287g

—An end to all racial profiling and the criminalization of our communities

—No ethnic cleansing or cultural genocide

—No border patrol encroachment/sweeps on sovereign native land

—No Deportations

—No Raids

—No ID verification

—No Checkpoints

—Yes to immediate and unconditional regularization ("legalization") of all people

—Yes to human rights

—Yes to dignity
—Yes to respect
—Yes to respecting Indigenous Peoples inherent right of migration.[1]

As their statement indicates, they articulate not migration but the nation-state and its reliance on control and ownership of territory as the problem. They are arguing that immigration is an Indigenous issue because settler colonialism ultimately depends on an exclusivist concept of nation based on control and ownership of land and territory that is demarcated by borders.

Thus, a liberatory vision for immigrant rights is one that is based less on pathways to citizenship in a settler state, than on questioning the logics of the settler state itself.

Harsha's very important text shows a way forward for building a holistic movement to oppose anti-immigration oppression. Solidarity work between immigrant peoples, nonimmigrant people of color, and Indigenous peoples must go beyond coalition politics based on the assumption that we are all "oppressed." Rather, Harsha asks us to look at how anti-immigrant xenophobia, white supremacy, and settler colonialism are mutually reinforcing in ways that actually prevent us from seeing how these logics are fully connected. Only by doing the kind of careful intellectual and activist work needed to understand how these logics are interrelated can we be in a position to dismantle them.

—Andrea Smith

Introduction

this is the year that those
who swim the border's undertow
and shiver in boxcars
are greeted with trumpets and drums
at the first railroad crossing
on the other side;
this is the year that the hands
pulling tomatoes from the vine
uproot the deed to the earth that sprouts the vine,
the hands canning tomatoes
are named in the will
that owns the bedlam of the cannery;
this is the year that the eyes
stinging from the poison that purifies toilets
awaken at last to the sight
of a rooster-loud hillside,
pilgrimage of immigrant birth;
this is the year that cockroaches
become extinct, that no doctor
finds a roach embedded

> in the ear of an infant;
> this is the year that the food stamps
> of adolescent mothers
> are auctioned like gold doubloons,
> and no coin is given to buy machetes
> for the next bouquet of severed heads
> in coffee plantation country.
> —Martin Espada, "Imagine the Angel of Breads"

This book is about undoing borders—undoing the physical borders that enforce a global system of apartheid, and undoing the conceptual borders that keep us separated from one another. Such visions are in the service of stubborn survival, and hold the vehement faith that there are millions subverting the system and liberating themselves from its chains. Just over the year that this book was written, hundreds of thousands have defiantly taken to the streets and won victories as part of the Idle No More movement, Quebec student strike, Tar Sands blockade, Arab Spring uprising, European-wide antiausterity strike, Undocumented and Unafraid campaign, and Boycott Divest Sanctions movement.

This work is a humble project; a modest effort born out of a decade of social movement organizing, for which no single individual can take credit or attempt to objectively describe. Writing this book has been a journey of overcoming my trepidation in documenting and sharing experiences related to a movement in which I have been deeply involved, yet in which I am not alone. I have had countless mentors and comrades who have challenged and influenced my thinking. I want to be explicit about these relationships given the individualistic nature of writing and the tendency toward celebrity culture in activism. There is no liberation in isolation; indeed, there is no liberation *possible* in isolation. This book reflects the collective and collaborative nature of social movements, and is the achievement of all those who informed its content, those who helped to edit and mold it, those whose voices and artwork are contained within these pages, and most important, those who daily self-determine and inspire rebellions and resurrections that are worth writing about.

Undoing Border Imperialism is also the piecing together of my own exiled living. My commitment to fighting state-imposed borders, which divide the rich from the poor, white bodies from brown/black bodies, the West from the Orient, is etched in blood. My mother's family is a product of the 1947 partition of India and Pakistan—a colonially created border that displaced twelve to fifteen million people within four years. My father spent most of his adult life as a migrant worker subsisting on a daily diet of sweat, prayers, once-a-week long-distance phone calls, and the indignity of always being a "foreigner." I have lived with precarious legal status for years and have seen the insides of an inhumane detention center. Though this book is not an autobiography, these personal experiences, memories, and stories are inseparable from the movements I am a part of and shape much of the analysis that I present in this book.

Undoing Border Imperialism

> Borderlands, the ultimate Achilles' heel of colonialism and imperialism.
> —Roxanne Dunbar-Ortiz, "Invasion of the Americas and the Making of the Mestizocoyote Nation"

The experiences of my family and other displaced migrants—what to Chicana feminist Cherríe Moraga is actually indescribable: "to gain the word, to describe the loss, I risk losing everything"—take place in the context of broader systemic forces.[1] Mainstream discourses, and even some segments of the immigrant rights movement, extol Western generosity toward displaced migrants and remain silent about the root causes of migration. But as Nobel laureate Amartya Sen explains, "Increased migratory pressure over the decades owes more to the dynamism of international capitalism than just the growing size of the population of third world countries."[2] Capitalism and imperialism have undermined the stability of communities, and compelled people to move in search of work and survival.

Capital, and the transnationalization of its production and consumption, is freely mobile across borders, while the people displaced as a consequence of the ravages of neoliberalism and imperialism are constructed as demographic threats and experience limited mobility. Less than 5 percent of the world's migrants and refugees come to North America.[3] When they do, they face armed border guards, indefinite detention in prisons, dangerous and low-wage working conditions, minimal access to social services, discrimination and dehumanization, and the constant threat of deportation. Western states therefore are undoubtedly implicated in displacement and migration: their policies dispossess people and force them to move, and subsequently deny any semblance of livelihood and dignity to those who can get through their borders.

Border imperialism, which I propose as an alternative analytic framework, disrupts the myth of Western benevolence toward migrants. In fact, it wholly flips the script on borders; as journalist Dawn Paley aptly expresses it, "Far from preventing violence, the border is in fact the reason it occurs."[4] Border imperialism depicts the processes by which the violences and precarities of displacement and migration are *structurally* created as well as maintained.

Border imperialism encapsulates four overlapping and concurrent structurings: first, the mass displacement of impoverished and colonized communities resulting from asymmetrical relations of global power, and the simultaneous securitization of the border against those migrants whom capitalism and empire have displaced; second, the criminalization of migration with severe punishment and discipline of those deemed "alien" or "illegal"; third, the entrenchment of a racialized hierarchy of citizenship by arbitrating who legitimately constitutes the nation-state; and fourth, the state-mediated exploitation of migrant labor, akin to conditions of slavery and servitude, by capitalist interests. While borders are understood as lines demarcating territory, an analysis of border imperialism interrogates the modes and networks of governance that determine how bodies will be included within the nation-state, and how territory will be controlled within and in conjunction with the dictates of global empire and transnational capitalism.

Borders are, to extrapolate from philosophers Michael Hardt and Antonio Negri, concurrently *transgressed* (when extending the reach of empire) and *fortified* (when policing the territorial center).[5] Border controls are most severely deployed *by* those Western regimes that create mass displacement, and are most severely deployed *against* those whose very recourse to migration results from the ravages of capital and military occupations. Practices of arrest without charge, expulsion, indefinite detention, torture, and killings have become the unexceptional norm in militarized border zones. The racist, classist, heteropatriarchal, and ableist construction of the legal/desirable migrant justifies the criminalization of the illegal/undesirable migrant, which then emboldens the conditions for capital to further exploit the labor of migrants. Migrants' precarious legal status and precarious stratification in the labor force are further inscribed by racializing discourses that cast migrants of color as eternal outsiders: *in* the nation-state but not *of* the nation-state. Coming full circle, border imperialism illuminates how colonial anxieties about identity and inclusion *within* Western borders are linked to the racist justifications for imperialist missions *beyond* Western borders that generate cycles of mass displacement. We are all, therefore, simultaneously separated by and bound together by the violences of border imperialism.

Discussing border imperialism also foregrounds an analysis of colonialism. Colonially drawn borders divide Indigenous families from each other. Just as the British Raj partitioned my parent's homeland, Indigenous communities across Turtle Island have been separated as a result of the colonially imposed Canadian and US borders. Indigenous lands are increasingly becoming the battleground for settler states' escalating policies of border militarization. In southern Arizona, for example, the O'odham have been organizing against the construction of the US-Mexico border wall, part of which would run through the Tohono O'odham reservation and make travel to ceremonial sites across the border more difficult. Alex Soto, a Tohono O'odham arrested for occupying US Border Patrol offices in 2010, states that the

> Department of Homeland Security, U.S. Border Patrol, Immigration Custom Enforcement, and their corporate backers such as Wackenhut, are the true criminals. . . . Indigenous Peoples have existed here long before these imposed borders, and Elders inform us that we always honored freedom of movement. . . . The impacts of border militarization are constantly being made invisible in and by the media, and the popular culture of this country. . . . Border militarization destroys Indigenous communities.[6]

Borders also factionalize heterogeneous communities and rigidify allegiances to artificially homogenized statist nationalisms. Multiracial Indigenous feminist Jessica Danforth writes, "What the border has done to far too many of our First Nations communities is horrific and atrocious on so many levels—and it has poisoned our minds to think in singular factions, instead of a full circle. . . . We belong to Mother Earth in whom no one has claim over— and where there aren't any borders."[7]

Rather than conceiving of immigration as a domestic policy issue to be managed by the state, the lens of border imperialism focuses the conversation on the systemic structuring of global displacement and migration through and in collusion with capitalism, colonial empire, state building, and hierarchies of oppression. These interrelated and overlapping forces of political, economic, and social organization shape the nature of migration, and hence inform the experiences of migrants and displaced peoples. Australian author McKenzie Wark reminds us, "Those who seek refuge, who are rarely accorded a voice, are nevertheless the bodies that confront the injustice of the world. They give up their particular claim to sovereignty and cast themselves on the waters. Only when the world is its own refuge will their limitless demand be met."[8] From May Day marches of millions of undocumented migrants in the United States and riots of immigrant youths in France to weekly detention center protests in Australia and daily mobilizations against the Israeli apartheid wall, localized resistances are manifestations of a global phenomenon affirming the freedom to stay, move, and return in the face of border imperialism. Indigenous Secwepemc artist Tania Willard observes, "Fences and borders can't stop the flow of rivers, migration of butterflies, or the movement of people, and won't stop the spirit of freedom."[9]

Undoing border imperialism would mean a freer society for everyone since borders are the nexus of most systems of oppression. While this book focuses on mobilizing against state borders, borders and the violences they enforce surround us. Much like immigration laws criminalizing migrants for transgressing state borders, trespass and private property laws outlaw squatting and the common use of space, while legalizing the colonial occupation and division of Indigenous lands. Interrogating such discursive and embodied borders—their social construction and structures of affect—reveals how we are not just spatially segregated but also hierarchically stratified. Whether through military checkpoints, gated communities in gentrified neighborhoods, secured corporate boardrooms, or gendered bathrooms, bordering practices delineate zones of access, inclusion, and privilege from zones of invisibility, exclusion, and death. Everywhere that bordering and ordering practices proliferate, they reinforce the enclosure of the commons, thus reifying apartheid relations at the political, economic, social, and psychological levels. Palestinian scholar Edward Said writes, "Just as none of us is outside or beyond geography, none of us is completely free from the struggle over geography. That struggle is complex and interesting because it is not only about soldiers and cannons but also about ideas, about forms, about images and imagining."[10]

Decolonizing Movement Borders

> Maybe home is somewhere I'm going and never
> have been before.
> —Warsan Shire, "To Be Vulnerable and Fearless:
> An Interview with Writer Warsan Shire"

Beyond conceptualizing border imperialism, this book is about migrant justice movements undoing border imperialism. As queer black educator Darnell Moore remarks, "To live, we must put an end to those things that would, otherwise, be cause for our own funerals."[11] The process of grassroots community organizing—resisting together and building solidarities against the various modes of governance constituted through borders—leads to the generation of transnational relations, which novelist Kiran Desai calls "a bridge over the split."[12] It is through this kind of active engagement against imperialism, capitalism, state building, and oppression—along with the nurturing of emancipatory and expansive social relations and identities, forged *in* and *through* the course of struggle—that visionary alternatives to border imperialism can be actualized.

All movements need an anchor in a shared positive vision, not a homogeneous or exact or perfect condition, but one that will nonetheless dismantle hierarchies, disarm concentrations of power, guide just relations, and nurture individual autonomy alongside collective responsibility. In the prophetic words of black historian Robin Kelley, "Without new visions we don't know what to build, only what to knock down. We not only end up confused, rudderless, and cynical, but we forget that making a revolution is not a series of clever maneuvers and tactics but a process that can and must transform us."[13] This necessitates creating concrete alternatives and strengthening relations outside the purview of the state's institutions and its matrices of power and control. Such alternatives unsettle the state and capitalism by functioning outside their reach.

Decolonization is a framework that offers a positive and concrete prefigurative vision. Prefiguration is the notion that our organizing reflects the society we wish to live in—that the methods we practice, institutions we create, and relationships we facilitate within our movements and communities align with our ideals. Many activists argue that prefiguration involves envisioning a completely "new" society. But as a prefiguring framework, decolonization grounds us in an understanding that we have already inherited generations of evolving wisdom about living freely and communally while stewarding the Earth from anticolonial commoning practices, anticapitalist workers' cooperatives, antioppressive communities of care, and in particular matriarchal Indigenous traditions. As theorists Aman Sium, Chandni Desai, and Eric Ritskes forcefully assert, "Decolonization demands the valuing of Indigenous sovereignty in its material, psychological, epistemological, and spiritual forms."[14]

Enacting a politics of decolonization also necessitates an undoing of the borders between one another. Queer feminist philosopher Judith Butler unmasks and celebrates human vulnerability and interdependency: "Let's face it. We're undone by each other. And if we're not, we're missing something. If this seems so clearly the case with grief, it is only because it was already the case with desire. One does not always stay intact. It may be that one wants to, or does, but it may also be that despite one's best efforts, one is undone, in the face of the other."[15]

In the face of omnipresent physical and psychological colonialism, decolonization traverses the political and personal realms of our lives, and honors diverse articulations of nonhierarchical and nonoppressive association. Decolonization movements create an alternative to power through committed struggle against settler colonialism, border imperialism, capitalism, and oppression, as well as through concrete practices that center other ways of laboring, thinking, loving, stewarding, and living. Ultimately, decolonization grounds us in gratitude and humility through the realization that we are but one part of the land and its creation, and encourages us to constitute our kinship and movement networks based on shared affinities as well as responsible solidarities.

Why No One Is Illegal?

> What would be the implications of acting out of love rather than the dictates of the nationalistic mind?
> —Shivam Vij, "Of Nationalism and Love in Southasia"

I have been active in the migrant justice movement, specifically through No One Is Illegal (NOII) groups in Canada, for over a decade. NOII is a migrant justice movement that mobilizes tangible support for refugees, undocumented migrants, and (im)migrant workers, and prioritizes solidarity with Indigenous communities. Grounded in anticolonial, anticapitalist, ecological justice, Indigenous self-determination, anti-imperialist, and antioppression politics, NOII groups organize and fight back against systems of injustice through popular education and direct action.[16] NOII groups exist across Canada, but are organized autonomously as a loose network with shared values and some ad hoc coordination. It was only in 2012 that the existing NOII groups drafted a joint statement of unity, in which we describe ourselves as "part of a worldwide movement of resistance that strives and struggles for the right to remain, the freedom to move, and the right to return."[17]

Mapping the currents of NOII's mobilizing and movement-based practices is critical for five reasons. First, NOII offers a systemic critique of border imperialism. This stands in contrast to more mainstream immigrant rights movements that ignore the centrality of empire and capitalism to the violence of displacement, migration, and border controls. Second, NOII's systemic critique, as an organizing framework, facilitates a convergence of a range of social movements. Links are forged between antidetention and antiprison activists, between antipoverty movements and nonstatus communities to ensure public access to basic services, between local anticolonial organizing and anti-imperialist international solidarity organizing, and between gender justice movements' defense of our bodies and environmental justice movements' defense of the land.

Third, the work of NOII is multilayered. While organizing from an antistate framework, NOII also strategically
navigates the state apparatus in order to win tangible victories for those facing detention and deportation. This kind
of mobilizing cannot easily be dismissed as simply being
reformist since it ensures that we are engaging with people
who are directly impacted by the injustices of border imperialism. Being rooted and relevant in such a way amplifies
the struggle for structural change and collective freedom.
The careful and thoughtful balance of strategies is explored
throughout this book as it is foundational to earning trust
and respect for NOII's organizing among affected community members and radicals alike.

Fourth, the mobilizing of NOII provides lessons on
maintaining principled political positions while expanding
communities of resistance through effective broad-based
alliances. A major corporate newspaper begrudgingly
acknowledges the force of NOII: "The once fringe community group . . . has grown in popularity. . . . Its crusade
for undocumented migrants have made headlines and
earned it recognition in the mainstream."[18] In a time of the
expansion of the nonprofit-industrial complex, NOII is an
example of all-volunteer, radical, and grassroots community
organizing that is sustainable, with a growing ability to
capture people's imaginations and a capacity to win victories. After nine years of grassroots organizing, for example,
NOII-Toronto has not only popularized migrant justice
issues but also mobilized to make Toronto the country's
first Sanctuary City, where city services are guaranteed
to all regardless of their citizenship status. In an effort to

discredit the cross-country popularity and effectiveness of NOII, Minister of Citizenship and Immigration Jason Kenney recently denounced NOII in Parliament as "not simply another noisy activist group but hard-line anti-Canadian extremists."[19]

Finally, returning to the words of Kelley, NOII offers a prefigurative vision for a different kind of society. The very name and its various invocations, such as "No Human is Illegal," "Personne n'est illegal," and "Nadie es illegal," emphasize that all humans are inherently worthy and valuable, and that policies that illegalize human beings are legal and moral fictions. Undoing border imperialism requires that we undo power structures, while prefiguring the social relations we wish to have and the forms of leadership we wish to support. Within NOII, we take leadership from marginalized communities, particularly communities of color and Indigenous nations impacted by state controls and systemic oppression. Such methods of organizing within NOII aim to reflect our vision of antioppressive, egalitarian, and noncoercive societies.

For these reasons, an analysis of NOII's decade-long history offers relevant insights for all organizers on effective strategies to overcome state-imposed borders as well as the barriers within movements in order to cultivate fierce, loving, and sustainable communities.

About This Book

> I came to theory desperate, wanting to compre-
> hend—to grasp what was happening around and
> within me. Most importantly, I wanted to make
> the hurt go away. I saw in theory then a location for
> healing.
> —bell hooks, *Teaching to Transgress*

Undoing Border Imperialism merges different forms of
theory that tend to be relegated to separate spheres: academic, movement, and experiential theories. While societal
structures legitimize academic discourse as the most rigorous and objective type of theory, all three kinds of theory
are invaluable. Together these forms help us to understand
systemic injustice from different angles, and empower us to
take action against authoritarian and oppressive systems.
This book is primarily embedded in movement theory,
which stems from the praxis of organizing, and experiential
theory, which is based in lived realities and resistances.

The first chapter, "What Is Border Imperialism?" relies
on academic theory. Drawing on critical race theory, feminist studies, Marxist analysis, and poststructuralism, this
chapter theorizes and evaluates border imperialism from
within intersectional pedagogy. I argue that the violence
of border imperialism is a direct result of the violence of
colonial displacements, capital circulations, labor stratifications in the global economy, and structural hierarchies of
race, class, gender, ability, and citizenship status. Rather
than victim blaming and racist stereotyping that punish

migrants for irregular forms of migration and render them "illegal," this chapter rigorously challenges the inhumane ideology of border controls that denies migrants their freedom and self-determination.

The second chapter, "Cartography of NOII," maps out NOII's response—as an anticapitalist, anticolonial, and antiracist migrant justice movement—to border imperialism. This is not a comprehensive history or even a summary of all NOII campaigns; rather, the chapter offers my perspective on some of the strongest formulations of NOII's movement-based analysis and practice over the past decade. I outline the analyses and practices of direct support work, regularization of legal status for all migrants, abolition of security certificates, Indigenous solidarity organizing, and collaboration within anticapitalist movements. The strategies described in this chapter are relevant to other social movements grappling with how to be accountable to communities that are impacted by the systems we are confronting, how to strengthen alliances, and how to expand movements to effect tangible as well as transformative change.

The third and fourth chapters rely on social movement theory. Describing social movement theorizing, radical queer activist Gary Kinsman notes, "Activists are thinking, talking about, researching and theorizing about what is going on, what they are going to do next and how to analyze the situations they face, whether in relation to attending a demonstration, a meeting, a confrontation with institutional forces or planning the next action or campaign."[20] In these chapters, I share the knowledge generated from these kinds of engagements within NOII. Rather than abstracting principles *onto* social movements, which can feel artificial and top down, these chapters generate principles *from* social movements, for a more grounded and pertinent discussion.

In the third chapter, "Overgrowing Hegemony: Grassroots Theory," I address social movement strategies and tactics, antioppression practice, and group structure and leadership. Within these three areas, I explore current social movement debates, including building broad-based alliances while maintaining radical political principles, fostering antioppressive leadership while opposing hierarchies, and affecting tangible change while prefiguring transformation.

The fourth chapter, "Waves of Resistance Roundtable," brings together fifteen grassroots NOII organizers to provide their own insights on some of these long-standing contentions. Their astute responses raise the level of consciousness on the nature of campaigning, organizational structure, alliances, and decolonization. Reflecting a diversity of (although not all) opinions within NOII groups, this roundtable disrupts conventional forms of writing that by privileging a single author, skew the collective and heterogeneous nature of movements. The roundtable holds the heart of this book.

The fifth and final chapter, "Journeys toward Decolonization," discusses decolonization as a liberatory and prefigurative framework on which to base not only struggles against border imperialism but all social movements. Decolonization is rooted in dismantling the structures of border imperialism, settler colonialism, empire, capitalism, and oppression, while also being a generative praxis that creates the condition to grow and recenter alternatives to our current socioeconomic system. Decolonization necessitates a reconceptualization of the discursive and embodied borders within and between us by grounding us in the fundamental principles of mutual aid, collective liberation, and humility—not in isolation, but instead within our real and informed and sustained relationships with, and commitments to, each other and the Earth.

This book also weaves together short narratives from thirteen powerful voices of color. For many racialized people, sharing our narratives means much more than having a personal outlet. Narratives and stories are foundational to keeping our cultural practices alive and to rekindling our imaginations. Leanne Betasamosake Simpson, an Indigenous Michi Saagiig Nishnaabeg scholar, describes storytelling as "a lens through which we can envision our way out of cognitive imperialism, where we can create models and mirrors where none existed, and where we can experience the spaces of freedom and justice. Storytelling becomes a space where we can escape the gaze around the cage of the Empire, even if it is just for a few minutes."[21] The stories throughout this book are not only challenges to the norms of border imperialism and settler colonialism; they are also glimpses into envisioning and actualizing egalitarian social relations.

The inclusion of these thirteen narratives, all authored by racialized and predominantly women activists and writers, is a political act. In one of the most poignant affirmations of women of color solidarities ever depicted, poet Aurora Levins Morales writes, "This tribe called 'Women of Color' is not an ethnicity. It is one of the inventions of solidarity, an alliance, a political necessity that is not the given name of every female with dark skin and a colonized tongue, but rather a choice about how to resist and with whom."[22] This describes more than a solidarity based on shared identity. Women of color solidarities are based on the recognition that since the subjectivities of women of color are the most impacted by systems of oppression and exploitation, we embody the pathways necessary to concurrently disrupt multiple layers of injustice.

The thirteen voices in this book refuse to be disappeared and defy surrender. These are the tongues that were never meant to survive, the stories that were meant to be stolen and silenced through centuries of annihilation and assimilation. The centrality of these voices to this book is an enactment of antioppressive leadership—a principle that this book calls on us to heed. Given that capitalist, white supremacist, and heteropatriarchal society has taught us to fear, judge, and compete with one another, facilitating space for other women of color warriors is an intentional political practice, an offering in the spirit of decolonization.

Acknowledgments

This book was written on Indigenous Coast Salish territories. The Musqueam, Squamish, and Tsleil Waututh peoples, who endure acts of genocide in order for us to live with amnesia about the histories of Turtle Island, have never surrendered these lands. This book also would not be possible without the toil of those, mostly immigrant workers locally and impoverished laborers across the globe, who daily work the fields and factories that produce my basic necessities, including my food and clothing. These are the founding conditions and violences of my intellectual labor.

I am indebted to Hari Alluri, Lisa Bhungalia, Fariah Chowdhury, Stefan Christoff, Nassim Elbardouh, Mary Foster, Harjap Grewal, Stefanie Gude, Alex Hundert, Andrew Loewen, Cecily Nicholson, Dana Olwan, Dawn Paley, Sozan Savehilaghi, Andréa Schmidt, Parul Sehgal, Naava Smolash, and Shayna Stock for their diligent comments and edits. Any errors within this book, however, are my own. Thank you to all the brilliant contributors for their wisdom, Andrea Smith for honoring the book with a foreword, Ashanti Alston, Roxanne Dunbar-Ortiz, Naomi Klein, and Vijay Prashad for humbling blurbs, Melanie Cervantes and Josh MacPhee of Justseeds for stunning design work, Zach Blue, Christa Daring, and Charles Weigl of AK Press for publishing this manuscript, and Chris Dixon and Cindy Milstein of the IAS for soliciting, encouraging, supporting, and editing this manuscript, and essentially being the backbone of this entire process. Gratitude to ancestors, family, comrades, elders, friends, and allies who light this journey. And to my brother, who always knew that living simply and loving deeply were interconnected.

"Pick One": Self-determination and the Politics of Identity(ies)

"Pick one," they said
North American. Indian?
But wait, I'm from Toronto.
Although that's not where my family is from
And I don't live there anymore
"Pick one," they said
Young. Woman?
But I'm not a woman like you might think I am
I'm Two Spirit beyond the acronym of LGBT
And it's more than a sexuality
"Pick one," they said
I work in sexual and reproductive health?
But it's about rights and justice over body and space
Even if we didn't want to include environmental violence
We have to since that's what's happening to us.

Don't worry—I'm not interested in winning the
Oppression Olympics
I know I'm complicit too
But this isn't a two-sided story
Since there aren't always two sides
There could just be the truth, the reality
The fact that there's a history to this continuing
The boxes, the borders, the lines being drawn

The refusal to accept that it's on purpose
The disguise that it's "so much better than it used to be"
While the roots remain too close for comfort

Now they say, "We're inclusive!"
Even though I'm not actually interested in being included
After I had to be included because I wasn't there to begin
with
They're not looking at the center where I was erased
To uphold what makes it easier to not deal with
Now they say, "I'm your ally!"
Even though I ain't *neva* seen them where I live
I don't remember being asked if that's what I want
There's this thing called free, prior, and informed consent
Which doesn't seem to apply when it's about titles
Now they say, "We'll get there someday!"
Even though the same patterns of oppression keep
repeating themselves
I don't want to keep swallowing the pill of having to
understand
It's not only about a better policy, law, or elected official
In the same system, it still hurts.

Unless things are dismantled and deconstructed where
there's pain
Regrounded and rebuilt where there's hope
It will still be messed up for some
Always that same sum
Who never fit nicely into an equal opportunity
I've failed applications, funding proposals, membership,

and residency tests
The same organizations and groups won't call me
 "You're just too mixed!" I'm told
But I don't feel mixed, I feel whole
And I'm not the only one.

Every explanation I have to give because my story isn't
shown in the mainstream
Every *but* I have to put in front of what I call myself in the
English language
Every discussion I have to get into because I will not allow
my ancestors' struggles for me to be here to be silenced
Takes away my self-determination of identity
If you want to stop the *us vs. them*
I just can't pick one.

—Jessica Danforth

Chile Con Carne

Manuelita walks slowly toward her desk. Music resembling the sound of a heartbeat plays.[1] MANUELITA: At school nobody knows I dance cueca. Nobody knows I work at the bakery and at the hair salon. Nobody knows my house is full of my parents' friends having meetings till really late. Nobody knows we have protests and rallies, nobody knows we have penas and cumbia dances, nobody knows my parents are going on a hunger strike. Nobody knows my dad was in jail. Nobody knows we're on the blacklist. Nobody from school, not even Lassie, comes over to my house. Nobody knows we have posters of Fidel Castro and Che Guevara on the walls. Nobody knows about the Chilean me at school.

Manuelita arrives at her desk. The man from the Royal Canadian Mounted Police is here to talk about safety. So stupid! MANUELITA: He's a huge gringo policeman, with a gun at his side. I bet he knows that me and Joselito broke the windows on the tractors that want to chop down Cedar, my favorite tree, and now he's come to get me. Then I'll be in jail. Just like my dad was. He's standing at the front of the class with a nice warm smile on his face. "Hi, kids," he says. I remember those nice grins, those are the same grins they wore when they raided our house and they tore my favorite doll's head off. I sit in the first row of desks so I can see the gun real clearly. It's real all right, but it's smaller than the ones in Chile. The man starts talking about dangerous men in the woods and never get in cars and never take money from strangers, but I'm thinking, I know. I know what you're really about. My mom explained to me once that the gringos helped to do the coup in Chile, that's why we always have protests outside the US consulate, so I know what you're up to, mister. You're trying to get us to trust you, but "No, sir." He takes his gun out slowly and holds it like this, flat in his hands; he's talking about how he never uses it, when all of a sudden I hear a kid screaming real loud. A few moments go by before I realize it's me that's screaming.

Manuelita stands on the desk and does a silent scream, turning in a circle. Then she sits back down. MANUELITA: There's a puddle of pee on my seat. Miss Mitten comes up to me with a frozen smile and eyes that are about to pop out. She hits me on the head with her flash cards.

Manuelita runs to Cedar. MANUELITA: I can hear the kids laughing 'cause I peed, but I run all the way home and here, to Cedar.

—Carmen Aguirre

The Bracelet

This is a dialogue between a father and his four-year-old son.[1]

"Dad, dad . . ."

"Yes, little one."

"What are you wearing around your neck?"

"Around my neck! Nothing."

"No, there."

"Oh, you mean around my ankle?"

"That's the neck of your foot, the annk . . . what?"

"Ankle, little one."

"But you didn't tell me what it is."

"Ah. That, that's a bracelet."

"How long have you been wearing it?"

"Three years."

"Why do you always wear it?"

"Because I'm attached to it; it was a present."

"Who gave it to you?"

"It was tonton."

"Who is tonton?"

"Er . . . it's Uncle Sam."

"Who is Uncle Sam?"

"Little one, you ask too many questions. It's just somebody who gave it to me . . . Uncle Sam, Uncle Stephen, Uncle Security. It doesn't matter; you don't know him."

"OK, but why is it black, your bracelet?"

"Because those who gave it to me have white faces but black hearts."

"Why isn't it gold, like mama's necklace?"

"Because those who gave it to me don't have a heart of gold, little one."

"But Dad, why are you the only person who wears it in Quebec?"

"Not for long, little one, don't worry. In not too long it'll be a style, like tattoos; everyone will have theirs. There are already ones in cell phones, in cars, for blue-collar workers, for grandfathers, for babies, for dogs.... Uncle Sam doesn't have a heart of gold but he doesn't miss anyone."

—Adil Charkaoui

Imposters

The world is made up of imposters. There is often a will towards authenticity, some semblance of the genuine. And yet, what might it mean to consider the figure of the imposter, not as an aberration or crime but as a standard. To play a part is to perhaps hold a role in the increasingly neoliberal global economy.

In Delhi, Bangalore, Hyderabad, Lahore, she will smile into a headset. Her voice will chirp with the intonations of *Friends* actresses whom she has learned to mimic. Her English intonation and slang is more precise than many Middle Americans she talks to. She will talk to Chris in Detroit. Grandchild of slaves, he wears a carving of the map of Africa around his neck and has been laid off for months. "Yes," he stammers, voice rough from days of Parliament cigarettes and the worries of the perpetually unemployed, "I'm an American citizen."

She will talk to Judy in Calgary who will discuss her poor credit rating. Judy once attended a seminar about "the Imposter Syndrome," a self-help workshop teaching graduate students to self-diagnose their anxieties regarding the place of intellectuals in the neoliberal marketplace. Judy went for the free coffee and muffins. Anything she didn't have to pay for. Judy will remember inspirational maxims she was force-fed along with crusty baked goods, proclaiming that she is a doctoral student who is confident that she will find a well-paying job. She will stare at the "balance owing" on the screen and say a silent prayer for Judy.

She will talk to John in Brooklyn. With the sound of religious processions carried through the office window, she will yawn silently. It is her night and his day. She will smile into the headset. "Good morning, sir! How are you today?" John will have just told his mother that everything is fine, before carrying empties of beer to the trash bin, kicking aside used syringes, and glancing at the home-less and the hipsters. She will see his prison and hospital records flash on the screen. He will smile into his cell phone. "Yeah, fine thanks."

"Jen" smiling into a headset is not a trusted friend or confidant. When baptized by a Bank with her new out-sourced cheerleader pseudonym, she giggled, as it reminded her of a word in another language meaning ghost. She sees your credit rating, prison and hospital records. She says a silent prayer for America.

We are a world of imposters. The postures of authen-ticity are continually undercut by the elaborate produc-tions of civility and capital that construct a world of fakes. Abraham in Ethiopia cannot cross the border, but his beans carry the fragrant aromas of coffee down the sparkling Western city streets. The produce is picked by Mexicans, the children fed by a Filipina, and the waiter is from Baghdad. To obtain a UK visa one no longer talks to the British, but to "World Bridge," a private business that now processes all applications. Heitsi greets you with a thick North American accent and dark hands that clink with wooden bangles. A British flag emblazoned on her chest, she flew through London once on her way to Nigeria.

"That's a crazy airport." The authenticity of production, the production of authenticity is undercut by stages of capital—assembly line, office banter, Internet wires upon which people stammer and strut.

Ron shortened his Sanskrit name to make it translatable over emails sent to and from Silicon Valley. He crosses the Indian border with a newly purchased Person of Indian Origin card that conceals his grudging disdain for the nation's poor, and his Lonely Planet accent. Ron skips across electronic sidewalks from New Jersey to New Delhi, the clip of his Italian leather shoes impatiently tapping in border security lines.

Faraz sees India from the rooftops of Pakistan. Delicate Ghazal heard across fault lines of nations resonate with him, like the songs of mothers singing mother tongues. At the border his name is translated into an electronic ledger of suspects and detainees. Curves of prophetic name turns to hard English letters and prison numbers, as unforgiving as passport photos and the harsh lights of shopping malls and interrogators.

The irony of our time perhaps lies in efforts to tighten borders and fix authenticity, while bodies and voices change, exchange, and multiply, leaving little trace or truth of origin. The world is made up of imposters.

—Tara Atluri

WHAT IS BORDER IMPERIALISM?

What Is Border Imperialism?

> The world was born yearning to be a home for
> everyone.
> —Eduardo Galeano, "Through the Looking
> Glass: Q & A with Eduardo Galeano"

For the past several years, Indigenous organizations in Australia have been issuing "Original Passports" to asylum seekers who have been detained or denied legal status by the Australian government. Most recently, in May 2012, passports were issued to two detained Tamil asylum seekers. During the ceremony, Ray Jackson of the Indigenous Social Justice Association said, "The Australian Government must stop imprisoning Indigenous people, and they must stop imprisoning asylum seekers. I am proud to welcome people in need into our community." Indigenous elder Robbie Thorpe commented, "The Australian Government has no legitimate right to grant or refuse entry to anyone in this country, let alone lock up people fleeing war and persecution."[1]

Such moments of solidarity between Indigenous people and migrants represent not only growing networks of understanding and alliance between marginalized communities, but also a fundamental challenge to the authority of settler-colonial governments and the sovereignty of Western statehood. Western governance and statehood is constituted through multiple modes, including the primacy of the border that delineates and reproduces territorial, political, economic, cultural, and social control. As activists Alessandra Moctezuma and Mike Davis write, "All borders are acts of state violence inscribed in landscape."[2] Constantly being redefined, borders represent a regime of practices, institutions, discourses, and systems that I define as border imperialism.

In this chapter, I establish the broad theoretical groundwork for conceptualizing border imperialism and its four overlapping structurings referenced in the introduction. Border imperialism is characterized by the entrenchment and reentrenchment of controls against migrants, who are displaced as a result of the violences of capitalism and empire, and subsequently forced into precarious labor as a result of state illegalization and systemic social hierarchies.

Border imperialism is a useful analytic framework for organizing migrant justice movements in North America. It takes us away from an analysis that blames and punishes migrants, or one that forces migrants to assimilate and establish their individual worth. Instead, reflecting Thorpe's words, it reorients the gaze squarely on the processes of displacement and migration within the global political economy of capitalism and colonialism. I argue that circulations of capital and labor stratifications in the global economy, narratives of empire, and hierarchies of race, class, and gender within state building all operate in tandem to lay the foundation for border imperialism.

An analysis of border imperialism encapsulates a dual critique of Western state building within global empire: the role of Western imperialism in dispossessing communities in order to secure land and resources for state and capitalist interests, as well as the deliberately limited inclusion of migrant bodies into Western states through processes of criminalization and racialization that justify the commodification of their labor. Western states thus are major arbiters in determining if and under what conditions people migrate.

I use the term West not only to denote the geographic site of the global North (that is, Europe, Australia, and North America) but also to reference the dominance of Western political, economic, and social formations and ideologies that have led to the foundation of other settler-colonial states such as Israel, and that are increasingly adopted by neoliberal states in Latin America, Africa, and Asia. Though political and economic governance are not uniform across these states, as Japanese scholar Naoki Sakai comments about the West as an ideology, "Unlike all the other names associated with geographic particularities, it also implies the refusal of its self-delimitation or particularistic determination. . . . In short, the West must represent the moment of the universal, which subsumes the particular."[3] Border imperialism works to extend and externalize the universalization of Western formations beyond its own boundaries through settler colonialism and military occupations, as well as through the globalization of capitalism by imposing financial agreements and exploiting human and natural resources. Simultaneously, the reinforcement of physical and psychological borders against racialized bodies is a key instrument through which to maintain the sanctity and myth of superiority of Western civilization.

Displacements and Secured Borders

> The itinerary was stamped in our palms at birth.
> —Monika Zobel, "The Immigrant Searches the
> Map for Countries Larger Than His Palm"

Butterflies have always had wings; people have always had legs. While history is marked by the hybridity of human societies and the desire for movement, the reality of most of migration today reveals the unequal relations between rich and poor, between North and South, between whiteness and its others. As the Frassanito Network observes, "To speak of autonomy of migration doesn't mean to remove from the center of the political debate the mechanisms of domination and exploitation which determine the migrants' life."[4] The International Organization for Migration and the United Nations (UN) estimate that there are a billion migrants around the world, 740 million of who are migrant workers inside or outside their own countries.[5] According to figures published by the UN

High Commissioner for Refugees, there are 43.7 million forcibly displaced people in the world, including 27.5 million people who are internally displaced within their own countries.[6] Half the world's refugees are women, and approximately 45 percent of forcibly displaced people are under the age of eighteen.[7]

The first defining process within border imperialism is displacements as a result of the coercive extractions of capitalism and colonialism, and the simultaneous fortification of the border—often by those very same Western powers that are complicit in these displacements—which renders the migration of displaced people as perilous. Large-scale displacements and the precarious conditions into which migrants are cast are not coincidental but rather foundational to the structuring of border imperialism.

Western imperialism is a major cause of mass displacements and migrations. Due to the dispossession of 750,000 Palestinians from their homelands in 1948 and the ongoing illegal Israeli occupation of Palestine, stateless Palestinians form one of the world's largest refugee communities, now numbering almost five million people.[8] Following two invasions and subsequent military occupations, the world's largest recent refugee populations come from Afghanistan and Iraq.[9] With decades of foreign intrusion, including the US and NATO occupations that began in 2001, these two countries have been subjected to the destruction of their infrastructure, privatization of their economies, interference in their governance, and military missions that have killed and tortured over one million people.[10] These interventions are best described as imperialist, defined by Said as "the practice, the theory and the attitudes of a dominating metropolitan center ruling a distant territory."[11] Border imperialism, then, represents the extension and imposition of Western rule, with the current dynamics of global empire maintaining unequal relationships of political, economic, cultural, and social dominance of the West over its colonies.

Border imperialism not only makes possible the transgression and violation of non-Western communities' autonomy in order to maintain the interests of Western empire, it also denies any accountability for its own victims. For example, despite its incessant rhetoric of humanitarian intervention, which political geographer Derek Gregory characterizes as the "velvet glove wrapped around the iron fist of colonialism," the United States accepted only 328 refugees from Afghanistan in 2009.[12] This is a shockingly low number, and even more so considering the direct responsibility of the United States in displacing Afghans. Of a staggering total of 4.7 million displaced people in Iraq and Afghanistan, the majority of refugees crossed into bordering countries such as Pakistan and Iran.[13] Contrary to popular belief about Western generosity and openness to refugees, over 80 percent of the world's refugees reside in neighboring countries within the global South.[14]

Capitalism is another root cause of mass displacements and migrations. A salient example of the impact of capitalist mobility on migration trends in North America is the effects of the 1994 North American Free Trade Agreement (NAFTA), which has displaced millions of Mexicans, and the parallel fortification of the U.S.-Mexico border against migrants. Under NAFTA, the Mexican government was forced to eliminate subsidies to corn while corn produced in the United States remained subsidized, thus making US corn cheaper to buy inside Mexico than Mexican corn. As a result, over 15 million Mexicans were forced into poverty, and 1.5 million farmers who lost their farms migrated to the United States to work in low-wage sectors.[15] Professor William Robinson summarizes this dynamic: "The transnational circulation of capital and the disruption and deprivation it causes, in turn, generates the transnational circulation of labor. In other words, global capitalism creates immigrant workers. . . . In a sense, this must be seen as a coerced or forced migration, since global capitalism exerts a structural violence over whole populations and makes it impossible for them to survive in their homeland."[16]

While such conditions push millions of Mexicans into low-paid work in the United States, the migration from Mexico into the US southwest (itself illegally annexed territory since 1846) is made perilous. Similar to the lack of hospitality toward Afghan and Iraqi refugees, displaced Mexican migrants contend with a heavily fortified border. "We never thought that we'd be in the business of helping to identify remains like in a war zone, and here we are," says Isabel Garcia, cochair of Tucson-based Coalición de Derechos Humanos.[17] Since millions of dollars were put into increasing border patrols and surveillance on the U.S.-Mexico border through Operation Gatekeeper, which went into effect the same year as NAFTA, the American Civil Liberties Union estimates that 5,600 migrants have died while attempting to cross that border.[18]

Geographer and critical race theorist Mary Pat Brady describes border deaths as "a kind of passive capital punishment," where "immigrants have been effectively blamed for their own deaths."[19] Women are particularly vulnerable to sexualized violence at the border. According to a representative of the Latin America and the Caribbean section of the UN Development Fund for Women, at least 60 to 70 percent of undocumented women migrants who cross the border experience sexual abuse.[20] The unfreedom for migrants and concurrent freedom of capital across borders is a defining element of the constant warfare of border imperialism. For example, immediately after 9/11, the Canadian and US governments signed the Canada-US Smart Border Accord to ensure that border restrictions on migrants would not impair the economic necessity of ensuring the free flow of goods, services, and capital across the border.

These instances highlight how mass displacements and precarious migrations are not random but rather largely a result of structural dictates. Within border imperialism, the dual processes of displacement and migration are *manufactured* through the specific trajectories of colonialism and capitalism. Wark points to the injustice of the system that creates displacement and migration: "Migration is globalisation from below. If the 'overdeveloped' world refuses to trade with the underdeveloped world on fair terms, to forgive debt, to extend loans, to lift trade barriers against food and basic manufactured goods, then there can only be an increase in the flow of people."[21] Border imperialism also illuminates the *management* of these migrations.

Political geographer Reece Jones documents how, under the guise of fighting "illegal immigration" and "terrorism," three countries alone—United States, India, and Israel—have built over 3,500 miles of walls on their borders.[22] Border controls are used to deter those for who migration is the only option to the plundering of their communities and economies due to the free license granted to capital and militaries.

Capitalism destroys land-based subsistence cultures and concentrates wealth and property into the hands of a select few. Production within capitalism is disconnected from human need, collective creativity, and the natural world—all of which become commodities to be bought and sold on the market. As the dominant global economic system, capitalism is based on a model of private property, production for profit, waged labor, and private ownership of the means of production and distribution. During the Industrial Revolution in late eighteenth-century England, peasants were displaced from their farmlands and forced to migrate to cities and work for scant wages in growing privately owned industries. Neoliberal capitalist globalization, as the current formation of capitalism, intensifies these processes of dispossession and impoverishment.

A central feature of neoliberalism is the increased mobility of capital across borders. The mobility of capital is aided by the multinational nature of corporations, which defy and evade labor and tax regulations through subcontracting, outsourcing, and transnational banking systems. Global economic regimes such as multilateral trade agreements and structural adjustment programs also facilitate the mobility of capital by imposing measures such as privatization, austerity cutbacks, and user-pay social services.

While guaranteeing capital flows, neoliberalism concurrently guarantees labor flexibility. Waged labor is evermore synonymous with labor flexibility, which necessitates creating a pool of precarious workers. Precarious labor is characterized by poor wages, insecurity in the continuity of work, and lack of protection by even minimal labor regulations. Casual, part-time, and contract labor—which have been termed the "Walmartization" of labor—are increasingly stratified further from more formal and secure forms of employment, and instead are stratified toward indentured and sweatshop labor. The precarity of both labor and social organization are intertwined and cyclic: capitalism requires precarious and exploitable workers to facilitate capital accumulation, and creates those precarious lives through hierarchies of systemic oppression along with its extractions of labor and land. As discussed later in this chapter, a fundamental feature of border imperialism within neoliberalism is to facilitate capital flows across borders while also ensuring labor flexibility by legalizing an exploitable migrant labor workforce.

Analyses of capitalism have generally ignored the central role of land and the colonization of Indigenous societies in the development of capitalism. In Karl Marx's theory of primitive accumulation, capitalist modes of production explicitly require conquest, enslavement, and the dispossession of communities from the lands on which they subsist. Glen Coulthard, an Indigenous scholar, explains that colonialism "forcefully opened-up what were once collectively held territories and resources to privatization (dispossession), which, over time, came to produce a 'class' of workers compelled to enter the exploitative realm of the labor market for their survival (proletarianization)."[23] Colonial and capitalist interests continue to expropriate Indigenous lands, dispossessing Indigenous nations of their territorial base and livelihood, particularly within but not limited to settler-colonial states. Within Canada, there has been a recent push to convert communally held reserve lands—what capitalists refer to as "dead capital"—into fee simple private proverty.[24] This privatization of Indigenous lands would ensure both the colonial state's interests in extinguishing Aboriginal title, and corporate capitalist interests in extracting and commodifying natural resources.

Such analysis reveals a critical connection between the Western state and capitalism, with the state serving as a key instrument to accumulate capital. Contrary to the suggestion by some analysts that the Western state's jurisdiction is withering under the power of multinational corporations, I would contend that the state is not *eroding* under transnational capitalist globalization. The state, along with its forms of governance including through border imperialism, is *evolving* to continue to meet the needs of capitalist expansion through more flexible means of governance and accumulation.

The state maintains an economic infrastructure for capital flows, including stock exchanges, tax regulations, and banking systems. The state also creates the political and legal framework that protects private property, enables the status of corporations as legal entities, sanctions the extraction and commodification of natural resources, and guarantees support for disciplining the workforce. Financial analyst Mike Konczal describes this succinctly: "When the state intervenes in the functioning of markets, it isn't to rectify injustices but instead to further create and maintain the rigor of the economy itself."[25] The Western state thus can be characterized as organizing, facilitating, and in many instances, enforcing capitalism.

The Canadian economy, for example, is largely based on the expropriation of natural resources internally, while the state-corporate nexus also profits from capitalist development projects imposed globally. Canadian mining corporations, which represent 75 percent of the world's mining and exploration companies, are protected and enabled by the Canadian state in Asia, Africa, Latin America, and the Caribbean, even though they have been responsible for, and in some cases charged with, environmental destruction, human and labor rights violations, and the forced displacement of surrounding communities.[26]

Likewise, multinational corporations are welcomed by the Canadian state to exploit and export tar sands, the world's most environmentally destructive industrial project that disproportionately impacts Indigenous nations. In a submission to the United Nations, the Indigenous Yinka Dene Alliance writes, "Canada has indicated that it is contemplating conduct that would infringe our Aboriginal Title and Rights. . . . [I]t is manifestly clear that the Canadian government has already reached a decision to push through this project regardless of the serious adverse effects on Indigenous peoples and lands and without their free, informed and prior consent."[27]

In settler-colonial states such as Canada and the United States, the encroachment on Indigenous lands is compounded by genocidal attempts to subjugate Indigenous governance and assimilate Indigenous cultures. Diné scholar Jennifer Nez Denetdale notes how Indigenous women have been intentionally targeted. "The rape and prostitution of Native women," she explains, was "integral to colonial conquest," as was "the imposition of a modern state formation . . . [which] reconfigured gender roles to mirror American gender roles."[28] This annihilation of Indigenous societies is justified through racist civilizing discourses, such as the discovery doctrine and *terra nullius*, which uphold the political and legal right for colonial powers to conquer supposedly barren Indigenous lands.

The world over, Indigenous communities are at the forefront of resisting dispossession while facing the brunt of displacement, particularly from rural areas into urban centers. The forced privatization and neoliberalization of subsistence farming has resulted in the loss of rural land for millions across Asia, Africa, and Latin America. These displacements bring astounding numbers of people to the centers of capital in order to survive. Forced to endure grinding poverty and stigmatization, displaced people make up the mass in urban slums and low-income neighborhoods. UN figures reveal over one billion slum dwellers across the world in 2005.[29] Women are overrepresented in these statistics, forced into the informal economies of sex work, domestic work, and street vending. This is what

border imperialism, embedded in colonialism and capitalism, engenders.

The Canary Islands, off the coast of Morocco, are a
critical convergence of colonial displacement, forced labor,
capitalist circulation, and border securitization within
border imperialism. Spain colonized the Indigenous
Guanches of the Canary Islands in the fifteenth and six-
teenth centuries, and imposed a plantation economy that
used forced labor to produce sugarcane and cochineal as
cash crops. Today, as the outermost region of the European
Union, the islands are a major gateway for African migrants
into Europe. Migrants from the western regions of Africa—
born of a legacy of slavery, civil wars fueled by Western
geopolitical interests, and the colonial Scramble for Africa
with its contemporary expression of landgrabs—flee to the
Canary Islands in the tens of thousands every year. This is
one of the most dangerous and heavily patrolled migration
routes in the world, with a Spanish official estimating that
40 percent of those attempting the journey die en route.[30]
Even according to conservative estimates cited by the Red
Cross, approximately fifteen hundred migrants died trying
to reach the Canary Islands in just a five-month period in
2005.[31]

Border securitization operates not at a fixed site but
rather through structures and technologies of power across
geographies. On the Canary Islands and elsewhere in
Europe, the border is pushed outward to secure an external
border around what has been called "Fortress Europe."
Created in 2004, Frontex is a European Union regula-
tory agency tasked with integrated border security and

fortification of the European Union's external border. As noted by Marxist philosopher Étienne Balibar, "Borders are vacillating . . . they are no longer at the border," and surveillance measures, including military aircrafts, are employed offshore to deter migrants from leaving Africa.[32] Border imperialism therefore excludes migrants through the diffusion of the state's jurisdiction *beyond* its actual territorial borders. The European network UNITED for Intercultural Action has documented 16,264 refugee deaths across Europe, most due to drowning at sea and suffocation in containers.[33] Like migrant deaths at the US-Mexico border, this number represents the human face of border militarization policies as people are forced to seek out more clandestine and perilous routes.

The ecological crisis is another recent manifestation of how capitalism propels migration. According to statistics by the American Association for the Advancement of Science, by the year 2020 there will be fifty million climate refugees displaced by climate-induced disasters including droughts, desertification, and mass flooding.[34] It is well documented that climate change correlates directly with carbon and greenhouse gas emissions, with the industrialized, consumption-based economies of the United States, Australia, the United Kingdom, and Canada topping in emissions per capita and consumption per capita emissions.[35]

Tuvalu is one of dozens of low-lying Pacific Island nations threatened with total submersion as climate change and global warming cause ocean levels to rise drastically. Since 2007, the government of Tuvalu has been urging countries within the UN Framework Convention on Climate Change in Kyoto and the UN General Assembly to heed the impending disaster in Tuvalu. Over one-fifth of Tuvaluans have already been forced to flee their country, many to poor neighboring islands such as Fiji, and others to New Zealand.[36] Despite having the world's highest emission per capita at 19.6 tons of carbon dioxide per person, Tuvalu's other neighbor, Australia, has so far refused to accept Tuvaluans as climate refugees.[37] Border imperialism again denies justice to migrants who are its own casualties.

The effects of Western colonialism and capitalism have created political economies that compel people to move, and yet the West denies culpability and accountability for displaced migrants. Liz Fekete of the Institute of Race Relations sums up the argument against borderlines that normalize protectionism within the West: "This isn't a separate world. Globalization isn't a separate world. I'm using words like 'First World' [and] 'Third World' as easy ways into this argument, but they're a lie—there is one world and there is one economic system. And that economic system is dominated by Europe, the United States and Japan. This economic system is creating these huge displacements of people, it's rampaging through the world."[38] Border imperialism, marked by forced displacements and precarious migrations from rural peripheries to urban cores as well as within and across state borders, is inextricably linked to the global circulations of capital and Western imperial dictates, even as the West seals itself off from these bodies.

Criminalization and the Carceral Network

> all around, and creeping
> self righteous, let's say it, fascism,
> how else to say, border,
> and the militant consumption of everything,
> the encampment of the airport, the eagerness
> to be all the same, to mince biographies
> to some exact phrases, some
> exact and toxic genealogy.
> —Dionne Brand, "Inventory"

The second defining process of border imperialism is the criminalization of migration and the deliberate construction of migrants as illegals and aliens. The celebrated multiculturalism of Western governments' carefully handpicked (professional elite or investor class) diaspora exists parallel to what migration researcher Peter Nyers terms the "deportspora"—a vastly larger and more diverse group of migrants.[39] According to US Immigration and Customs Enforcement statistics, deportations under President Barack Obama skyrocketed to a total of 1.4 million people.[40] As researcher and author Anna Pratt writes, "Detention and deportation and the borders they sustain are key technologies in the continuous processes that 'make up' citizens and govern populations."[41]

Migrants, particularly undocumented migrants or asylum seekers arriving irregularly, are punished, locked up, and deported for the very act of migration. In order to justify their incarceration, the state has to allege some kind of criminal or illegal act. Within common discourses, the victim of this criminal act is the state, and the alleged assault is on its borders. The state becomes a tangible entity, with its own personhood and boundaries that must not be violated. Butler describes the policing of the state and its national subject as a "relentlessly aggressive" and "masculinist" project.[42] Within this concept of sexualized nationhood, borders are engendered as needing protection, or as cultural theorist Katrina Schlunke puts it, "vulnerable shores that must be kept intact and secured against the threat of un-negotiated penetration by strangers."[43]

By invoking the state *itself* as a victim, migrants *themselves* are cast as illegals and criminals who are committing an act of assault on the state. Migrants become prisoners of passage; their unauthorized migration is considered a trespass, and their very existence is criminalized. In a telling representation, one of the principal detention centers in Canada is the Canadian Immigration Prevention Center (Laval). Migrants are not seen for their actual humanity but instead as a problem to be prevented, deterred, managed, and contained. They become stereotyped by politicians, media, and within popular consciousness as floods of people from "over there" who are "disease ridden," "fraudulent," or "security threats." These narratives buttress moral panics about "keeping borders safe and secure" from poor and racialized migrants.

Migrant detention regimes are a key component of Western state building and its constitutive assertion of border controls. According to research conducted by the Global Detention Project, "Migration-related detention is the practice of detaining—typically on administrative (as opposed to criminal) grounds—asylum seekers and irregular immigrants. . . . Migration detainees often face legal uncertainties, including lack of access to the outside world, limited possibilities of challenging detention through the courts, and/or absence of limitations on the duration of detention."[44]

Practices of incarceration and expulsion, often shared across Western states, demarcate zones of exclusion and mark those deemed undesirable. Philosopher and social theorist Michel Foucault contends that "we should not . . . be asking subjects how, why, and under what right they can agree to being subjugated, but showing how actual relations of subjugation manufacture subjects."[45] The words of Nader, an Iranian asylum seeker held in a Canadian detention center for six years, sheds light on such structures of subjugation: "The length of my detention has not been predicated on any evidence that I am a 'threat to national security' or that my release poses any 'risk to the public safety.' Yet I have endured the psychological trauma of confinement and the emotional suffering and anxiety of being separated from my son, who has since been granted asylum in Canada."[46]

Migrant detention centers are part of the expanding prison system. In the United States, undocumented migrants comprise one of the fastest-growing prison populations with over two hundred detention facilities, representing an 85 percent increase in detention spaces, and approximately three million detentions since 2003.[47] Detained migrant women in the United States report routine abuse by male guards including the shackling of pregnant detainees.[48] Australia's offshoring of detention centers to remote islands and the internationally condemned mandatory-detention-first policy has resulted in an average of three incidents of attempted self-harm per day as well as countless hunger strikes and prison riots.[49] Legal organizations and refugee groups have called this dire situation of six thousand detainees in Australian detention centers "a national emergency."[50] Canada detains approximately nine to fifteen thousand migrants every year, more than one-third of whom are held in provincial prisons.[51] A new Canadian law has introduced mandatory detention for many refugees including children over the age of sixteen. Migrant women in detention in Canada report being denied basic services such as access to translation services that male detainees are provided.

Some miles away, Israel is constructing the world's largest detention center. With a capacity of eight thousand people, this detention center is geared toward the incarceration of Eritrean, Sudanese, and other African asylum seekers who are deemed infiltrators under the recently amended 1954 Prevention of Infiltration Law. For "threatening to change the character of the state," refugees can be detained without trial for a period of three years, and could even be held indefinitely.[52] As part of the Zionist logic to keep Israel an exclusionary national home for Jews, this law was originally intended to imprison Palestinian refugees who were returning to their homes after the 1948 Al-Nakba. The law therefore simultaneously criminalizes Palestinians who defy dispossession and the illegal occupation of their homelands by asserting their right to return, as well as African refugees fleeing Western imperialism and structural poverty. Drawing the links between these parallel forms of expulsion and exclusion, Palestinian commentator Ali Abunimah observes that to Israeli apartheid, "Palestinians and Africans are a 'threat' merely because they live, breathe."[53]

The systemic lens of border imperialism sheds light on how state practices of migrant detention create huge corporate profits. Within weeks of 9/11, Steve Logan, a chief executive of the former prison company Cornell Corporations, which is now owned by GEO Group, told stock analysts, "It's clear that since September 11th there's a heightened focus on detention, both on the borders and in the U.S. . . . What we are seeing is an increased scrutiny of tightening up the borders. . . . More people are going to get caught. So I would say that's positive."[54] Corporations that run private prisons and detention centers made over five billion dollars in combined annual profits in the United States over the past decade. According to Detention Watch Network, five prison corporations that hold contracts with the US Immigration and Customs Enforcement have poured twenty million dollars into lobbying efforts.[55] Arizona's controversial SB 1070, which legalizes racial profiling based on "suspicion of being an illegal immigrant," was drafted during a meeting between state legislators and the Corrections Corporation of America, the largest private prison corporation in the United States.[56]

This is part of what Naomi Klein calls "a privatized security state, both at home and abroad," as she outlines how the War on Terror has maximized profitability for security markets.[57] In this lucrative market of migrant detention and border securitization, the value of Israeli exports in security technologies has almost quadrupled.[58] A notable example is the contract for the border fence between the United States and Mexico going to a consortium of companies including Elbit. One of the world's biggest defense electronics manufacturers and Israel's largest arms manufacturer, Elbit also has a contract for electronic detection along the illegal apartheid wall in Palestine.[59] State securitization of borders and corporate profiting from migrant detentions are the practices of imperial democracies, which postcolonial feminist theorist Chandra Talpade Mohanty describes as those practices that are sustained by "overly militarized, securitized nation states," where "the militarization of cultures is deeply linked to neoliberal capitalist values."[60] The state and capitalism are again in mutual alliance: state criminalization of migrants directly feeds capitalist profits in ever-expanding security markets.

The "tough on illegals" narrative, which justifies increased border patrols, armed border guards, migrant detention, immigration enforcement raids in homes and workplaces, and vigilante programs like the Minutemen in the United States or deportation tip lines in Canada, is not new or unique. Such narratives and material practices are linked to that which predates them, including the "tough on crime" narrative deployed in the 1980s, and the more recent "tough on terror" rhetoric. These discourses have justified the oversurveillance and overincarceration of Indigenous people, black people, sex workers, homeless people, Muslims, and migrants of color.

Largely unnoticed, the imprisonment of women has skyrocketed over the past two decades. As the world's largest jailer, the United States, with only 5 percent of the world's population but 25 percent of the world's prisoners, has increased its incarceration rate of women by 832 percent over three decades.[61] The incarceration rate of black women in the United States has increased by 828 percent over a five-year period, and black women now constitute one-half of the US female prison population.[62] In Western Australia, the number of incarcerated women doubled between the years 1995 and 2001, with Indigenous women comprising 54 percent of the female prisoner population although consituting only 2 percent of the state's population.[63] In Canada, the representation of Indigenous women in prison has increased by nearly 90 percent over the past decade and has been declared "nothing short of a crisis."[64]

Though informed by different logics, the incarceration of all these "undesirables" is interrelated. Migrant detention centers, prisons, secret torture facilities, juvenile detention centers, and interrogation facilities are all part of the growing prison-industrial complex. As former political prisoner and prison abolitionist Angela Davis points out,

> Homelessness, unemployment, drug addiction, mental illness, and illiteracy are only a few of the problems that disappear from public view when the human beings contending with them are relegated to cages. . . . Taking into account the structural similarities of business-government linkages in the realms of military production and public

punishment, the expanding penal system can now
be characterized as a "prison industrial complex."[65]

Foucault further explains the expansion of prisons as the
self-perpetuation of power: the constant creation of prisoners in order for the state to keep exercising coercive and
disciplinary power. He describes this as the carceral network, an inescapable and increasingly internalized network
of "discourses and architectures, coercive regulations and
scientific propositions, real social effects and invincible uto-
pias, programs for correcting delinquents and mechanisms
that reinforce delinquency."[66]

The construction of illegals within border imperialism
is part of a broader logic that constructs deviants in order
to maintain state power, capitalist profiteering, and social
hierarchies. Within mainstream narratives, criminals are
never imagined as politicians, bankers, corporate criminals, or war criminals, but as a racialized class of people
living in poverty. The word criminal becomes synonymous
with dehumanizing stereotypes of ghettos, welfare recipients, drug users, sex workers, and young gang members.
Similarly, the term illegals is imagined as referring to poor
migrants of color, even though many white tourists often
illegally overstay their visas. As Davis writes, "Regardless
of who has or has not committed crimes, punishment,
in brief, can be seen more as a consequence of racialized
surveillance."[67] In North America, we can look to the
countless police killings of Indigenous and black men, such
as Dudley George and Oscar Grant, since the enduring
violences of genocide and slavery, and also the more recent

illegal detentions of over eight hundred Muslim men and boys in Guantanamo Bay to understand that these bodies are disciplined by being cast as suspicious even before any so-called criminal act has been committed.

Therefore, the social control and criminalization that delineates the carceral network and disappears undesirables is the frequently invisible yet entrenched racist colonial belief that incarceration is a legitimate response to communities that are constructed and characterized *innately* as being illegals, deviants, criminals, terrorists, or threats.

Racialized Hierarchies

The third constituent structuring within border imperialism is the racialized hierarchy of national and imperial identity, which anchors and shapes the understanding of citizenship and belonging within the nation-state as well as within the grid of global empire.

Racialization comprises the social, political, economic, and historical processes that utilize essentialist and monolithic racial markings to construct diverse communities of color. Whiteness, as a dominant and dominating structuring that is more than a fixed identity, is able to escape these markings of identity while determining the markings of its racial others. The enduring centrality of whiteness rests in white supremacy, which Challenging White Supremacy Workshop facilitators define as a "historically based, institutionally perpetuated system of exploitation and oppression of continents, nations, and peoples of color by white peoples and nations . . . for the purpose of maintaining and defending a system of wealth, power, and privilege."[68] Language such as "racial equality" and "multicultural diversity" are described by anthropologist Elizabeth Povinelli as the optics of liberal democracies parading "social difference without social consequence," thus becoming effective color-blind cloaks for the maintenance of a racial hierarchy that situates whiteness as pervasive and hegemonic within state building, global empire, and border imperialism.[69]

Racial profiling has received much attention in post-9/11 discourse, but must be understood within the broader phenomenas of global white supremacy and racialization that underwrite border imperialism. Racialization enables the conditions for racial stereotypes to be inscribed onto racialized individuals as an *inherent* marking of their racial community. Yasmin Jiwani of Researchers and Academics of Colour for Equity writes,

> The racialization of these Others is maintained and communicated through a focus on the inferiorization, deviantization and naturalization of difference. While overt and explicit forms of racism are no longer condoned by the liberal state, colour-blind racism permeates institutional rhetoric and through the mediation of inferential referencing, cordial tonality and culturalized modality, focuses on difference as the site of the abject and contemptible.[70]

For example, Islamophobia in the post-9/11 era is predicated on the ability to designate and vilify the "dual"
citizen (such as Arab Canadian or Muslim American) as a
potential terrorist threat, rendering every Muslim, Arab,
and/or South Asian as an eternal other and outsider to
the nation-state. The 2011 massacre in Norway by Anders
Behring Breivik and 2012 shooting by Wade Michael Page
in the Oak Creek gurudwara in Wisconsin were considered
the acts of "lone" white men, rather than an indictment
of whiteness, white supremacy, or right-wing libertar-
ian culture. As commentator Juan Cole derisively blogs,
"White terrorists are random events, like tornadoes. Other
terrorists are long-running conspiracies. White terrorists
are never called 'white.' But other terrorists are given ethnic
affiliations."[71]

Theorist Sherene Razack argues that race thinking not
only depicts racialized people as deserving a different type
of humanity but also constructs them *as* a different type
of humanity.[72] This casting out *within* the nation-state is not
new or unique; it is evident in the experiences of segregation, internment of Japanese Canadians and Japanese
Americans, the War on Drugs, and reserve system. These
lived experiences of otherness are shaped by imaginings
about who is entitled to protection *from* the nation-state
because they represent the national identity, and who faces
violence *by* the nation-state because their bodies are deemed
not to belong. The material structures of the Western
state have killed, tortured, occupied, raped, incarcerated,
sterilized, interned, robbed land from, pillaged, introduced
drugs and alcohol into, stolen children from, sanctioned

vigilante violence on, denied public services to, and facilitated capital's hyperexploitation of racialized communities.

Dangerously, racism is increasingly legitimized through the rhetoric of rights, freedoms, and protections for women. From the earlier "yellow peril" myth that warned of migrant Asian men ensnaring white women with opium to the more contemporary justifications of the occupation of Afghanistan as a mission to liberate Muslim women, such putatively feminist causes have been perennially seductive, and many feminists are implicated in shaping these counters of racialized empire. Postcolonial theorist Gayatri Chakravorty Spivak bluntly portrays the cheerleading of civilizing crusades masked as feminist solidarity as "white men saving brown women from brown men."[73]

Razack notes that three figures have come to symbolize the current War on Terror: the dangerous Muslim man, the imperiled Muslim woman, and the civilized European.[74] This racist and sexist construction is played out ad nauseam in the mainstream media with the dangerous Muslim man embodying the threat that Islam poses to all oppressed Muslim women, who lack the agency to accept or challenge their heterogeneous cultures and religions, and thus must be rescued by progressive white civilization.

The architecture of these representations is an intentional ideology that normalizes racialization and justifies its impacts on racialized bodies. Far from supporting Muslim women, attacks on Islam as innately fundamentalist, conservative, barbaric, and heteropatriarchal have increasingly targeted Muslim women within the West for public scrutiny, hate crimes, and state surveillance. The most palpable example of this is the debates over, and in some cases the laws banning, the niqab throughout North America and Europe, which scholar Juanid Rana describes as a means to "discipline bodies into an imperial racial order."[75] Muslim women's clothing becomes a racialized and gendered marker that immediately identifies their bodies as not only outside the social boundaries of whiteness but also as disruptive to the disciplinary logic of adherence and assimilation to whiteness, along with its acceptable aesthetic of how one clothes the body.

Anxieties about tainting the nation-state's normative heteropatriarchal whiteness are linked to the racist justifications for the violence of economic and military imperialism globally and the violence of settler colonialism locally. The racist denial and violation of Indigenous self-determination is part of the colonial project to, on the one hand, annihilate Indigenous communities through overt violence, and on the other hand, assimilate them through residential boarding schools and legislative control. In Canada, until 1985, Indigenous women who married non-Indigenous men were entirely stripped of their legal status as "Indians" and lost all corresponding rights, such as the rights to live on the reserve, inherit family land, and be buried on reserve land. As Indigenous scholar Bonita Lawrence notes about such racialized and gendered policies of population control, "To be federally recognized as an Indian either in Canada or the United States, an individual must be able to comply with very distinct standards of government regulation."[76]

In addition to sanctioning such state and societal violence within its borders, racism justifies imperialist wars abroad that kill, torture, and displace millions of women, children, and men. Theorist Gargi Bhattacharyya argues that the discourse of racialized empire "enables the cruelty and carnage of imperial adventures—because these people are not like us, are not people at all, and their otherness proves that they are lesser, unworthy, dangerous, and to be contained by any means possible."[77] The logic of racism and inferiority that drives Western imperial wars is inextricably connected to the logic of racism and exclusion within the West. The racialization that anchors national identity and state building therefore comes full circle through an analysis of global racialized empire and border imperialism.

Labor Precarity

> The very act of dividing the earth and the sea surface by tracing borders whether they are physical, virtual, or legal also allows for the appropriation of its resources. However, the resource which borders appropriate is not simply the portioned territory. Rather, it is also the subjective claim of people to freely choose the territory in which to settle and the kind of relation they wish to establish with this territory. In other words, borders transform people's claims to movement into a resource which can be appropriated and exchanged.
>
> —Frassanito Network, "Borders Are There to Be Undermined"

The fourth and final structuring of border imperialism is the legalized, state-mediated exploitation of the labor of migrants by capitalist interests. While workers of color generally contend with underemployment, low wages, and long hours, workers without legal citizenship constitute a distinct category of labor in relation to border imperialism—what author Justin Akers Chacón describes as "displacement accompanied by disenfranchisement and often internal segregation in host countries."[78] Workers without legal citizenship include undocumented/nonstatus workers as well as guest/temporary migrant workers. This section focuses on undocumented workers and migrant workers to draw attention to the constellation of neoliberal globalized capitalism, racialized hierarchies of citizenship, and state building within border imperialism.

The International Labor Organization estimates that there are eighty-six million migrant workers across the world.[79] To highlight one migration pattern, migrant workers are recruited from rural areas in South Asia and Southeast Asia to work in low-wage jobs in the oil economy, domestic sphere, and construction industry in the states of the Gulf Cooperation Council (Bahrain, Kuwait, Oman, Qatar, Saudi Arabia, and the United Arab Emirates). Migrant laborers represent almost 40 percent of the total population in these countries, and in some countries make up to 90 percent of the total population.[80] These workers are rarely granted citizenship despite decades of residency. Additionally, they are forced to live in labor camps; face routine abuse including wage theft and, particularly for domestic workers, sexual violence; and disproportionately face death sentences in countries such as Saudi Arabia that practice the death penalty. Their working conditions are frequently fatal.

In the United Arab Emirates, approximately nine hundred migrant construction workers died in 2004.[81] Sahinal Monir, a migrant worker from Bangladesh in Dubai, told journalist Johann Hari,

> To get you here, they tell you Dubai is heaven. Then you get here and realise it is hell. . . . You have to carry 50 kg bricks and blocks of cement in the worst heat imaginable. . . . You become dizzy and sick but you aren't allowed to stop, except for an hour in the afternoon. You know if you drop anything or slip, you could die. If you take time off sick, your wages are docked. . . . Nobody shows their anger. You can't. You get put in jail for a long time, then deported.[82]

His experience is representative of the precarity of migrant workers within border imperialism: impoverished people forced to migrate to centers of capital in order to survive end up enduring horrific working and living conditions that are supported, and in many cases facilitated, by the state.

In Canada and the United States, migrant workers are most commonly associated with the infamous US Bracero programs of the 1940s to1960s, the current H-2A visa program for agricultural workers in the United States, and Canada's Seasonal Agricultural Worker Program. The labor of these migrant workers has secured billions of dollars in profit for agribusiness and is a major subsidy to the economy. Temporary migrant workers are brought on state visas for short periods of time to work for a specific employer. The indentured nature of these state-mediated migrant worker programs, tying workers to their employers, has been described by workers as a form of modern-day slavery. Workers are paid low (often less than minimum) wages with no overtime pay. They labor long hours in dangerous working conditions, frequently leaving their families behind, and are regularly held captive by employers or contractors who seize their identification documents.[83]

Unlike temporary migrant workers who come on employer-lobbied state visas, undocumented workers have no legal authorization to reside or work in the country, and hence have no (theoretical) legal recourse in the face of violence and exploitation. Migrants, and often their children such as the DREAMer students in the United States, are undocumented either because they crossed the border irregularly, they failed an asylum claim, or their visas expired. It is estimated that there are a half million undocumented people in Canada, and eleven million undocumented people in the United States.[84] Many have worked, studied, lived, and built community in Canada and the United States for generations.

Despite differences in the two legal regimes, a defining characteristic of both is the lack of full and permanent legal status. This lack is exactly what makes the lives of migrant and undocumented workers insecure and precarious. They live in isolation with minimal access to basic social services, despite paying into them through their taxes, and are extremely vulnerable to employer abuse, since any assertion of their labor rights can lead to deportation by the state. As scholar Nandita Sharma argues, "The social organization of those categorized as non-immigrants works to legitimize the differentiation of rights and entitlements across citizen lines by legalizing the indentureship of people classified as migrant workers. . . . Their vulnerability lies at the heart of the flexible accumulation process."[85] In other words, the state denial of legal citizenship to these migrants ensures legal control over the *disposability* of the laborers, which in turn embeds the *exploitability* of their labor.

Despite antimigrant exclusionary rhetoric, it is not in the interests of the state or capital to close down the border to all migrants. Activist and academic David McNally observes that "it's not that global business does not want immigrant labor to the West. It simply wants this labor on its own terms: frightened, oppressed, vulnerable."[86] Consequently, the violence enacted on those bodies that have been *displaced* by imperialist and capitalist foreign and trade policy is further enabled through the deliberate making of migrant and undocumented workers as perpetually *displaceable* by colonial and capitalist immigration and labor policies. The state processes of illegalization of migrant and undocumented workers, through the denial of full legal status that forces a condition of permanent precarity, actually legalizes the trade in their bodies and labor by domestic capital. This strengthens the earlier contention that the state is evolving its structures to protect neoliberal transnational capitalism.

Capitalism's drive to maximize profit requires a constant search for cheap labor and effective mechanisms to control workers. Historian Harold Troper notes that the denial of legal citizenship to temporary migrant and undocumented workers allows states to accumulate domestic capital via the "in-gathering of off-shore labor" in order to compete in the global market.[87] Theorists Carlos Fernandez, Meredith Gill, Imre Szeman, and Jessica Whyte write, "Without the border, there would be no differential zones of labor, no spaces to realize surplus capital through the dumping of overproduction, no way of patrolling surly populations that might want to resist proletarianization, no release valve for speculative access."[88] Migrant and undocumented workers thus are the flip side of transnational capitalist outsourcing, which itself requires border imperialism and racialized empire to create differential zones of labor. These workers represent the ideal workforce, particularly in the recent era of austerity: commodified and exploitable; flexible and expendable.

Migrant and undocumented workers, especially women, are overrepresented in low-wage sectors such as garment and domestic work. Under the Live-In Caregiver Program (LCP) in Canada, for example, predominately Filipina migrant workers enter Canada as domestic workers. They are required to work for twenty-four months within a window of four years in order to qualify for permanent residency. During this period, the women must work only in the home of the employer whose name appears on the work permit. Although the program calls for a maximum in the workweek, the live-in aspect of these jobs allows employers to call on the caregivers at any time.

This exposes the women to labor violations including unpaid or excessive work hours, additional job responsibilities, confiscation of travel documents, disrespect of their privacy, and sexual assault. As one migrant domestic worker remarks, "We know that, under the LCP, we are like modern slaves who have to wait for at least two years to get our freedom."[89] In addition to the supply of cheap labor provided by migrant women under the LCP, the program serves a critical function in the capitalist economy. By facilitating the replacement of domestic labor for middle-class and rich women through the LCP, the state is absolved of the responsibility to create a universal child and elder care program that benefits *all* women and families.

Within border imperialism, migrant and undocumented workers are included in the nation-state in a deliberately limited way, creating a two-tier hierarchy of citizenship. The common naming of migrant workers as foreign, illegal, or temporary automatically signals their nonbelonging. For sociologist Himani Bannerji, these expressions are "certain types of lesser or negative identities" that in actuality are "congealed violence or relations of domination."[90] She reveals how such terminology has little to do with how long these workers have lived and worked within the nation-state; rather, it signals their permanent positioning on the bottom rungs of the socioeconomic ladder. The noncitizen status of these workers *guarantees* that they fall outside the realm of the state's obligations; they can be paid less than minimum wage, prevented from accessing social services, and deported during recessions without the elite having to worry about unemployment rates or social unrest. For this underclass, their selective inclusion within the nation-state as well as legal (un) national identity as foreign or temporary normalizes the status of their unfree labor and exclusion from the state's regime of rights.

The noncitizen status of undocumented and migrant workers also makes them vulnerable to abuse and stigma within society. Poor and working-class people are socialized through the media to view these workers as "stealing jobs" and "flooding neighborhoods," a divide-and-conquer strategy that Saket Soni of the New Orleans Worker Justice Coalition describes as "wedge" politics that pits people against migrant workers.[91] Sharma similarly expresses this when she comments, "Categories of legality and illegality are therefore deeply ideological. They help to conceal the fact that both those represented as foreigners and those seen as Canadian work within the *same* labour market and live within the *same* society."[92]

The classification of migrant workers as foreign, which embeds labor exploitability, is concurrently maintained through racialization. As noted earlier, people of color are already otherized within the Western nation-state, especially within settler-colonial states where whiteness has been necessary for the state's foundation. Subjugation and exploitation are normalized against those marked as racial outsiders, and then even more so against those legally branded as foreigners. As noted by political scientists Gargi Bhattacharyya, John Gabriel, and Stephen Small,

"Capitalist expansion has depended so heavily on mytholo-
gies of race and their attendant violences that the double
project of racial economic subjugation is a constitutive
aspect of this expansion."[93] Racialization within capitalism
is therefore cyclic. Racism is itself a structuring discourse of
both the labor market and the regime of citizenship, and is
also an effect of the interrelationship between the state and
the social, political, and economic segmentation of labor.

While media panics attribute large numbers of noncitizens to a "broken" immigration system, Western policy-
makers are touting the legalized exploitation and racism of
migrant worker programs as the model of the future. These
programs are a form of managed migration that fulfills
capitalism's needs for cheap labor, while concurrently
retaining the racialized national identity of the nation-state
by legally disenfranchising migrant workers. Therefore,
within border imperialism, the state-capital nexus relies on
the apartheid nature of citizenship status to expand a pool
of disposable migrant and undocumented labor that lowers
the wage floor for capitalist interests without disturbing the
normative whiteness of the nation-state.

A Counternarrative

1,950 mile-long open wound
    dividing a pueblo, a culture,
    running down the length of my body,
    staking fence rods in my flesh,
    splits me, splits me

me raja me raja
This is my home
this thin edge of
barbwire.
—Gloria Anzaldúa, *Borderlands La Frontera:*
The New Mestiza

Border imperialism can be understood as creating and reproducing global mass displacements and the conditions necessary for the legalized precarity of migrants, which are inscribed by the racialized and gendered violence of empire as well as capitalist segregation and differential segmentation of labor. As I have described in this chapter, within the matrix of racialized empire and neoliberal capitalism, border imperialism is underwritten by, first, the free flow of capitalism and dictates of Western imperialism that create displacements, while simultaneously securing Western borders against the very people who capitalism and empire have displaced; second, the process of criminalizing migrants through their construction as deviants and illegals, which also ensures profits for companies that receive contracts for border militarization and migrant detention; third, the entrenchment of a racialized national and imperial identity with its gendered contours that has specific embodied and material impacts locally as well as globally; and fourth, the legal denial of permanent residency to a growing number of migrants to ensure an exploitable, marginalized, and expendable pool of labor.

The constant imagining of the nation-state—the ideology of "who belongs"—is best understood within the context of border imperialism and its linkages to the incessant violences of both global racialized empire and the transnational circulation of capital. The physical, social, discursive, and metaphoric dimensions of border imperialism have an undeniable effect in producing a two-tiered apartheid system of citizenship. As Anzaldúa, a queer Chicana feminist, declares, "Borders and walls that are supposed to keep the undesirables out are entrenched habits and patterns of behavior"—an emphatic call to reject the social landscapes and material complexes of exclusion and domination.[94]

Over the past century, the universalization and proliferation of the Western state as the defining political institution as well as citizenship as the defining political community is a consequence of Western imperialism. European powers drew arbitrary borders, dividing communities in order to serve political and economic interests. It is therefore critical to challenge state-centric framings, such as "Immigrants are American too" or "Refugees want to enjoy the freedoms of Canada," that buttress the legitimacy of the state and its illegitimate foundations in settler colonialism, imperialism, capitalism, and oppression. Such framings rely on a regime of state-sanctioned rights, state-perpetuated myths of tolerance and benevolence, and state-enforced assimilation into racialized social formations. Additionally, these framings invisibilize the nature of the neoliberal state as the political and legal jurisdiction that allows for the expansion of capitalism. Finally, they obfuscate the state's role in perpetuating social, economic, and political violence, including the incarceration and expulsion of those migrants deemed "undeserving." As Balibar reminds us, we must critically question "what the state is tending to become, how it is behaving, and what functions it is fulfilling."[95]

In contrast to state-centric framings of migrant justice, two of the most popular slogans within radical migrant justice movements are "We didn't cross the border, the border crossed us" and "No one is illegal, Canada is illegal." These slogans reflect an understanding of border imperialism as a key pillar of global apartheid, and borders as cartographies of anticapitalist, antiracist, anticolonial, and antioppressive struggles. As geographers Henk Van Houtum, Olivier Thomas Kramsch, and Wolfgang Zierhofer depict it, a "border is not so much an object or a material artefact as a belief, an imagination that creates and shapes a world, a social reality."[96]

A systemic analysis of borders, as sites of both the diffusion and concentration of power, informs the basis of NOII's transnational anticapitalist, antiracist, anticolonial, and antioppression analysis: the freedom to stay and resist systemic displacement, the freedom to move in order to flourish with dignity and equality, and the freedom to return to dispossessed lands and homes. NOII movements, described in subsequent chapters, challenge the social Darwinian constructions of good/desirable/real migrant (read: English-speaking, employed, and/or conforming to heteropatriarchal norms) versus bad/undesirable/bogus migrant (read: unemployed, without formal education, and/or with a criminal record). Such dichotomies reinforce state controls on self-determination, strengthen the capitalist exploitation of labor, and maintain social hierarchies based on race, class, gender, sexuality, and ability.

Instead, the expansive vision of NOII-Vancouver (Indigenous Coast Salish territories) is as follows: "We envision and actively strive for a humanity where everyone has the right to sustenance and the ability to provide it, where we are free of oppression, misery, and exploitation, and are able to live meaningfully in relationship to one another and in reverence for Mother Earth that sustains us."[97] Or in the words of Gungalidda elder Wadjularbinna, who articulates a similar global vision of undoing border imperialism through collective solidarities and responsibilities to each other rather than to the state or systems of power: "Before Europeans came here illegally, in the Aboriginal world we were all different, speaking different languages, but we all had the same kinship system for all human beings, in a spiritual way. Our religion and cultural beliefs teaches us that everyone is a part of us and we should care about them. We can't separate ourselves from other human beings—it's a duty."[98]

The Door of No Return

Everyone in my family has run from something. Some of us run halfway across the world. Crossing a border's less like a family secret and more like a family tradition. Filling out paperwork, getting an immigration sponsorship, pretending we were 99 percent white, and flirting or saying "yes, ma'am" to the guard—all that stuff came to my family as natural as tears and sweat. Easy. It wasn't that far a leap from my grandparents sneaking into White Australia for to me to decide to leave America, Giuliani, and $4.25 minimum wages for Canada in 1996.

> *It's time, girl.*
> Time for what?
> *Time to be free.*

When you apply for Canadian immigration through marriage, your sponsor has to sign an undertaking that for the next ten years they're financially responsible for you. You can't go on welfare, you can't really go on disability. The government makes sure immigrants don't get to use any of the lovely Canadian social safety net that your taxes pay for. A lot of husbands tell their wives that that means they can't get divorced, telling them if they leave they will be deported. There's a law that makes that illegal, but the system doesn't always pay attention to it and the women don't always know. When my partner signs the undertaking, I know it is a problem but I also don't have an alternative.

Lining up in the snow. A line of migrants snaking
out of the downtown immigration office when it was still
on Dundas Street. Line out the door from before when it
opened, but I was sick so I never got there before two or
three. Long line of people afraid, clutching forms, talking
softly in our own languages. Mean-ass barking lady telling
us to speak up, telling us, "I DON'T UNDERSTAND
YOUR ACCENT, DO YOU SPEAK ENGLISH?" Hour
or two wait, me English speaking and American citizenship, but brown skinned, poor and queer and sick, and they
still gave me the wrong form two or three times. That long
line of pain and fear.

Soon they would move the office out to Etobicoke and
strongly encourage everyone to shift to calling the 1-800
lines instead, so no one working or living downtown had to
see the physical face of immigration, so we couldn't see each
other, just alone waiting on the damn hold on the 1-800
number. I remember taking four buses out to Mississauga
to the immigration consultant, who took a hundred bucks
from us to explain the forms and tell us where to sign.

Sometime later, two winters and a spring and summer
and two falls of poverty, off the books, shoveling snow,
handing out flyers, landscaping paid in cash, packing food
for the Afri-Can food basket in exchange for tokens and
a meal and a big food box, a huge amount of bulk food I
bought via a credit card scam, and living off the rice and
dhal and falafel mix that I had told the health food store
was for a new chapter of Food Not Bombs, I get that
narrow faded piss-yellow letter in the mail from immigration. The one that says I am landed in principle. Then the

one that says I need to show up at the immigration center at 8:00 a.m. on a certain day. When I talked about how hard it was and how broke we were, I remember my lover's mother saying, "But you know, it won't always be that way." I could see her remembering being just like us—twenty-two, broke, and immigrant. And here it was, that day. The day when things were no longer quite so hard. The day when I got a health insurance card, a social insurance number, the ability to rise out of the basement apartment to that world I'd been looking at through a smeared window.

When the postcard with the date and time showed up, I got up early. Dressed in my least patched-up best and took the subway all the way to Kipling to get there on time. The waiting room was that shit-diarrhea yellow of all institutional waiting rooms, filled with folks who looked just like some variation of me. The ones who had finally made it. When my name was called, I went to my Plexiglas cubicle. The lady there looked at my forms, and then looked at me. She handed me a long pale piss-yellow form through the slot. It said "FAMILY CLASS LANDED IMMIGRANT STATUS" on it.

I looked at her. "Um, this is the wrong one. I'm supposed to have a Humanitarian and Compassionate." I had gotten my free counselor in the partner abuse program to fill out all the forms and write a support letter so I wouldn't be bound to my partner and the undertaking for the next decade. I was still looking over my shoulder every time I left the house.

"Dear, I don't see anything about that. What do you mean?"

"Humanitarian and Compassionate. It's for when your sponsor was abusive."

"Well, dear, I'm not seeing anything about that here. And I have your landed. Do you want it or not?" She paused. "Dear. Don't break up a marriage over something like that."

What could I do? I had been waiting for this, this piece of paper. The one that would open the door to doctors and jobs, tax returns and bank accounts, ID and health insurance cards, a maybe easier time at the Greyhound border crossing. I nodded.

BAM. Stamp on the passport. Coveted, coveted document stapled into coveted, coveted passport. "Take the elevator downstairs, you can get your SIN number and OHIP application there."

I was silent. I'd passed through. But what now?

—Leah Lakshmi Piepzna-Samarasinha

Enemy Alien

My family was interned in Greenwood, British Columbia, in 1942, along with twelve hundred other Japanese Canadians. We lost our hardware store, home, and all our possessions. My mother was pregnant with her seventh of twelve children. After surviving the harsh conditions of a labor camp in a neighboring town, my father was allowed to move back to Greenwood. My father became a trouble-shooter for Japanese Canadians, and fought hard to get shelter and health care for the community. My mother's refuge was her beautiful vegetable and fruit garden, and we grew up eating all fresh vegetables and fruits before organic was fashionable. We grew up poor, but my mother's cooking nurtured my body and soul. It was through experiencing the survival and struggles that my family endured that I naturally learned about political activism.

There is sadness and grief when I think of the internment's negative impact on my family; it created so much dysfunction in our family. My father was very angry and bitter about the internment and having to work in a sawmill for the rest of his years after having his hardware store confiscated. During and after the internment, his political activism supporting the Japanese Canadian community meant he was neglecting his family.

Growing up, we experienced many incidences of racism—for example, having to attend Catholic school. Then at public school in grade three, I was asked to read a textbook that had the word "Jap" in it. I refused to do it. I was detained after school, and the teacher came in every half hour asking me to apologize. I asked her to apologize instead. I told her that my parents had taught me that "Jap" was a bad word. I was sent home with a note saying I was "insolent." My father read the note, slapped me across the face, and told me that I was stupid for defying authority and that this could be dangerous. However, I was proud of standing up for myself. When I was ten years old, I had to fight off three white girls with a baseball bat because they bullied me unmercifully about my eyes and the food I ate. When I was older, there was a lot of discrimination in the workforce. I worked at a garment sweatshop, putting darts in dresses, and as an elevator operator.

I am a firm believer that protest and political dissent are necessary. In the 1970s and 1980s, I got involved in the redress movement for Japanese Canadians to seek justice for us being labeled "enemy aliens," forcibly expelled from the West Coast, and interned from the year 1942 until 1949. The federal government finally redressed us with monetary compensation and an apology on September 1988. When we were fighting the federal government for redress and an official apology, it was the *sanseis* (third generation) who were able to keep up the struggle because the *niseis* (second generation) were silenced by the internment experience. Internalized racism and fear has paralyzed and killed their spirit. Sometimes I get frustrated with them and their apathetic silence, but I think that the internalized racism is like a nail in their heart. Pulling out that nail is more painful, but we have to do it in order to heal.

—Lily Yuriko Shinde

Grassroots Wet'suwet'en

Ancient oral histories and contemporary archaeological evidence trace our presence on Wet'suwet'en lands to more than thirteen thousand years ago. Over all these years, our people have protected the integrity of our lands. Since the first invader fur traders made their way into our territories, we have faced down the illegal occupation of our lands. We dealt with biological disease epidemics deliberately forced on us through the Hudson Bay Company's smallpox blankets. The economic disease of capitalism was the next wave of destruction to sweep through our territories. The commodification of all the Creator's creatures skewed the worldview of the Wet'suwet'en, including our matrilineal form of government, and began to feed the sorrowful process of spiritually disconnecting us from our natural world. We were further overrun by arrogant missionaries who were hell-bent on opening the way for miners of the gold rush, loggers, and settlers wanting to exploit the lush lands and precious resources of our ancestors. Many of our communities were quickly converted to Christianity and adopted subservient attitudes.

The next hundred years brought the forced incarceration of our people into the first federal Indian reservations. Our people speak of starvation, and begging from a police officer for special permits to leave the reservation. The children were then taken from their homes and placed into distant Indian residential schools, where many were raped, psychologically manipulated, and brutally killed by priests and nuns, who in the name of God were intent on killing the Indian. A new railroad was also forced on to our lands and brought with it further droves of white men who roamed on what they saw as unoccupied lands. Any resistance from my people at that time meant quick imprisonment.

The second half of the twentieth century brought an acceleration of resource extraction. Equity Silver Mine, for example, has killed entire ecosystems. Similarly, the southern territories of the Unist'ot'en and Likhts'amisyu clans of the Wet'suwet'en were flooded for a hydroelectric project. Habitat that nurtured seemingly unlimited natural resources was turned into wastelands. Today, the Wet'suwet'en are faced with even more forced industrialization. Pipeline companies are lining up to force their way from the fracking fields of the Peace River area and tar sands of the Athabasca region to the coastal community. The international markets that hope to be the recipients of the oil and gas rush are pouring unimaginable amounts of funds into the pockets of corrupt governments and Indigenous leadership as well as deliberately ignorant settler populations.

Thankfully, beneath the layers of Westernized rule there remain many grassroots people who remember their old teachings; they remember the stories, songs, and dances; they remember the hopes and dreams of those who fell victim to the first diseases; they remember that they are still warriors. In Wet'suwet'en country, the grassroots warriors are the "Lhe Lin Liyin." We are committed to stopping all pipelines, and working closely with others who fight the injustices of illegitimate governments and multinational corporations. The Lhe Lin Liyin will win, like so many of our ancestors before us. Alongside people around the world, we will win this war waged on our Mother Earth.

—Toghestiy, Mel Bazil, and Freda Huson

Chronologies

Chronologies
with no purpose
just dates upon dates and dates
to remind us we once existed over There.
Years are only names for massacres
48
67
2013 and waiting
the dead are numbered
listed, graphed, mapped
and clustered in phosphorus
wrapped neatly in statistic for the evening news

2013 and waiting
long enough in visa lines
to carve out a home of fake smiles and documents
to know I am from There and unwanted anywhere else.
The There they accuse us of
The There of stories told in shelters in Beirut
by grandparents
voices trembling
not knowing if they will see There again.
"the Oranges There taste different, *ya benti*"

2013 and waiting
to negotiate or not negotiate
to apologize for our own Nakba
accept exile and pray forgetfulness

and be "practical" child
be "pragmatic" child
"the refugees are the last stumbling block"
so they negotiate us away
"they will never let you return" child
as if we need permission to be from There
or had a choice to be from somewhere else.

2013 and waiting
for another boat to break another siege
for mothers to make miracles raising children
only on water and lentils and no shoes for school
for some to let us be human and work
others to just let us be.
Palestinian and return.

There will be more boats
I will sit in one—curled up in a memory
that still smells of lead and concrete
my children will learn to play
by a beach in Yaffa, they will tell stories
of how long we waited
to come back There.
2013 and waiting.

—Rafeef Ziadah

Seeking Refuge

Fear, silence, distrust, isolation, mental distress, poverty, debts, helplessness, sleepless nights, and self-doubt—these are the characteristics of being a refugee in Canada. I am a Mexican writer and journalist, but I could be a Palestinian refugee running from violence and occupation, or a Latin American migrant farmworker who has had to leave her motherland because of starvation-level poverty. My husband and I came in 2008 to Vancouver as refugees after I uncovered corruption in the federal cultural institution in Mexico. I fled harassment, intimidation, and death threats.

When I arrived, as is the situation for many refugee claimants, I looked for support through agencies. My husband and I had to wait a long time to get a temporary work permit; it was even harder trying to find a job. We were struggling to adapt to Canadian society, and spent our time volunteering while juggling bureaucratic requirements for immigration and preparing our case. We hired a lawyer who said my evidence was strong enough to meet the strict test in Canada and that I would get protection. But soon I realized how difficult it was; I think I can better describe it as *torment*.

After almost two years, while I was six-months pregnant, we faced our hearing at the Refugee Protection Division in front of a female judge and a tribunal officer. I will never forget the scene: the so-called honorable judge was yawning and drinking coffee, and the tribunal officer was sarcastically questioning our credibility and doubting the validity of our fears. The tribunal officer kept trying to paint Mexico as a "safe place" where President Felipe Calderon provides "safety to his citizens." To these immigration officials, Mexico is just what they see on a tourist leaflet with beautiful beaches and delicious food. Our lawyer could not even finish presenting our case because the judge asked him to send the arguments via mail!

We received a negative decision on our refugee claim in June 2010. We jumped through a few more bureaucratic hoops, and then we decided to make our situation public in 2011. At the time, I was pregnant with my second daughter and had just published my book *El talento de los farsantes* (The Talent of Charlatans). I solicited the help of friends and organizations in the Latin American community, such as Latino Soy and Vancouver South Cultural Project. I also read about an organization called No One Is Illegal that was helping immigrants and refugees. The course of our struggle changed when my family and I were supported by them. With their help, we organized a public support campaign and press conference. It was then and there that we finally defeated the internalized fear to talk about our life and pending deportation.

We captured media attention and the attention of immigration authorities, and almost two months later we were accepted to remain on Humanitarian and Compassionate grounds. We are the lucky ones, but we could have been one of the tens of thousands of families deported each year by the Canada Border Services Agency.

—Karla Lottini

CARTOGRAPHY OF NO ONE IS ILLEGAL

Cartography of NOII

Walls turned on their sides are bridges.
　　—graffiti on the US-Mexico border wall

In 2005, Ali Reza Monemi was detained by immigration enforcement in Vancouver and faced deportation within the week. Members of his family, the International Federation of Iranian Refugees, and NOII announced an indefinite hunger strike until his release. For four days, in subzero temperatures, over twenty hunger strikers and hundreds of supporters camped outside the immigration offices. Less than twelve hours prior to his scheduled deportation, Ali was granted a stay. During a victory rally, his elderly mother chanted, "Stop the Deportations! No One Is Illegal."[1] The next year, Farah Kulmiyeh Abdil, an HIV-positive Somali refugee living in limbo for sixteen years and under a deportation order, chained himself to the Immigration and Refugee Board headquarters in Montreal. Supported by migrant justice activists, he declared his refusal to be invisible.[2] These specific struggles connect to a broader NOII movement that actively confronts border imperialism through the individual as well as collective power of defiance, subversion, and prefiguration.

NOII groups were initiated in Canada during heightened racist national hysteria and escalating attacks on immigrant and refugee communities after the incidents of September 11, 2001. The first NOII group formed that year in Montreal. Groups have since formed in Calgary, Halifax, Kingston, London, Toronto, Ottawa, Winnipeg, Vancouver, Victoria, and Quebec City. NOII is concurrently an ideological framework to counter border imperialism, as described in the previous chapter, and an extended network of grassroots migrant justice groups without any overarching centralization, "rooted in anticolonial, anticapitalist, ecological justice, Indigenous self-determination, anti-occupation, and antioppressive communities."[3]

NOII organizing practices are founded on a commitment to interconnected analysis and a political vision aimed at growing resistance beyond our own organizational boundaries. This means that although migrant justice is our emphasis, NOII groups are more than a single-issue group. NOII movement building takes place with an understanding that NOII is inherently a part of other movements, and vice versa. NOII groups have been pivotal in contributing to anticapitalist, Indigenous solidarity, feminist, antioppression, Palestinian self-determination, and workers movements. The relationships between NOII and these varied movements are not simply those of parallel allied movements; rather, they are linked and interwoven in a web of movements. Another critical strength of NOII groups is the emphasis on empowering and supporting organizers from immigrant and racialized backgrounds. The personal experience of racialization and colonialism becomes a site for enacting movement leadership. Our lived experiences and political analysis provides a critical foundation to anchor mobilizing efforts and through which to envision the nature of solidarities across communities.

Sustaining a connection between the daily grind of community organizing and broader Left struggles is necessary in order to maintain an expansive political perspective and to stay inspired. These connections are fostered across multiple layers and are a testament to the strength of NOII groups. First, we operate within migrant communities to raise awareness about the impact of immigration policies, and provide support for those facing detention and deportation. Second, we organize in a network of service providers, legal organizations, academics, and community groups that are part of a more mainstream immigrant rights movement that tends to organize against specific policies and for specific reforms. We are also part of a network of anticolonial Indigenous solidarity groups that prioritize responsibility to Indigenous land defense movements. In addition, NOII groups mobilize within the broader Left to strengthen the linkages between the migrant justice movement and antiwar, student, labor, antipoverty, and environmental justice movements by highlighting the disproportionate impact of war, austerity, and environmental degradation on displaced, Indigenous, and migrant communities. Finally, we are active within the antiauthoritarian Left that identifies with principles of anticapitalism, anti-imperialism, and direct action.

This chapter serves as both an observation of NOII's strongest movement-based practices and an illumination of strategies that are useful for other radical social movements within North America to consider. It is a reflection of NOII's commitment to five key movement-based practices: community organizing and antioppressive leadership through direct support work, advocating status for all migrants and prefiguring safe spaces for undocumented migrants, building broad alliances toward a systemic abolition of the security apparatus, the centrality of Indigenous self-determination within anticolonial migrant justice struggles, and strengthening anticapitalist resistance. These five forms of praxis provide useful insights for other social movement organizers.

To begin with, I examine the concept of direct support, which ensures that our campaigns are informed by antioppression practice and the experiences of migrants impacted by the systems we confront. The second formulation is the Status for All campaign that pushes for a regularization program for all migrants without full legal status. Demanding status for all and creating zones of safety for nonstatus migrants is a tangible way to articulate our rejection of, and simultaneously prefigure alternatives to, border imperialism. I then discuss the campaign to abolish security certificates. Although this campaign is not led by NOII, NOII groups are heavily involved in shaping its trajectory. One of the persistent questions for movement organizers is how to strike a balance between maintaining a principled message while working with groups that may not share our full analysis. The campaign to abolish security certificates provides some critical insights into this dilemma.

Next I consider NOII's long-standing priority to ally with Indigenous struggles for self-determination. I argue that as migrants of color, taking up our end of the responsibility to dismantle settler colonialism on the lands we now reside on is necessary in the fight against border imperialism and the move toward decolonization. The final practice I explore is the role that NOII has played in integrating local community resistance within broader anticapitalist movements. The chapter ends with a brief sketch of some of the specific events, actions, and initiatives undertaken as part of these five key movement-based practices and strategies.

A few acknowledgments about the limits of this chapter are necessary. The radical migrant justice movement includes a diverse range of community groups and campaigns. I remember one of the first meetings of NOII-Montreal at the Immigrant Workers Center (IWC) with older Filipino immigrant and labor activists. In Vancouver, Direct Action against Refugee Exploitation predated NOII and brought together primarily women of color to organize against mass detentions. In Toronto, the Ontario Coalition against Poverty, Headsup Collective, and Project Threadbare mobilized against antiterror arrests and deportations prior to the formation of NOII in that city. This chapter is not an analysis of this wide-ranging migrant justice movement. Given the highly decentralized and heterogeneous nature of NOII organizing, this chapter is not intended to supply any kind of definitive history of NOII either. Rather, this chapter revolves around my involvement in the migrant justice movement as a current member of NOII-Vancouver (Indigenous Coast Salish territories) and previous member of NOII-Montreal. The strength of this chapter comes from an analysis based on actual experience and active participation as opposed to an abstract sociological study of the entire movement.

Direct Support Work

Over the past decade, NOII has fought against hundreds of cases of detention and deportation. Direct support work is a daily aspect of NOII's community organizing, and encompasses the practical advocacy needed to defend migrants from detention, deportation, immigration enforcement raids, and other forms of control and exploitation. The concept of direct support work in Canada can largely be attributed to the Ontario Coalition against Poverty, which uses direct action casework to effectively protect low-income people from landlords and social assistance bureaucracies. Responding to lived realities, NOII's support work involves drafting legal submissions, coordinating group delegations to immigration offices, providing child care, mobilizing court support, raising funds, hosting press conferences, running errands, organizing public actions, and offering emotional support. Many migrants we have supported over the years have been torn from their communities and violently deported; many others have won their fight to stay.

As she mentioned in her "Seeking Refuge" narrative, Lottini, a Mexican refugee in Vancouver, recently won her fight to stay based on a campaign by NOII. She spoke to media about the values that motivated how support work was organized for her: "I respect NOII very much—they acted very quickly. They worked fast, and were very organized. It wasn't just a relationship of sending memos or just writing letters. We talked and reviewed our words until midnight some nights. They came and brought me a lot of food. I have two daughters to care for. It goes beyond organization or community work—that's love and it's very human."[4]

Direct support work is based on five tenets that Lottini alludes to. Direct support is premised on the notion that supporting people in fighting for their most basic needs, especially to live in safety, is necessary in advancing the struggle. Second, the practice of antioppression encourages people with privilege to take on tangible responsibilities in ensuring a more dignified survival for those without full immigration status. Even though many of us, as racialized immigrants, come with our own histories of border imperialism, we recognize that we must offer support to those migrants who are currently caught within the system's tentacles. The third tenet is to mobilize on the basis of solidarity not charity, which means that support is mobilized alongside rather than on behalf of people. Chris Ramsaroop of Justice for Migrant Workers has often reminded well-intentioned activists who want to work with migrant workers to listen to the workers and their own articulations of their needs and demands.[5]

Direct support work also encourages us to name and confront political systems in order to break through the psychological isolation that is intended to silence, blame, shame, and ultimately disempower people. Direct actions such as group delegations or disruptions of bureaucracies are key processes to flip from the internalized logic of being an "ungrateful" or "unworthy" migrant to laying the blame squarely on the system of border controls. Finally, direct support is explicitly political, and part of a process of empowerment, consciousness-raising, and movement building. Migrant justice organizer Sarita Ahooja notes the critical difference between social worker or nongovernmental organization (NGO) models of service provision and NOII's models, where support work "is done as part of a long-term struggle for a radical restructuring of society."[6]

A persistent question has been how to keep support work politicized, and avoid its devolution into a form of radical social or paralegal work that off-loads responsibility from the welfare state and paid service providers on to volunteer community activists. In my experience, the most powerful forms of support work are those that are part of political campaigns that force the struggles of migrants into the public realm and thus ignite the spirit of resistance rather than replicate a dynamic of charity. In Montreal between 2003 and 2006, self-organized committees of refugees in alliance with NOII activists laid the terrain for monumental victories and provided an inspirational model for the migrant justice movement. The Action Committee of Nonstatus Algerians, the Coalition to Stop the Deportation of Palestinian Refugees, and the Pakistani

Action Committee against Racial Profiling all had similar demands to stop the deportations of their members and to regularize their legal status as permanent residents. In Vancouver in 2004, Refugees against Racial Profiling likewise brought together groups of refugees to collectively organize against deportations.

Emerging from invisibility and breaking the silence, these refugees and nonstatus migrants regularly spoke to media and at community events. They gave voice to the violence of living with precarity and in poverty. These committees utilized a number of strategies and tactics: general assemblies, weekly pickets, mass mobilizations including coordinated national days of action, lobbying, delegations to immigration offices, women- and children-led marches (the Action Committee of Nonstatus Algerians and the Pakistani Action Committee against Racial Profiling both had active women's committees), educational forums, press conferences, occupations, legal advocacy, taking sanctuary in churches in defiance of deportation orders, and more.

In an astounding victory, after nine months of meetings, petitions, educational forums, workshops, demonstrations that brought thousands to the streets, delegations to immigration offices, and a family taking sanctuary in a Montreal church, Immigration Canada and Immigration Quebec announced the regularization of a large majority of the nonstatus Algerians. This regularization program, however, excluded many, including those who lived outside the province of Quebec and those with any criminal record. In a gesture of solidarity that rejected state divisions, many of the nonstatus Algerian activists who qualified for the regularization program continued to mobilize for full regularization alongside those who were still excluded. They campaigned to ensure that those who lived outside the province or had criminal records were not left behind.[7]

These collective committees of refugees and nonstatus migrants were pathbreaking for several reasons. They brought together migrants who were able to share their collective experience and build strength in numbers to organize against detentions and deportations. Given that the inherent nature of the system serves to individualize one's experiences, the process of coming together is crucial in and of itself. These committees also stressed the necessity of political struggle and furthered a systemic analysis of the violence of border controls, while also fighting to stop individual deportations. As nonstatus Algerian activist Mohamed Cherfi often stated, "We need to be radical. That is the best way we are going to grow and be effective."[8] Finally, these committees were able to build mass mobilizations and disruptive resistances by fostering multiracial and multilingual alliances among diverse migrant communities as well as among labor unions, antiwar groups, anticapitalists, women's centers, and others.

This powerful organization of those directly impacted working in alliance with migrant justice activists became a primary model that was replicated for several years. Several weaknesses started to become apparent, though. As some people won status, while others were deported or began to feel defeated, the weight of facilitating organization among groups of migrants became tremendous. As someone who was involved in daily support work for the Pakistani Action

Committee against Racial Profiling in Montreal and
Refugees against Racial Profiling in Vancouver, it became
evident to me that organizing among people in different
phases of the legal process was generally perceived as a
burden by those just trying to survive. Collective organization was most possible in the case of the Action Committee
for Nonstatus Algerians because all those involved were
simultaneously affected by the same legal regime; the lifting
of a five-year moratorium on Algerian deportations in May
2002 meant that thousands of Algerians all faced deportation at the same time. There were no legal avenues left and
collective political action was the only available recourse.
Collective organization was also most powerful in the case
of the Action Committee for Nonstatus Algerians because
it was the first of the committees to form, and so delegations, mass protests, and taking sanctuary had political
punch. The more routinely these strategies were used, the
more predictable they became to the authorities. Their
effectiveness was lost; sanctuary cases dragged on for years,
immigration offices shut down to prevent delegations,
police were increasingly used to repress and deter.

Political organizing requires us to assess changes in
conditions and adapt accordingly. Direct support work
should be seen less as a definitive model and more as a
system of values to guide how we work alongside those
facing deportation. In its most potent form, support work
is expressed through the organization and mobilization
of thousands of migrants joining forces to subvert border
imperialism. But it also takes the form of patiently organizing alongside migrants and offering support—ranging from

emotional to legal support—to break isolation and shame, and instead affirm dignity and choice. Since 2006, most of NOII's support work takes this individualized form. In many cases, public campaigns have developed around these cases of detention or deportation. Stopping one deportation at a time makes a significant difference in people's lives and helps build movement morale.

An example of a public campaign focused on fighting an individual deportation was the struggle to prevent the deportation of Laibar Singh, a paralyzed refugee from India. Between 2007 and 2008, NOII-Vancouver (Indigenous Coast Salish territories) organized intensely including speaking daily on Punjabi radio shows, writing commentaries in multilingual newspapers, building alliances at campus and union meetings, leafleting at gurudwaras to connect with other immigrants, coordinating national days of action, facilitating community meetings and debates, and lobbying. We did all this while navigating complicated dynamics of gender, caste, class, and community protocols within the South Asian community. The latter included, for example, conversations with some allies who were also staunchly antireligion about respecting the gurudwara, a space that we were entering into to show support and seek guidance from, and therefore should not be railing against while present there.

I remember feeling squeezed from all directions: racist diatribes in the mainstream media that personally attacked me, Punjabi businesspeople denouncing me for "ruining the community's image," aunties telling me that I should step aside and "leave this work to the men," white supremacists showing up and threatening me at my workplace. NOII organizers felt that the odds were stacked against us because few people seemed supportive of an irregularly arrived refugee with a permanent disability. Given the campaign's highly polarized nature, a few NOII organizers of color also received numerous death threats. Yet we persisted—unsure of whether our strategies were helping or hindering and tentative about what to expect, but knowing that community organizing is often messy yet always necessary.

One of these messy debates was on the issue of how to work with (or not work with) the few politicians who were jumping on board with the campaign. It was obvious that they were just using the campaign as an opportunity to gain votes within the South Asian community, but they were also our primary access point within government to receive crucial updates. NOII agreed to not invite politicians to any events that we were taking the lead on, but we would not block the decisions of other community groups to invite them as part of the campaign. We also made a calculated decision for some NOII members to maintain channels of communication with these politicians, and other NOII members to actively speak against them and condemn their opportunism. This was a risky strategy and could easily have led to politicians breaking away from the campaign, but we assessed that the stakes were too high for these politicians. More fundamentally, we felt that although lobbying politicians was a necessary strategy for our support campaign, to do so without a simultaneous and vocal critique of that same system was antithetical to our principles.

After months of such intense internal consternation and external scrutiny on top of day-to-day mobilizing, we were stunned when two thousand people, mostly Punjabi elders and aunties, showed up at the Vancouver International Airport to create a blockade preventing the deportation. Many of the aunties who had previously chastised me were suddenly telling me how proud they were that a South Asian immigrant woman was leading the fight. The entire international terminal was shut down, and dozens of flights were canceled throughout the day. After hours of thousands of us forming a protective circle around Singh, immigration enforcement backed away. This historic blockade in December 2007 is the only documented time in recent North American history that the violence of deportation has been prevented through the power of a mass mobilization and direct action.

NOII centers direct support work in our mobilizing because it grounds our work in migrant communities. What form it will take—whether launching a large-scale public campaign or helping to fill out paperwork—depends on the specific political context and specific needs of those affected by the systems we are confronting. The greatest value of support work comes from building relationships of respect, trust, and accountability. Providing migrant communities with the necessary advice and support facilitates skills and capacity for migrants to lead their own struggle. This enables us to grow our movements by being more responsive to migrant communities, and simultaneously, politicizing and empowering migrants through the process of building relationships.

Status and Access for All

NOII groups across the country have laid the ground for a comprehensive regularization program. We advocate for full regularization, also known as legalization or amnesty, for all undocumented, nonstatus, and temporary migrants. Regularization is an extension of the demand for an end to all detentions and deportations, and means that migrants can live without constant fear. Regularization brings migrants out of invisibility. Regularization is a step toward ensuring that bosses can no longer so casually and callously exploit undocumented and migrant labor. Regularization facilitates access to health care, education, child care, social assistance, labor protection, housing, legal aid, and antiviolence services. Demanding full regularization is a humanizing force in the face of border imperialism's dehumanizing trend toward criminalization and precarity.

NOII's framework for regularization is drawn from our basic belief that no one person is more deserving of a self-determined life than another person. Because we refuse distinctions and divisions between good/deserving migrants and bad/undeserving ones, our principles for regularization are inclusive. Regularization cannot discriminate or exclude based on race, class, educational background, national origin, faith, gender, mental or physical disability, sexual orientation, medical condition, or criminal record. The framework for regularization that NOII advocates for, therefore, is fundamentally equitable in its call for status for *all* those without full immigration status.[9]

One of the most common retorts to NOII is that we would "let anyone stay, including criminals and rapists." This reveals a form of double racism or double punishment that Steve Cohen of NOII in the United Kingdom describes as "an exercise in imperial arrogance," where the "offending conduct is merely being shipped overseas."[10] On top of dealing with the injustices of the criminal justice system and prison-industrial complex that oversurveils and overincarcerates racialized communities, noncitizens are punished further with deportation. As described in the first chapter, challenging border imperialism necessitates challenging criminalization, which is a key form of social control of racialized and poor communities. NOII's position against double punishment is rooted in this political analysis of border imperialism and criminalization, as well as our experiences supporting migrants and their loved ones personally affected by the double punishment processes of incarceration and deportation.

Many labor unions and mainstream immigrant rights groups support the regularization of nonstatus workers employed in certain trade sectors. However, advertently or inadvertently, this reinforces the idea that migrants are only worth their labor. NOII believes that regularization must not be contingent on a person's participation in the labor force, and should not exclude the poor, unwaged, unemployed, or disabled. It must also be ongoing, meaning that it does not exclude migrants who have lived in Canada for a short period of time, or temporary workers whose transient status is enforced by the state and an inherent part of their labor exploitation and social stigmatization.

In addition to advocating and popularizing a No One Is Illegal, Status for All People campaign, various NOII groups have worked to actualize and prefigure regularization from the ground up. As NOII-Toronto organizers explain, "We need to take back our community centres, schools, health centres and neighbourhoods by declaring them as sanctuary zones free of immigration controls."[11] This means organizing to create community spaces and neighborhoods where undocumented migrants can access critical services without the threat of deportation. Such campaigns are prefigurative in their aim to ensure that undocumented migrants, despite lacking full legal immigration status, can have their basic needs met and be supported in creating semiautonomous spaces of safety. Sanctuary zones for nonstatus migrants, also known as solidarity zones, take power away from the state because their very existence represents nonparticipation in and subversion of an exclusionary apartheid system of citizenship.

These campaigns have many iterations: Sanctuary City, Solidarity City, Access without Fear, and Don't Ask Don't Tell. Over thirty US municipalities have been pressured to adopt a Don't Ask Don't Tell policy that prohibits municipal employees from asking or sharing information about immigration status when providing city services.[12] In Canada, powerful and effective campaigns to ensure that people accessing city and social services are not discriminated against based on immigration status have been led primarily by NOII in Toronto, the city with the largest number of nonstatus migrants in the country. In 2013, the city of Toronto declared that all city services would be accessible to undocumented migrants and migrant workers. I describe below some of the persistent mobilizing that built toward this historic Sanctuary City victory.

In 2006, after two years of advocating for Don't Ask Don't Tell policies within various municipal and governmental bodies, NOII-Toronto concentrated on building an Education Not Deportation campaign. This was precipitated by the removal of two undocumented children by immigration enforcement officers from a Toronto school. Within a month, the Toronto District School Board was swamped with official submissions from parents, teachers, migrant justice activists, and educators (including the largest teachers' union in Ontario) calling on the school board to welcome all students and defend schools from immigration enforcement. Shortly thereafter, the Toronto District School Board passed a Don't Ask Don't Tell policy stipulating that all students under the age of eighteen had a right to access education without the fear of detention or deportation. The campaign then shifted to ensure that every local school was informed about how to meaningfully implement this policy. In 2010, the Toronto School Board was pressured to provide appropriate trainings to teachers and administrative staff. Over five hundred schools were given educational posters about the policy to ensure that they were truly becoming safe spaces for all elementary and secondary school students.[13]

In a similar vein, the Shelter Sanctuary Status campaign was initiated in 2008 to prevent immigration officers from entering women's shelters in Toronto. For two years, the campaign emphasized outreach to women and trans resource centers. Over 120 groups endorsed the main campaign demand: ensuring that antiviolence services are accessible to undocumented survivors of violence, and barring immigration enforcement from entering or waiting outside these centers. One might assume that women's shelters would be natural allies in a campaign to ensure safety for undocumented women fleeing abuse. Yet Farrah Miranda, a NOII-Toronto organizer, points to divisions within the feminist antiviolence movement, citing roadblocks put up by senior management in a number of women's shelters against this campaign. She writes, "We were told that if undocumented women found out that certain spaces were accessible to them, they would show up in larger numbers at their gates. These ideas smacked of racism and anti-immigrant hysteria, similar to the lies about immigrants showing up in western countries and availing of services without pay."[14] The campaign continued, pushing an analysis of women's safety inclusive of undocumented women's experiences.

In 2010, the Shelter Sanctuary Status campaign won a significant victory when the Canadian Border Services Agency (CBSA) was pressured to issue a directive that enforcement officers would not enter women shelters or other spaces for women who are experiencing violence. Nor could the CBSA make inquiries of staff or other shelter residents about the identity and legal status of any non-status women seeking these services. Noting how critical this victory is, Miranda comments, "Forcing this policy through is an indication that enough women understand and agree that deportation is violence against women, that deportation is violence and must be stopped."[15] This policy was abruptly reversed in 2011 with a new CBSA policy authorizing enforcement officers to enter antiviolence centers. And so the campaign persists with the understanding that our victories can never be taken for granted and must always be actively defended.

The Education Not Deportation and Shelter Sanctuary Status campaigns are impressive as they have ensured that some of the most marginalized within our communities can live more freely. Alliances between migrant justice organizers, undocumented migrants, high school and university students, women and trans activists, and neighborhood associations have led to significant and concrete victories. The victories within schools and women's shelters laid the foundation to force a larger victory with Toronto City Council declaring that all city-operated spaces were accessible to undocumented migrants. These are also struggles to reclaim public space and social services by holding increasingly bureaucratized institutions and service providers accountable to those they are supposed to serve.

More important, these campaigns illustrate how NOII is creating a de facto grassroots regularization program from the ground up. We are fighting for—and in many cases winning—access for undocumented migrants to women's shelters, food banks, schools, and hospitals. As NOII-Toronto organizer Fariah Chowdhury describes it, "Solidarity City is a way of organizing as well as a goal. It is a way to get access to services for non-status people right now, and to involve people in the control and organization of the places they work, live, and receive education, healthcare, and basic services. . . . We know that this is only possible when all grassroots movements in the city collaborate, connect, and commit to a politic based on autonomous power that is separate from state power."[16] Beyond just demanding a regularization program from the state, these prefigurative campaigns demonstrate the necessity *and* possibility of movements to organize zones of safety for undocumented migrants beyond the state's authority. The logic of border imperialism, which relies on the hegemonic control of the state to determine who has the right to citizenship and access to basic services afforded through it, is undone through the prefiguration of solidarity zones for nonstatus migrants.

Abolish the Security Apparatus

The post-9/11 era has furthered racist anti-immigrant hysteria through the particular discourse of "national security." This has entrenched state securitization and border militarization in Canada through, for example, the creation of the CBSA, the implementation of a number of antiterror provisions that legalize extensive surveillance and lengthy interrogations, and a multibillion-dollar joint border security plan with the United States that includes biometrics and armed border guards. In an essay on race and national security, Razack draws attention to how race thinking "becomes embedded in law and bureaucracy so that the suspension of rights appears not as a violence but as the law itself."[17] Canada, along with other Western states, has utilized the War on Terror to justify draconian sanctions under the jurisdiction of intelligence services as well as criminal, tax, and immigration laws that target Muslim, Arab, and South Asian communities.

One such measure within immigration law is a security certificate. Security certificates are prepared by the Canadian Security Intelligence Service (CSIS) and issued by the Government of Canada against noncitizens, including legal permanent residents, who are deemed "inadmissible on grounds of security" and who thereby could "be detained without the issue of a warrant."[18] While existing in various forms since 1976, this measure was reintroduced as an amendment to the 2002 Immigration and Refugee Protection Act. Under this Kafkaesque law, detainees can be imprisoned indefinitely without any charges ever being laid against them and face possible deportation to torture. In the cases of the men against whom security certificates were issued, secret evidence and vague allegations—including hearsay—were admissible but never revealed to them in an open court of law. In the words of one of the detainees, Charkaoui, who contributed "The Bracelet" narrative above, these certificates are "a mixture of McCarthyism and Islamophobia. . . . And you can't win. If you have a beard, you're a fundamentalist. If you shave your beard, you are trying to blend in, you're a sleeper agent."[19]

While security certificates were already being used to unjustly detain and deport migrants prior to 9/11, a particularly heightened and demonizing post-9/11 media focus on security-related investigations created the political context for the development of a national campaign in support of security certificate detainees. The five men held on security certificates, also known as the Secret Trial 5, were Mohammed Mahjoub, Mahmoud Jaballah, Mohamed Harkat, Hasan Almrei, and Charkaoui. Four of the detainees were held in a maximum security facility notoriously known as Guantanamo North. From 2002 onward, a well-coordinated movement to abolish security certificates and support the detainees emerged in almost every major city across the country. Committees such as the Justice Coalition for Adil Charkaoui, Justice for Mohamed Harkat, and Justice for Mahjoub Network consisting of migrant justice activists, family members, Muslim organizations, and antiracists sprung up to support individual detainees while also mobilizing broader public support against security certificates.

There have been significant victories in this campaign. None of the five men have been deported. No new certificate has been issued since the campaign gained national prominence in 2003. Detainees were released, though on stringent conditions, after years of harrowing incarceration. While a limited victory since the legislation was reformed instead of completely scrapped, the post-9/11 security certificate regime was struck down by the Supreme Court of Canada in 2007. Two of the detainees had the cases against them completely quashed in 2009, and Guantanamo North was eventually shut down in 2011.

I remember attending the initial meetings and gatherings in Montreal to denounce Charkaoui's arrest on a security certificate in 2003. The first few rallies brought out only a handful of people, led by Hind Charkaoui,

Adil's sister, and Mary Foster, an anticapitalist and migrant justice activist who would end up being one of the many indefatigable organizers within the campaign. There was a climate of fear that inhibited mass involvement in the case of a "terror suspect" who was being vilified on the front pages of every local and national newspaper. Muslim community members were legitimately concerned about the heightened surveillance within mosques and about becoming targets through guilt by association if they spoke out. Mainstream NGO and legal organizations, on the other hand, wanted to first determine if Charkaoui was "innocent" (that is, deserving of support) before getting involved in the campaign.

Slowly but surely, over the next six years—and to some degree, continuing today—a national campaign developed to highlight the injustices of security certificates. In collaboration with family members, including Sophie Lamarche Harkat, Hind Charkaoui, Latifa Radwan, Mona El-Fouli, and Ahmad Jaballah, Muslim and other faith-based organizations, and migrant justice groups including every NOII group from Victoria to Kingston, the grassroots Campaign to Stop Secret Trials became a formidable force. At the peak of the campaign between 2005 and 2006, critics of security certificates included Human Rights Watch, Amnesty International, three UN committees, politicians from every level of government, the Canadian Bar Association, and the International Civil Liberties Monitoring Group.

A key strategy in this campaign has been to highlight the impact of the detentions on family members and amplify the voices of the detainees, particularly when they have been on almost-fatal hunger strikes. The popularization of phrases such as Secret Trials and Guantanamo North was a crucial strategy in challenging and countering the unsubstantiated and vague allegations. A range of tactics brought the issue of security certificates to the forefront of media outlets and public discourse, such as countless legal battles, outreach to student, faith, artist, and labor groups, media advocacy, allying with antiwar, community, and immigrant rights groups, producing feature documentaries, lobbying nationally and submissions to the UN internationally, gathering celebrities to offer bail support, and national days of action including sit-ins, vigils, and walks.

All these diverse actions were possible due to a widespread, multipronged grassroots campaign to empower and support detainees and their families to lead this struggle while building as many alliances as possible. This is the principle of uniting all who can be united. Radicals are often skeptical of moving beyond our own ideological and political circles. There is a valid concern about lowest-common-denominator coalition politics, wherein aligning with others who have a more mainstream analysis will necessarily change the message to a minimalist one that everyone can agree to. Effective campaigns, however, do require us to bring in and work alongside those who may not share our systemic analysis.

So how do we build alliances without devolving into a race to the bottom that dilutes our principles? One approach is to build strategic alliances to meet others where they are comfortable, while maintaining the autonomy to shape our own work. In this campaign, instead of a formal coalition, groups are loosely aligned through the overarching framework of End Secret Trials. This creates the momentum for a diversity of strategies that allows groups to contribute what they are best suited for—legal submissions, petitioning, lobbying, educational forums, or actions—without having to be responsible for others' tactics or messaging.

Co-optation of the campaign toward mainstream legal reform has not been a significant issue because grassroots migrant justice activists alongside family members of the detainees were able to establish a firm foundation for the antisecurity certificates campaign. As Foster notes, relations with more mainstream groups and politicians were "cultivated by the grassroots (and not vice versa)."[20] The sustained consciousness-raising and careful leadership of radicals unexpectedly brought many mainstream allies into the campaign for complete abolition of security certificates, rather than mere legal reform. Under the new reformed legislation, three men continue to have outstanding security certificates. The veneer of fairness exhibited by the new law masks the fact that these Muslim men are still facing possible deportation to torture, are living under draconian conditions of house arrest, and have to defend themselves against vague allegations without being charged. Sophie Harkat, Mohamed's wife, calls this "out with the old, in with the old!"[21] While some argue that the new process has alleviated the most egregious legal excesses of the prior law, the orientation of the campaign as a whole has not lost its bearings and remains focused on abolition.

Another notable aspect of the campaign has been the emphasis on antiracism as a key analytic framework through which to oppose security certificates. The main demands of the campaign are the abolition of security certificates, an end to all deportations to torture, and an end to the racist scapegoating of Muslim and Arab communities. This stands in contrast to the dominant discourse in the United States to shut down Guantanamo Bay that stresses the exceptional legal nature of the detentions. As scholar Luke Vervaet asserts, "Even if Guantánamo eventually closes, the problem that Guantánamo symbolizes—the lawlessness, racism and imperialist mentality of the powerful—remains."[22] While the particular civil liberties violations of security-related detentions are abhorrent, the suggestion that they are arbitrary or exceptional obscures the fact that they are a deliberate extension of the torture, killings, Islamophobia, and colonial crusading that marks the current global War on Terror.

The main effectiveness of this campaign, therefore, has been the consistent call for the abolition of security certificates, forwarded through a principled analysis of systemic racism along with widespread education to build support for this position. There is now an extraordinary understanding within much of the broader Left that mere legal reform through "fairer" trials misses the mark. Legal instruments such as security certificates are selectively deployed against certain noncitizen communities caught in the tentacles of racialized global empire. During the June 2006 Freedom Caravan, when dozens of events were organized leading up to the Supreme Court constitutional

challenge to security certificates, there was focused attention on grassroots, radical, and antiracist struggles beyond
the courtroom. Matthew Behrens of the Campaign to Stop
Secret Trials wrote at the time, "Although the Supreme
Court hearings will be a significant moment, they are not
the end of the road. Indeed, no matter how the Court rules,
spy agency CSIS and the cruel bureaucracy of Canadian
Immigration are likely to continue their harassment of
immigrant and refugee communities."[23] The campaign to
end secret trials and abolish security certificates has been
critical in highlighting the dehumanizing experiences of
security certificate detainees as part of a wider struggle to
dismantle the racism inherent in state securitization and
border imperialism.

Canada Is Illegal

Racialized communities face interlocking and connected
conditions of marginalization within the settler-colonial
state. Victims of a global political economy built on our
dispossession, communities of color are further disciplined
into normative whiteness and hegemonic neoliberalism.
The power of state control and the insidious nature of
racism force us to metabolize our own oppression, and
many of us become "the good Indian" or "good immigrant"
who is silent, complicit, and grateful to the colonial master.
Some even become the system's greatest cheerleaders. The
reality, though, is that people of color face legislated racism
from immigration laws to policies governing Indigenous

reserves; are discriminated against and excluded from equitable access to health care, housing, child care, and education; are disproportionately victims of police killings and child apprehensions; fill the floors of sweatshops and factories; and are overrepresented in head counts on poverty, incarceration, unemployment, and high school dropout rates.

It comes as no surprise, then, that diverse racialized communities across North America have built coalitions for racial justice that are at the forefront of resistance to systemic oppression, capitalism, state repression, global empire, and ecological destruction. NOII has been involved in many of these coalition efforts, with a particular emphasis on building alliances between migrant and Indigenous struggles. The slogan No One Is Illegal, Canada Is Illegal was popularized at a rally during the 2005 International Indigenous Youth Conference in Vancouver. NOII-Vancouver (Indigenous Coast Salish territories) was involved in supporting this conference by providing logistical assistance, translation, and child care. Through this process, we built relationships with the Indigenous youth organizers as well as shared stories about our homelands, the idea of "belonging" within Canada, and global resistance to imperialism. At the end of conference, a rally took to the streets, and we suddenly heard the emcee chanting "No One Is Illegal, Canada Is Illegal." Since then, we have been using that slogan as a key framework toward decolonization and our collective liberation.

Smith, who introduces this book, has written extensively about how white supremacy in North America is constituted through interrelated but separate logics: "slaveability/anti-black racism, which anchors capitalism; genocide, which anchors colonialism; and orientalism, which anchors war."[24] Under Smith's first pillar, black people are constructed as property of the state and capital due to the legacy of slavery and current conditions of mass incarceration. The second pillar is the assimilation and attempted disappearance of Indigenous people through genocide and settler colonialism in order to illegally claim land and resources. The final pillar is Orientalism—a term theorized by Said that casts certain communities, especially Arab and/or Muslim, as permanent internal and external threats to empire. Orientalism justifies imperialist occupations globally and anti-immigrant rhetoric locally.[25]

Smith's landmark analysis illuminates how racialized people are victims of one or more of these pillars of white supremacy, and are simultaneously complicit in oppression through the other pillars.[26] Low-income communities of color and Indigenous communities in North America, for instance, are recruited into the army and become complicit in empires' wars against people of color across the global South. Examining another pillar illuminates how nonnatives become embedded within settler colonialism. Migrants, many once Indigenous to their own lands, but often displaced due to Orientalist crusading and corporate plundering, are thrown into capitalism's pool of labor and, in a cruel twist, violently inserted into the political economy of genocide: *stolen labor on stolen land*. Many immigrant workers in the North are low-wage laborers within corporate industries that extract resources by encroaching on Indigenous lands, or equally ill fated, work as support staff for the army.

Within the migrant justice movement, there has been much discussion on how we understand the positioning of migrants of color within settler colonialism. On the one hand, as argued by antiracist scholars Bonita Lawrence and Enakshi Dua, migrants of color frequently point toward the Canadian state's racism against themselves in order to claim innocence in the dispossession of Indigenous lands.[27] Many mainstream immigrant rights groups largely perpetuate this notion by framing our struggle in terms of "integration," thereby disconnecting us from a more systemic analysis of border imperialism. In their seminal work, Lawrence and Dua offer the challenge to immigrant rights movements to "think through how their campaigns can pre-empt the ability of Aboriginal communities to establish title to their traditional lands."[28] On the other hand, antiracist scholars Nandita Sharma and Cynthia Wright contend that migration cannot be conflated with colonialism and challenge the divides between Indigenous people and migrants. They forcefully suggest that these divides are perpetuated by state categorizations and the colonial language of "minority rights," which lead us to mistakenly believe that the demands of Indigenous people and migrants are in competition, or necessarily at odds with one another.[29]

Looking through a lens wider than that of migrant justice, antiracist Beenash Jafri has been theorizing the particular relationship between racialized nonnative and Indigenous communities. She differentiates between racialized communities being *privileged* within settler

colonialism and racialized communities being *complicit*
in settler colonialism.[30] Rather than conflating complicity
with privilege, she encourages us to think about them as
distinct frameworks. Jafri posits that racialized communities are complicit in the matrix of racial and colonial power
that marginalizes Indigenous communities, while recognizing that racialized communities are not necessarily privileged subjects within the nation-state. She writes,

> When people refer to "settler privilege," they are
> referring to the unearned benefits to live and work
> on Indigenous lands, and to the unequal benefits
> accrued through citizenship rights within the settler
> state. . . . When we account for systemic inequities,
> underemployment and the racialization of poverty,
> for most people of color there are few "benefits"
> associated with being a settler. . . . Complicity is a
> messy, complicated and entangled concept to think
> about; it is not as easy to grasp and, because of this,
> it requires a much deeper investment on our part.
> This would demand, for example, that we think
> about settlerhood not as an object that we possess,
> but as a field of operations into which we become
> socially positioned and implicated.[31]

NOII, without explicitly theorizing as such, embraces
a similar analysis. While I cannot speak to the diverse
personal understandings that NOII members have, I want
to elaborate on my experiences with and interpretations of
the relationship between migrant and Indigenous struggles.

I use the phrase migrants of color because it is more specific
than the term racialized. Rather than homogenizing the
experiences of, say, descendants of slaves or indentured
laborers within a presumed pan-people of color experience,
NOII primarily organizes with those who are racialized immigrants, refugees, or undocumented migrants.
Admittedly, immigrants, refugees, and undocumented
migrants have diverse lived realities, including varying
degrees of choice in migration, varying class backgrounds,
and varying access to services based on immigration status.
Still, there is a basic experience of migration that allows us
to delve into the specific relationship between the structurings of precarious migration and settler colonialism.

While I believe that migrants of color are inevitably
implicated in settler colonialism and have a responsibility to ally with Indigenous struggles, I do not believe that
migration as a process in and of itself, especially in this
late period of capitalist globalization and global neo-
colonialism, can inherently be understood as a form of
settler colonialism. Settler colonialism is an ideology that
seeks to dominate, control, and commodify communities
and lands, while migration—largely characterized as precarious migration—is an expression of self-determination.
Displacement and precarious migration are products of
colonialism and capitalism, and it would be a mistake
to identify all those who migrate, whether as refugees or
immigrant workers, as those seeking to colonize. Smith
notes that "without a critique of the settler state as simultaneously also white supremacist, all 'settlers' become morally
undifferentiated."[32] NOII-Montreal member Jaggi Singh

similarly maintains that "settlement is as much an ideology as a practice, and the only way to escape complicity with settlement is active opposition to it. I do organize on the basis of a vision for no borders and free movement. But, I have never heard of an Indigenous theory of decolonization that is about expulsion—expulsion of a corporate mine perhaps—but never of people who migrate to achieve dignity in their lives."[33]

As a migrant myself, I realize that migrant justice will be short lived if gained at the expense of Indigenous self-determination. Many other members of NOII are also cautious to not call for a simple unity between migrants of color and Indigenous communities. Despite the violence of deportation and detention against nonstatus migrants along with the racialization of immigrant communities as eternal outsiders, oversimplifications that suggest our struggles are the same as those of Indigenous peoples are irresponsible. The founding violence of settler colonialism is, by definition, against Indigenous people. We cannot ignore or minimize the reality of genocide of Indigenous peoples and the ongoing erasure of Indigenous sovereignty on these lands. Given the devastating cultural, spiritual, economic, linguistic, and political impacts of colonialism on Indigenous nations across Turtle Island, all social and environmental justice movements, including migrant justice movements, must involve nonnative solidarity in the fight against colonization.

Cultivating an ethic of responsibility among migrants of color toward Indigenous struggles is essential. We have to understand ourselves as those displaced victims of global empire and capitalism who enter into, and hence become complicit in and benefit from, the processes of colonization in North America. This means we have to go beyond a politics of optional alliance. We cannot debate the merits of whether or not to align with Indigenous communities; we are *obligated* to educate ourselves and each other about the histories of the illegal settlement and appropriation of Indigenous lands. NOII members have, for example, consistently translated and included Indigenous communiqués into immigrant community publications, appeared on multilingual radio stations to increase the understanding of Indigenous issues within immigrant communities, hosted discussions within community and faith centers about Indigenous histories, and frequently facilitated the travel of migrant and refugee delegations to Indigenous land reclamations to hear firsthand from Indigenous communities. This awareness leads to the active participation of migrant communities in the struggle for decolonization.

Engaging in decolonization struggles also involves tangible solidarity with Indigenous communities. All NOII groups have prioritized support for Indigenous struggles, both urban and land based, for the past decade. These efforts have been most noticeable in Vancouver. NOII-Toronto organizer and scholar Craig Fortier believes that "the significant work exerted by organizers in Vancouver has provided a model example for migrant justice organizers throughout Canada with respect to the long-term and committed nature of Indigenous solidarity."[34] The organizing of NOII-Vancouver (Indigenous Coast Salish territories) is based in a province where only a few treaties or agreements have been signed. Despite the provincial and federal governments' assertions otherwise, legal title has never been ceded and remains with Indigenous nations.

Since 2003, NOII-Vancouver (Indigenous Coast Salish territories) has been supporting the Skwelkwek'welt Protection Centre against tourism, mining, and real estate development on Secwepemc lands, located in the interior of the province. This has included monthly pickets, public events, court support as well as fund-raising to support speaking tours, community land reclamation, and language revitalization efforts. NOII was also involved in organizing a historic convergence against the Sun Peaks Resort that brought hundreds of migrant justice activists, Palestinian refugees, environmentalists, and anticapitalists into the community to construct a Secwepemc resistance camp on the land.

Many solidarity activists enter Indigenous communities during moments of crisis—for instance, to support a blockade against development—and exit shortly thereafter. But as feminist writer bell hooks reminds us, "Solidarity is not the same as support. To experience solidarity, we must have a community of interests, shared beliefs and goals around which to unite, to build Sisterhood. Support can be occasional. It can be given and just as easily withdrawn. Solidarity requires sustained, ongoing commitment."[35] The relationship between Secwepemc land defenders and NOII has continued for ten years, with frequent delegations, meetings, strategizing workshops, and a deepening of personal trust and respect. It has been a central experience in informing my own learning about the depth and breadth of resistance and resilience within Indigenous communities—from stewardship of the land to cultural resurgence, from affirming natural laws to learning the centrality of prophecies and ceremonies.

Similarly, NOII-Vancouver (Indigenous Coast Salish territories) has prioritized annual delegations and support for the Sutikalh Protection Camp that, since being constructed in 2000, has become one of the longest-standing camps against corporate development in the country. More recently we have been supporting the efforts of the Lhe Lin Liyin, who have been preventing oil and natural gas pipelines from operating in Wet'suwet'en territory. Along with other allies, we have participated in four annual action camps, hosted speaking events, disseminated information, coordinated national days of action and media support, and helped with fund raising.

Over the years, different NOII groups have supported struggles in Akwesasne, Barriere Lake, Cheam, Grassy Narrows, Kahnasatake, Kitchenuhmaykoosib Inninuwug, Six Nations, Tyendinaga, Secwepemc, St'ati'imc, Wetsuweten, and other communities. We have also prioritized support for urban struggles such as justice for missing and murdered Indigenous women as well as inner-city housing for Indigenous peoples. Rather than campaign-based or NGO approaches to working with Indigenous communities—approaches that can seem manipulative and goal oriented—our focus has been on building relationships and trust with no ulterior motive other than learning Indigenous histories, offering support to frontline communities, and sharing visions for our futures.

The Indigenous Defenders of the Land network recently brought together grassroots land defenders from dozens of Indigenous communities across Canada. As part of these historic Defenders of the Land gatherings, NOII groups and a few other allies were invited to participate in and support the network. We worked with other nonnative activists to develop a Supporters Declaration, which in part reads,

> As non-Indigenous supporters, we have come from different places and we have come for different reasons. As multiracial settlers, migrants, refugees, and descendants of slaves, we came across many oceans or continents, four hundred years ago or yesterday. Many of us feel deeply attached to places across Turtle Island, but we recognize that our homes are built on the ruins of others. We are on the lands of Indigenous peoples: lands unjustly seized, unsurrendered lands, treaty lands, and urbanized lands. This reality is visible in the names of our streets, our towns, our monuments—erasing the genuine identity of the Original Peoples of this land.[36]

This declaration and the process that led to it are significant for two reasons. First, it highlighted that migrant justice activists have been identified by Indigenous communities themselves as having worked on Indigenous solidarity efforts, which usually tend to be dominated by white solidarity activists. Second, it articulated a shift in nonnative solidarity discourse toward understanding the layered, differential dynamics of settlement to include oppressed peoples who are differently complicit in settler colonialism than those with white settler background and privilege.

Steady relationship building, mutual learning and sharing of experiences, and solidarity delegations to Indigenous communities have led to powerful reciprocities between migrants of color and Indigenous people. One of my first experiences of the revolutionary possibility of such alliances was at a march in 2003 by the Action Committee for Nonstatus Algerians, where Tyendinaga Mohawk activist Shawn Brant expressed his support for the fight against deportations. Brant, himself imprisoned numerous times for his stand against corporate and colonial development on Indigenous land, stood outside the Citizenship and Immigration offices and welcomed nonstatus Algerians on to Turtle Island. He not only expressed solidarity but also affirmed Indigenous jurisdiction over the land as a direct challenge to the Canadian state's authority to execute deportations. The hairs on my arms again stood up when, years later, I watched Melissa Elliott, the cofounder of Young Onkwehonwe United, give a powerful speech at a NOII rally. She proclaimed to a crowd of thousands of migrants and allies that "the Canadian government has no jurisdiction in our lands to be deporting you people, to be treating you the way that they are, or us the way that they are."[37]

I have been humbled by the gestures of Indigenous communities to consistently welcome displaced migrants and refugees on to their lands. On numerous occasions, legendary former political prisoner Wolverine has talked

to NOII members about asserting Indigenous laws to
protect refugees who are facing deportation. In 2010, when
492 Tamil refugees aboard the *MV Sun Sea* arrived on the
shores of the West Coast and faced immediate incarceration, Indigenous elders opened the weekly demonstrations outside the jails by welcoming the refugees. As their
contributions toward a national day of action to support
the detained Tamil refugees, the Lhe Lin Liyin of the
Wet'suwet'en nation hung a banner affirming, "We welcome refugees." And as part of this same national day of
action, Pierre Beaulieu-Blais, an Indigenous Anishnabe
member of NOII-Ottawa, declared, "From one community of resistance to another, we welcome you. As people
who have also lost our land and been displaced because
of colonialism and racism, we say Open All the Borders!
Status for All!"[38] Such public affirmations subvert state controls and colonially imposed divisions in profound ways.

In describing Indigenous host laws that are still alive
on these lands, Indigenous feminist writer Lee Maracle
articulates how Indigenous laws offer a clear counter to
colonial immigration laws. She says:

> You [migrants] have a counter-law. It is my law. It is
> the host law of Indigenous people. Everybody eats,
> every woman has a right to a house, and everyone
> has access to the wealth of the land. . . . As you
> respect and honour Indigenous sovereignty, you
> also take on the law and the legal framework of
> our people here. . . . We are all here to conjure up
> a living with each other. . . . No one is illegal, no

one is a bastard child, no one is an illegal alien. We
have to get that very clear in our minds, and in our
hearts, and in our bodies, and move with it. . . . So
if you support Indigenous sovereignty, you are also
supporting No One Is Illegal, there is no disconnect
between those two things.[39]

As Maracle suggests, there is nothing contradictory about supporting struggles for migrant justice and
Indigenous self-determination; our liberation is interconnected. As migrants of color, understanding ourselves as
complicit within settler colonialism, taking up the responsibility to educate our communities about Indigenous
histories on the lands we reside on, and prioritizing active
support for Indigenous self-determination are three critical
steps in building long-term alliances with Indigenous communities. Simple calls for racial unity between migrants of
color and Indigenous people obscure the matrix of differential racial power within settler colonialism, particularly as some immigrant communities are becoming class
mobile. Anti-imperialist scholar Vijay Prashad describes
how immigrants' "license to accumulate economic wealth
through hard work" is leveraged in exchange for their
willingness to be used as symbols of discipline—that is, as
model minorities—against other marginalized communities of color.[40] Instead, through engaged relations based on
solidarity and respect, NOII-Vancouver (Indigenous Coast
Salish territories) has started to identify and organize as an
explicitly *anticolonial* migrant justice group. This reflects
our belief that our visions must steer away from seeking

greater recognition from a colonial system and go beyond demanding citizenship rights from a settler state. Slowly, we are negotiating a decolonized path toward relations based on dismantling settler colonialism through the affirmation of Indigenous self-determination and the welcoming of migrants to live in respectful relationship to existing communities and the land.

Anticapitalist Resistance

Canada has one of the highest proportions of low-paid workers in the industrialized world.[41] Labor precarity under capitalism is most acute for migrant and undocumented workers, and is evident in the state's thrust to expand temporary worker programs. Canada now accepts more migrants under temporary permits than those who can come permanently.[42]

Accordingly, NOII groups have been working within the labor movement to link immigrants' rights to workers' rights. In Vancouver, one of the dialogue sessions between union delegates and migrant justice organizations resulted in a set of resolutions that vows to "work to build solidarity between unionized workers, non unionized workers— recognizing that (im)migrant and nonstatus workers often fill non unionized, precarious jobs and that the struggle of (im)migrants encompasses the movement against neoliberal exploitation and against war, occupation, poverty, and displacement."[43] Annual May Day (International Workers' Day) marches also provide a critical framework to link workers' struggles and movements against neoliberal capitalism to migrant justice. As stated by Parambir Gill of NOII-Toronto, which mobilizes thousands for May Day each year, the importance of these marches is "to make the invisible seen, to make the silent heard, to make the absent felt, and to show that even though many in our communities may be undocumented, we are also unafraid."[44]

The influence of NOII groups within anticapitalist and antiauthoritarian movements is also noteworthy. In 2000, with her influential piece "Where Was the Color in Seattle?" Elizabeth Martinez sparked conversations within the antiglobalization movement about examining the phenomenon of "summit hopping"—and the privileges associated with it, such as traveling across the continent—and instead, prioritizing local resistance. Being grounded in local community struggles is critical; however, I believe that as a strategy, megamobilizations against the global elite should not outright be dismissed as symbolic rituals of privileged protest. These actions are necessary to assert and be invigorated by our collective power of refusal, to delegitimize and disrupt the institutions of capitalism and imperialism, to increase the social and financial costs for elites at these summits, to strengthen our networks of resistance across often-disparate movements, and to stretch the bounds of our strategies and actualize freer social relations through the process of engaging in struggle.

NOII-Montreal member Singh captures the dilemma grassroots anticapitalist community organizers have been grappling with since the anti-World Trade Organization (WTO) protests in Seattle in 1999. He states,

> The enduring challenge of the post-Seattle moment
> remains to link mass mobilizations and direct
> action against global capitalism to the on-the-
> ground day-to-day struggles against colonialism,
> poverty, racism, and police brutality—to root them
> in long-standing struggles for dignity and survival.
> We need, at the very least, to conceive of the move-
> ment against global capitalism in such a way that
> those who are on the frontlines of resistance can
> actually recognize it.[45]

Movements such as NOII, along with Indigenous as well as poor and working-class movements, help bridge anticapitalist movements with the strength of local resistance. In 2002, the anticapitalist Take the Capital convergence was announced in Ottawa to oppose a meeting of the G8 leaders taking place in Kananaskis, Alberta. Coordinated through People's Global Action, a decentralized network of anticapitalist groups across Ontario and Quebec, a NOII march endorsed by over a hundred groups was held on the first of these days of action. "No One Is Illegal: A March of 1,000 Flags of Resistance" expressed opposition to racism, imperialism, and genocide as well as affirmed solidarity with global self-determination struggles and Indigenous sovereignty. As the notice for the march emphasized, "The new 'war on terror' is really something very old—the continuance of systematic policies of exploitation and dispossession."[46]

This march brought together local immigrant community organizations, Palestinian refugee and Latin American diasporic groups working on international solidarity campaigns, and grassroots Indigenous land defenders from the region. It was one of most diverse and genuinely representative anticapitalist marches that I had witnessed at the time. While the tone of the march did not involve direct action, it expressed solidarity with separate, more confrontational actions. This marked the first of many similar NOII actions and contingents during anticapitalist convergences, including against the WTO mini-ministerial meeting in Montreal in 2003, the Security and Prosperity Partnership summit in Montebello in 2007, the 2010 Winter Olympics in Vancouver, and the G20 meetings in Toronto in 2010.

NOII groups in Vancouver and Toronto were involved in cofounding the Olympic Resistance Network in 2008 and Toronto Community Mobilization Network in 2010. These networks organized the cross-country No Olympics on Stolen Native Land campaign and anti-G20 convergence. These convergences had three notable achievements. First, they served to successfully link anticapitalist movements to community resistance. Beyond articulating an ideological opposition to capitalism, these convergences explicitly named—and did active outreach to—those most impacted by capitalism: migrants, workers, Indigenous and rural communities, poor and homeless people, and diasporic communities from the global South. This allowed local community groups to see their specific issues mirrored within an anticapitalist movement. Alliances strengthened between migrant justice, Indigenous, antiwar, queer and trans, environmental, anarchist, labor, disability rights, and antipoverty groups. Geographer David Harvey observes that "the unities beginning to emerge around these different vectors of struggle are vital to nurture for within them we can discern the lineaments of an entirely different, non-imperialistic, form of globalization."[47]

This is organizing that goes beyond coalition building; it is the politics of linking movements to the everyday experiences of oppressed peoples and inviting these communities to take leadership. This is not easy. In my experiences organizing a few major convergences, the biggest hurdle was overcoming the resistance among many radicals to bridge with community organizing. While no one opposed, in principle, taking leadership from poor and racialized communities, comments in meetings reverted to "well, they are not at the meeting so they must not be interested." This led to somewhat-strained conversations about how many traditional methods of anticapitalist organizing—such as long meetings, haphazard outreach, and goal-oriented task lists—are unwelcoming to many. Despite the tiresome burden on activists of color to keep bringing these issues up, the ongoing dialogues were successful in persuading many radical anticapitalist activists to transform the methods and strategies of organizing, as well as shift the movement's leadership toward marginalized communities. By articulating and enacting a politics that is relevant across communities, while also facilitating an anticapitalist basis of unity across struggles, we create a potentially potent and revolutionary movement.

Second, both convergences were organized on an anticapitalist *and* anticolonial basis. This reflects the oft-repeated call by Indigenous communities that Indigenous self-determination must become more central within social and environmental struggles. Rather than being a single issue within a longer laundry list, the recognition of Indigenous self-determination was the foundation for mobilizing against the Olympics, as No Olympics on Stolen Native Land became the rallying call for the campaign over four years. Indigenous land defenders, especially those from the St'at'imc and Secwepemc communities, and Indigenous people residing in low-income urban neighborhoods in Vancouver led a groundswell of popular resistance against the Olympics. On the first day of the anti-Olympics convergence, a No One Is Illegal, Canada Is Illegal contingent walked alongside Indigenous elders and land defenders who were leading the march. In Toronto, one of the main days of action against the G20 was called Canada Can't Hide Genocide, an Indigenous-organized day of action. One of the long-term impacts of these mobilizations has been more widespread dialogue among movements at a national level about strengthening an anti-colonial politics as well as understanding the connection between capitalism and colonialism, and their impacts, as being mutually reinforcing.

Finally, despite preemptive infiltration of activist groups by state intelligence officers and intimidation of organizers by law enforcement, the anti-Olympics and anti-G20 convergences saw an escalation in confrontational tactics. Leadership of racialized, queer, disabled, and poor people's movements during these convergences is evidence of the commitment and courage of marginalized communities to participate in militant social struggle. Some of those

who risked arrest and faced charges lacked full citizenship
status. Like the Undocumented and Unafraid actions
and DREAM activists in the United States, they exhibited moral fortitude despite risking possible deportation.
Several NOII members faced lengthy trials on trumped-up,
politically motivated charges for being so-called ringlead-
ers in anti-G20 mobilizing. In response, NOII groups
in Halifax, Montreal, Ottawa, Toronto, and Vancouver
released a joint statement:

> The type of repression that has followed the G20 is
> symptomatic of the broader policies of exploitation
> that are the daily reality for Indigenous, poor, and
> racialized communities. The G8 and G20 leaders
> and their corporate masters erect borders, manu-
> facture weaponry, pillage the earth with industrial
> projects, and profit from war. . . . Daily, we stand in
> solidarity with those who are deemed "illegal" by
> the colonial state and are forced to live under the
> threat of detention and deportation. And daily, we
> organize against the racism and xenophobia that
> defines the history of colonization and displace-
> ment in Canada.[48]

Activists Clare O'Connor and Kalin Stacey write that
the challenge of revolutionary organizing is "to build a base
capable of not only appealing to constituted power but of
displacing it."[49] Migrant justice organizers, some without
full immigration status, remain on the front lines daily,
affirming our visions of and organizing toward a world free

of border imperialism, where people have the right to stay, freedom to move, and right to return, where liberated communities have control over their own lands, lives, and labor, and where each of us is able to self-determine and express our dreams and desires free of the coercive, oppressive, exploitative relations of capitalism and colonialism.

A Chronology

On many days, fighting for an end to border imperialism is like swimming in glue or grieving against gravity. But I remember all the battles we have won and the shifting terrain for migrant justice movements that has centered the voices and experiences of our immigrant, refugee, and nonstatus communities within broader social movements. In the words of Davis, "What we manage to do each time we win a victory is not so much to secure change once and for all, but rather to create new terrains for struggle."[50]

This chronology describes moments that serve to shed additional light on the five specific formulations of NOII's movement-based analysis and practice that I have been discussing. It is not a comprehensive history, or a summary of all major NOII campaigns or projects. By highlighting just some memorable events and victories, this chronology offers insights on how we have created new landscapes of struggle by taking antioppressive leadership from those directly impacted by border imperialism, strengthening alliances based on solidarity and mutual aid, cultivating and expanding anticolonial and anticapitalist networks of resistance, and growing strategic and effective movements that affect tangible social change in our communities on the path toward decolonization and liberation.

JUNE 2002: A mass, family-friendly NOII march takes place as part of the anticapitalist Take the Capital days of action in Ottawa against the G8 leaders meeting in Kananaskis. This march links the impacts of the War on Terror at home and abroad to the expansion of neoliberal capitalism.

OCTOBER 2002: An Algerian nonstatus family, the Bourouisas, takes sanctuary in a Montreal church. Within eleven days of an international campaign by NOII-Montreal and the Action Committee for Nonstatus Algerians, they are granted legal status. This is the first of over a dozen sanctuary cases, including Abdelkader Belaouni, the Ayoub family, Mohamed Cherfi, Menen Ayele, the Vega family, Ali Reza Monemi, Amir Kazemian, and Laibar Singh, that NOII groups in Montreal and Vancouver become involved in.

JANUARY 2003: A group of thirty activists swarm the deportation of an Iranian refugee and her son at the Vancouver airport. Kobra Natghi and her son escape the airport, but her son is later apprehended. A few months later, NOII-Vancouver is formed. In 2004, one anarchist is sentenced to three months in jail for his alleged role in the action.

FEBRUARY 2003: NOII-Montreal hosts a *consulta* for migrant justice groups from Quebec, southern Ontario, and Vancouver. The *consulta* concludes with demands for the

regularization of all nonstatus people, an end to deportations, dismantling detention centers, and justice for
migrant workers. An analysis of the colonial foundation of
Canada and connections between racism, capitalism, and
patriarchy are highlighted.

MAY 2003: Ten members of the Action Committee for
Nonstatus Algerians and two NOII-Montreal members
occupy the offices of the immigration minister to denounce
the exclusions of certain nonstatus Algerians from the
2002 regularization program. They are beaten, tasered, and
charged with mischief. They are acquitted in 2006, but two
of the nonstatus Algerians have since been deported. One
of the deportees is Cherfi, arrested while in sanctuary in
2004. A Canada-wide campaign by Cherfi's partner, the
Action Committee of Nonstatus Algerians, and NOII in
Montreal and Quebec City demand his return. Cherfi eventually succeeds in winning his return to Canada in 2009.

OCTOBER 2003: A pan-Canadian day of action, including in
Halifax, Edmonton, Peterborough, St. John, and Guelph,
against security certificates is held. Four people in Ottawa
are arrested for occupying the CSIS headquarters.

DECEMBER 2003: NOII-Vancouver begins a two-year campaign
to support the Skwelkwek'welt Protection Center against
Sun Peaks Resort and Delta Hotels.

FEBRUARY 2004: NOII-Vancouver supports a group of refugees from North Africa and the Middle East in forming

Refugees against Racial Profiling. Through successful direct support and actions over the next months, many of the deportation orders are overturned.

APRIL 2004: A national day of action to support Palestinian refugees facing deportations is announced by the Coalition against the Deportation of Palestinian Refugees and NOII-Montreal. At the year's end, one of the most active coalition members, Osama Saleh, wins a victory in the Federal Court of Canada. Later that year, as part of a large antiwar mobilization to protest President George W. Bush's visit to Ottawa, the coalition holds a demonstration to express solidarity with the Palestinian resistance to Israeli occupation as well as support Palestinian refugees facing deportation from Canada.

MAY 2004: NOII-Vancouver organizes the first of its annual delegations to Sutikalh, an Indigenous camp erected in St'at'imc territory to prevent the construction of a resort. Sutikalh is foundational to the 2010 No Olympics on Stolen Native Land campaign that will link urban anti-capitalist and anticolonial activists to Indigenous land defenders.

AUGUST 2004: Solidarity across Borders campaign is launched in Montreal with four principal demands: the regularization of all nonstatus persons, an end to deportations, an end to detentions, and the abolition of security certificates. The campaign brings together a range of refugees, migrant groups, community organizations, anticapitalists, and anti-imperialists. The next year, a two-hundred-kilometer walk from Montreal to Ottawa is organized by Solidarity across Borders, receiving support from the Canadian Auto Workers, Canadian Union of Postal Employees, and Quebec Women's Federation. The march is inspired by one of the leaders of the Pakistani Action Committee against Racial Profiling, Shamim Akhtar, who was deported along with her family in 2004.

OCTOBER 2004: Stateless Roma refugee Adrian Dragan goes on hunger strike after sixteen months in a detention center. He is placed in solitary confinement after refusing to sign documents consenting to his own deportation. NOII-Vancouver publicizes his situation to the media and the UN, resulting in high-level talks between Canadian and Romanian officials. In 2011, NOII-Vancouver publicizes a similar situation of prolonged detention of Nader, an Iranian refugee incarcerated for over six years. After six weeks of mobilizing, he is released from detention and granted legal status.

MARCH 2005: Toronto activist and artist Wendy Maxwell is arrested at the International Women's Day Fair and deported to Costa Rica. Attention to the gendered violence of border controls that punishes survivors of violence becomes core to NOII's analysis.

APRIL 2006: The maximum security $3.5 million Kingston Immigration Holding Center, dubbed Guantanamo North, opens for the purpose of security certificate detentions.

From 2006 onward, the Campaign to Stop Secret Trials in Canada, Justice for Mohamed Harkat Committee, Justice Coalition for Adil Charkaoui, and NOII-Kingston demand the closure of this new facility. The facility is finally shut down in December 2011.

APRIL 2006: Kimberly and Gerald Lizano-Sossa are apprehended in their high school by immigration officials and subsequently detained, sparking the Education Not Deportation campaign. A few months later, the Toronto District School Board passes a Don't Ask Don't Tell policy throughout Toronto public schools.

MAY 2006: Inspired by May Day in the United States, which brought millions of migrants into the streets, NOII groups and allies across Canada, including in Vancouver, Toronto, Ottawa, Montreal, Halifax, Fredericton, and Peterborough, organize under the banner of "Immigrant Rights Are Workers' Rights; Status for All." Large May Day marches, organized by NOII-Toronto, become a key annual event in Toronto.

JUNE 2006: As activists and family members prepare to attend the Supreme Court of Canada hearings on the constitutionality of security certificates, the Freedom Caravan from Toronto to Ottawa stops in over thirty communities, including Ajax, Kingston, Port Hope, Lindsay, Peterborough, Trenton, and Napanee. There is also a Canada-wide day of action to shut down Guantanamo North.

DECEMBER 2006: Mahjoub, Jaballah, and Almrei begin a hunger strike in Guantanamo North. This is not their first hunger strike. An open letter, widely circulated in alternative and mainstream media, reads: "We have been very patient and done our best to deal with a process where it is impossible to defend yourself. And we will remain patient, because we know that ultimately, we will be let out, because we are innocent men. But sometimes there is only so much human beings should be required to accept before they raise their voice in peaceful protest."[51] After approximately 90 days, Mahjoub and Jaballah are released on bail and cease their hunger strike. Almrei continues on a juice and water hunger strike for 156 days. He is released in 2009.

OCTOBER 2007: National day of action against the introduction of reformed security certificate legislation. This action is endorsed by over a hundred groups, including labor unions, international human rights organizations, and student associations.

OCTOBER 2007: The Commission of the Sixth Declaration of the Zapatista National Liberation Army and the Organizing Commission of the Gathering of the Indigenous Peoples of the Americas invite NOII-Vancouver to attend the Indigenous Peoples Gathering in Mexico.

MARCH 2008: NOII-Vancouver organizes its first antiracism march. This becomes an annual event during which racialized communities come together to oppose systemic racism, institutional discrimination, colonization of Indigenous lands, imperialist occupation, structural poverty, anti-immigrant measures, and law enforcement violence.

JULY 2008: NOII-Vancouver, anticapitalists, and anti-imperialists disrupt the Pacific Northwest Economic Region summit by preventing access to the delegates' luxury boat.

AUGUST 2008: Fredy Villanueva is shot dead by a police officer, and NOII-Montreal becomes heavily involved in a campaign to support the family. Two years later, Villanueva's brother Dany, who is scheduled to testify at the coroner's inquest into his brother's death, faces deportation to Honduras due to a prior criminal conviction. NOII-Montreal mobilizes support for Dany's immigration hearings and pushes the campaign against double punishment.

OCTOBER 2008: The Shelter Sanctuary Status campaign is coordinated nationally, and two hundred national, provincial, and Toronto women's groups and community organizations join the campaign. In Toronto, four hundred people join an emergency rally precipitated by the pending deportation of Isabel Garcia, who fled gender violence in Mexico. Two years later, the CBSA is forced to issue a directive that prohibits immigration enforcement officers from entering any resource center for survivors of violence.

MAY 2009: Akwesasne Mohawks take a stand against the arming of CBSA guards within their territory and effectively shut down a border crossing. NOII-Montreal offers support to the struggle, including being present on-site and disseminating updates. On July 1, Canada Day, NOII-Montreal sends an Anti-Canada Day solidarity statement to Akwesasne: "The CBSA, and the border they enforce, serve not only to divide Haudenosaunee peoples, and the community of Akwesasne, but also to enforce a racist immigration regime that deports and detains members of our communities. . . . We continue to try to practice our own decolonization, rooted in the traditions and under-standing of the Haudenosaunee—such as the two-row wampum treaty—and in a present and future where we can establish and re-establish relations."[52]

OCTOBER 2009: NOII-Vancouver initiates a Let them Free, Let them Stay campaign for the seventy-six Tamil refugees aboard the *MV Ocean Lady* boat. Almost a year later, 492 Tamil refugees aboard the *MV Sun Sea* arrive. NOII-Vancouver mobilizes a national response over eighteen months in support of the refugees, many of whom are incarcerated.

DECEMBER 2009: NOII-Halifax begins a two-year campaign to stop the deportation of the Chaudhry family to Pakistan. Through persistent direct support work, including letter-writing drives, press conferences, court support, outreach to community organizations and mosques, and legal advocacy, the campaign succeeds in preventing this deportation.

FEBRUARY 2010: NOII-Vancouver organizes a No One Is Illegal, Canada Is Illegal contingent within the 2010 No

Olympics on Stolen Native Land convergence "against the ongoing colonization of this land, resists the racist police state, opposes restrictive border controls and the exploitation of immigrant workers, denounces the imperialist occupations waged across the globe by the Canadian government and military, and combats the violence, poverty, and environmental devastation inflicted disproportionately on women and children by corporate profiteers and the capitalist system."[53]

JUNE 2010: NOII groups in Halifax, Montreal, Ottawa, Toronto, and Vancouver join the anti-G20 convergence. A cross-country meeting lays the ground for increased coordination and communication. A panel on "Colonialism, Capitalism, and Migration" furthers an analysis about the impacts of G20 policies on displaced and colonized communities. NOII groups also organize a "No Fences, No Borders" press conference with Indigenous Defenders of the Land, and mobilize contingents and affinity groups in all the actions. Over a thousand arrests take place during the G20 protests.

AUGUST 2010: NOII-Ottawa, along with Queers against Israeli Apartheid, march in the LGBT Pride Parade in support of the boycott, divestment, and sanctions movement against Israeli apartheid as well as queer refugees fighting deportation from Canada. In 2012, NOII-London organizes a similar contingent during Pride week.

SEPTEMBER 2010: As a result of the mobilizing of the Education Not Deportation campaign, the Toronto District School Board releases a poster to 558 elementary and secondary schools stating, "All children living in our community, including those without immigration status in Canada, are entitled to admission to our schools."[54]

OCTOBER 2010: Migrant agriculture workers and Justice for Migrant Workers, accompanied by allies from across Ontario, participate in a fifty-kilometer Pilgrimage to Freedom. On the heels of the deaths of two migrant workers at an organic foods apple orchard, the workers demand immigration status, an end to exorbitant recruitment fees, better housing, safe working conditions, and an end to discrimination in the workplace.

MAY 2011: Queer undocumented artist Alvaro Orozco is arrested and detained. This sparks a massive campaign, coordinated by Orozco's friends and NOII-Toronto, and unites migrant, artist, and queer communities. Due to the immense pressure, he is released from detention and granted legal status within Canada.

FEBRUARY 2012: NOII-Montreal actively participates in the historic Quebec student strike, and makes links between tuition hikes and the commodification of education to lack of access to education for nonstatus students. A Status for All casseroles is organized in June by NOII-Montreal, the IWC, and Solidarity across Borders.

MAY 2012: NOII-Toronto, May First Movement, and (de) Occupy Toronto join together for May Day under the slogan "No Banks! No Bombs! No Bosses! No Borders! No Broken Treaties! Capitalism is the Crisis."

DECEMBER 2012: Racialized immigrants across the country express support for Idle No More. A statement initiated by NOII members and immigrants in support of Idle No More reads, "Enduring decades, if not centuries, of colonialism, empire, racism, impoverishment, violence and displacement . . . many of us have struggled to find stability and to make homes here on Turtle Island. But we recognize that our homes are built on the ruins of others. . . . With humility and gratitude, we affirm our solidarity and support for the sovereignty not of the illegal Canadian government or its immoral laws but of those communities whose lands we reside on."[55]

FEBRUARY 2013: Ten years into the Don't Ask Don't Tell campaign, Toronto is successfully declared a Sanctuary City, and Toronto City Council commits to providing services to undocumented residents.

Working alongside Migrant Farmworkers

Scanning the restaurant job classifieds in a Toronto Chinese daily late in 2003, I find the ad I'm looking for: "Farm Hiring. Picking Tomatoes." I call the number, and within a week I'm whisked down the highway to a greenhouse in southwestern Ontario.

We're in the heart of the tomato industry. The conditions vary from farm to farm and greenhouse to greenhouse, but at this greenhouse—one of the region's biggest players—I know some specifics. In the summer, when the growers can bring in carefully selected, young, fit Mexican and Caribbean workers, they assign each of their workers personal digital assistants measuring how quickly they work and ranking them compared to their colleagues. The living conditions are clean, but cold and dehumanizing.

In the winter, the growers and contractors play a different game. Some workers are picked up as early as 3:00 a.m. They wait, unpaid, until the workday starts at 6:00 a.m. At the end of the day, some may get to bed at midnight, sometimes as late as 1:30 a.m. Why so late? Between ten and twenty farmworkers live in a dwelling, sharing one stove, fridge, and bathroom. Contractors pick up and drop off workers from and to scattered locales. Waiting dominates each day.

When we're roused at 6:00 a.m., a pay dispute has already erupted. A worker tells me he hasn't been paid in more than two weeks. The contractor had promised payment on the arrival of our crew; our driver would bring the cash from Toronto. Yet here we were, but no cash. Three

workers from his crew have already given up and left, for-
feiting two weeks' worth of pay.

The contractor drives six of us—three men, three
women—to a smaller nearby greenhouse. Two Bosnians
work for the same contractor here. A Mexican, a Mexican
Mennonite, and two Canadians are also at work, hired
directly by the greenhouse owner.

Everything we're working with is at floor level; after
a row I'm already aching. The greenhouse floor is covered
with thick white plastic. Steam pipes run along alternating
rows. We're warned to keep the plants from touching the
pipes, but I slip on the wet plastic and bump into a pipe,
receiving a slight burn.

Employment is precarious. When a worker at another
greenhouse is accused of taking a slightly longer afternoon
break, he is barred from continuing work that day and
forced to wait at the plant, unpaid, until the end of the
workday to go home.

I notice some graffiti written in Chinese on one of the
greenhouses' bathroom stalls. It reads, translated: "Worked
in this small town two and a half days. Tasted sour, sweet,
bitter, and heat. Looking to discover a bit of fortune. Only
to discover it's not here."

—Aylwin Lo

To Prevent a Deportation

(july 2007–october 2008)

calls

10:00 a.m. rally, parking lot of george pearson centre
                                           july 7, 2007
paralyzed punjabi refugee claimant has taken sanctuary
                                           july 7, 2007
dinner to support   july 28, 2007
arrested while in hospital   august 14, 2007
rallies held across canada   august 18, 2007
wins sixty-day stay of deportation   august 19, 2007
conditional release from detention   august 22, 2007
wins another temporary stay   october 20, 2007
deportation set   october 22, 2007
rally, on one of the coldest days in the lower mainland
                                           december 2, 2007
convergence of thousands, vancouver international airport
                                           december 10, 2007
4:30 a.m. emergency rally, surrey gurudwara sanctuary
                                           january 9, 2008
national days of action in eleven cities
                                           january 24–29, 2008
vancouver/surrey evening vigil   january 27, 2008
one year too many in sanctuary   july 13, 2008

actions

humanitarian and compassionate claim, community,
    sanctuary

rally, media, campaign, volunteer, free, taxis, pro bono,
    donation
public, petition, letters, twenty-five thousand signatures,
    prayers, people, vigils
delegations, information, education, crtc complaint, civil
    disobedience
cbsa physically and peacefully blocked, interviews,
    coverage, outreach
documentation, defiance, signs, urgent action, unity,
    supporters[1]

act in a world
primarily elderly, women, working-class grassroots
community mobilization a powerful inspiration
challenging unjust laws, policies of Immigration Canada
the idea that some migrants are more worthy than others
not just for him alone nor is it simply one case
how hard and long racialized migrants must fight
to assert their right to self-determination
and continue to actively organize

ii. *prior to suffering worked as a laborer*

as you all might   have heard by now
intends to present   for removal
thankful to supporters   their kindness
choice affirming how important   choice is
no longer able to endure   State of limbo
on many occasions   agents
attended despite   sanctuary

extreme immense "example"
scrutiny constant threat   self-doubt
about "being a burden" overwhelming
precarity faced with   unwavering courage
        Laibar Singh
dared demand dignity
the right to exist, to be recognized
commend him, condemn a government
they fear legitimate concerns of people
people moved coast to coast   beautiful
and unprecedented   mobilizing
model minority   direct action defiance

we used to be farmers   I will not forget your departure
to have been a part—carried forward
to stand undeterred—the point of a claim
to organize with greater dedication—alongside

—Cecily Nicholson

Serendipity

In August 2010, the *MV Sun Sea* ship arrived on the Northwest coast of British Columbia, on the territories of the Songhees First Nation, carrying 492 Tamil asylum seekers from Sri Lanka. Only two years after the Canadian government apologized for its racist and exclusionary history in turning back the *Komagata Maru* ship carrying 376 passengers from India in 1914, history repeated itself. After being greeted by a Canadian warship and declared "illegal," the children, women, and men aboard the *MV Sun Sea* were separated and forced to stay in detention centers across Vancouver.

We all felt the responsibility to do something, and decided that while it was important to counter the public discourse around the refugees being "queue jumpers," "terrorists," "illegals," and "criminals," it was equally important to show our solidarity in a way that could be felt. In addition to organizing public demonstrations, forums, press conferences, and national days of actions, we also produced a legal resource guide for the detainees and hosted noise demonstrations outside the detention centers.

We played Tamil music, held up a sign that said "We Support You" in Tamil, and banged pots and pans against the fence blocking us from the detention center. I will always remember the poignancy of the Indigenous elders who attended and opened many of the demonstrations by welcoming the asylum seekers to their territories and condemning the governments' draconian immigration policies. On several occasions, we saw children waving at us through one of the only visible windows. After over ten weeks of weekly demonstrations, the metallic letters that spelled out Burnaby Youth Detention Center began to fall off, and cracks born out of sheer persistence opened up the fencing.

A few weeks later, my roommate and I were able to enter the prison to conduct arts programming with the children. It was the first time that I had ever been inside of a prison, and I was shocked at the matrix of locked doors and swipe cards that led us to where the women and children were being detained. I remember my stomach clenching when the guards tried to explain that this wasn't really a jail, and that these mothers and their children were dealt a good set of cards. We did not want the guards to know that we had been organizing the noise demonstrations, but when we asked one of the mothers what she thought of all the music outside, she smiled discretely and whispered: "Nice." When it was time to leave, the children gave us the pictures that they had drawn as presents. All of the pictures were of boats.

Shortly after, my roommate and I were taking out the garbage, and we saw two young girls taking out the recycling across the alley. I felt like I knew them, but I couldn't place from where. My roommate asked them in Tamil what their names were, and one of them said: "Don't you remember us? We met you in the detention center!" They ran inside and moments later, as we stood in shock, the kids and two older women came outside to smile and wave at us from the balcony. We later found out that house they were in was a refugee house and that they would be living across from us for the fall.

That serendipitous moment will forever remind me that in 2010, a ship arrived on the Northwest coast, on the territories of the Songhees First Nation. Not a person on that ship was illegal.

—Nassim Elbardouh

No Easy Victories

Supporting nonunionized immigrant and migrant workers often seems like an impossible task, but at the Immigrant Workers Centre (IWC) we take on these cases because we believe that all workers, regardless of immigration status, deserve basic rights. The more we fight, the more we can win against employers and the Labor Standards Commission, and this helps to build confidence among workers.

This was true, for example, for Margaret. Margaret was a Caribbean mother who was laid off without severance from one of Montreal's most prestigious country clubs, where she worked as a cleaner. We organized with her to win two months of wages from her employer, who like many other employers, profits so heavily from low-wage immigrant workers.

Another victory was the case of Mousa, an undocumented car-wash worker who was denied his pay for over two months. Given his lack of legal immigration status, Mousa felt unable to exercise his basic right to his wages and was terrified when he first came to the IWC. When we began advocating for his pay, his employer backed off and Mousa received his outstanding wages.

But there really is no specific moment or particular victory that most defines the work of the IWC. So much of the injustice that people face is not just about policies; it is a constant feeling of being denied respect in the workplace and feeling devalued in society. These workers' lives become invisible, yet they are the ones who make our society run, by cleaning our homes, taking care of our children, and picking, serving, and packaging our food. While much of our work at the IWC is focused on specific cases and victories, we have collectively created a space that can be called home, a place that allows for immigrant and migrant workers to find family and love, and a movement where the little moments help to regain a sense of dignity.

Victor is a Mexican temporary migrant worker who left the United States due to heightened racist immigration enforcement, only to find himself in Montreal in a work situation where he was paid less than minimum wage, never paid overtime, and constantly harassed by his employer. He quit his job, but because he was a temporary migrant worker, he lost not only his income but also his immigration status.

Victor found support and courage from others at the IWC. Two of those people are Aadi, a community organizer at the IWC who was once a nonstatus migrant from Senegal, and Kader, a nonstatus Algerian refugee who spent four years in sanctuary in defiance of a deportation order prior to becoming an IWC organizer. Aadi's and Kader's own struggles are examples of living and fighting with dignity, and so the IWC wanted to provide them with employment and support them to inspire others. In a true embodiment of solidarity, Aadi and Kader supported Victor, who won a settlement, and regained some sense of justice for himself and his family. Victor now spends time at the IWC, playing music and dancing, which Kader often joins in on.

Another member who has changed the IWC and affected the lives of others is Noe. He is a friend who I can never really communicate with due to no common language. Noe used to be a migrant farmworker from Guatemala who got blacklisted, and is now fighting for both his immigration status and justice from his employer. Despite having his own struggles, he spends every day organizing for regularization with nonstatus Mexicans and with placement agency day laborers in the food processing industry. I remember Noe helping Rolando, another migrant worker, to file a grievance for his workplace accident when the union did not want to help Rolando.

These are just some of the faces of the IWC, friends I drink coffee with and complain about the state of affairs for nonstatus migrants and immigrant workers with over a heaping plate of fried rice. Because victories can be few and far between, creating the relationships of trust and an open space are critical steps toward building mass movements and more long-term change. So much of our activism is based on the idea of the perfect organizer who has the correct analysis and right skills that we end up leaving the people themselves out of our processes. There has been nothing like the IWC in the twelve years that I have been involved in radical activism, and the biggest victory has been the creation of a space where migrant and immigrant workers are empowered.

—Mostafa Henaway

OVERGROWING HEGEMONY:
GRASSROOTS THEORY

Overgrowing Hegemony: Grassroots Theory

> Perhaps the most radical act today is to speak the truth about a darkening sky and remain committed to organizing, knowing there is no guarantee we can endure, let alone prevail. . . . The potential power of social movements at this moment in history flows from this commitment to speaking the truth—not truth to power, which is too invested in its delusions to listen—but truth to each other.
>
> —Robert Jensen, "The Power—and Limits—of Social Movements"

Movement building requires reflexivity. And yet it is rare to find open spaces of debate and discussion, outside of insular networks, where movement practices can be rigorously analyzed. I attribute this rarity to a variety of factors: the crisis-oriented nature of community organizing, skepticism about intellectualism stemming from a misplaced conflation with the elitism and inaccessibility of academic institutions, and our own personal fears and defensiveness about unsettling existing movement practices in which we are invested or implicated. Rather than shying away from debate and dialogue, transformative and effective movement organizing requires us to kindle a consciousness within the Left that fosters deliberate thought aimed at effectively challenging exploitation and oppression beyond ritualized "petition to workshop to rally" activism. When I speak of the Left and social movements here, I am not referring to the entire Left but instead specifically to those North American movements that aspire to be radical yet accessible in pedagogy, mass based while militant in orientation, and are characterized as the antiauthoritarian, anticapitalist, nonsectarian Left engaged in grassroots community organizing.[1]

This chapter aims to offer a space for movement-based theorizing by indexing some universal concepts, debates, and challenges within Left social movements. I apply the specific principles of NOII organizing in the previous chapter to general social movement practices for the Left by providing an overview of key lessons on strategies and tactics, antioppression work, and group structure and leadership. The pitfalls and potentials of these concepts are also picked up in greater detail in the subsequent roundtable.

There are no definitive answers when theorizing about the transformation of hegemonic power relations; movement building cannot be imposed, and by its very nature, is a perpetual process of analysis, organizing, and reflection. As novelist Eduardo Galeano writes, "Utopia is on the horizon: when I walk two steps, it takes two steps back. I walk ten steps and it is ten steps further away. What is utopia for? It is for this, for walking."[2] By reflecting and theorizing on my on-the-ground experiences, I hope to contribute to the creation of sustainable and revolutionary movements that have a political and spiritual commitment to walking toward and winning social change.

Transformative movements mean something different to each of us, but we all know the feeling of being in a space because we *want* to be there. Although we are tired and the daily hustle is taking a toll, we are there because our whole selves are moved and called to be there. Ai-Jen Poon of Domestic Workers United says, "We need a culture that supports being centered, focused and connected to our sense of purpose."[3] Nourishing that sense of purpose, while enabling a culture that makes it possible for all of us to keep that sense of purpose alive, is what transformative movements strive toward and what transformative movement practices—through thoughtful strategizing, meaningful antioppression work, and empowering group structures—are ultimately about.

Transformative movement organizing not only transforms systems of power but as Eric Mann of the Los Angeles-based Labor Community Strategy Center also notes, transforms the consciousness of those participating in the movement.[4] We are structured socially by the material conditions of border imperialism and psychologically disciplined by its logic. It therefore requires tremendous commitment to steer movement strategies and relations toward collective liberation. The Horizontal Alliance of

Very Organized Queers (HAVOQ) in the San Francisco Bay Area describes transformative movement organizing as an intentional practice of undoing borders. The group's manifesto states, "We will make time to do the work of building ways of being with one another that do not replicate the hierarchies that marginalize us in the first place. . . . We want to create and maintain liberating and borderless spaces within which to meet and do work."[5]

In order to create movement spaces that are liberated and liberating, this chapter's discussion on strategies and tactics, antioppression practices, and group structure and leadership is interwoven with a more fundamental recognition of the need to undo all the ways in which border imperialism spills over into our social movement organizing. Given all the power-over we have internalized, traumas we have metabolized, and walls and hierarchies we have maintained between one another, it is imperative that we unravel and confront these effects of border imperialism within our movements as we work to dismantle the systems that propagate it.

On Strategies and Tactics

Given that what radical movements seek is systemic revolutionary change, it is often easy to avoid defining how we will actually get there. But it is imperative for movements to break out of our activist bubbles and identify what tangible impacts we can have within broader communities and what victories we can leverage that will bring us closer to our vision of freedom, liberation, and self-determination. This is the process of strategizing. Successful social movements incorporate several key strategies that I explore below, including building alliances through grassroots organizing, effectively campaigning without diluting political principles, and thoughtfully utilizing diverse tactics.

One of the hardest tasks in movement building is building alliances. Popular educators Joshua Kahn Russell and Harmony Goldberg draw attention to the necessity of reaching beyond our echo chambers to unite as many people as possible: "A genuine radical imagination holds space for those who have not yet come to adopt the entirety of our worldviews, and sees those close to us as potential allies, rather than enemies. If we really want to take on the power structures in our society, we're gonna need a lot of people."[6] Alliance building requires consideration and practice to navigate tricky terrain. Within NOII, for example, many questions arise around alliance building. How do we build a base of support within migrant communities without alienating people through our radical actions? How do we support our immigrant communities in crisis while also taking responsibility for educating immigrants about settler colonialism, capitalism, and oppression in order to build solidarity with other marginalized communities? How do we discuss migrant justice issues with the white middle class without resorting to simplifications such as "but immigrants are hardworking taxpayers"?

No alliance is free of such complicated dynamics, differences in ideology, and nuanced questions.

NOII-Vancouver (Indigenous Coast Salish territories) has, for example, spent many years organizing alongside refugees who fled Iran as political dissidents. The main slogan for this group of Iranian exiles is "Down with the Islamic Regime of Iran." Though they are leftists, they often join forces with anti-Iranian imperialists such as politicians of the Conservative Party of Canada to amplify their goals. For us, this has posed a complicated dynamic—supporting refugees fighting deportations to Iran and respecting their own articulations of their very real and horrific experiences at the hands of the Iranian regime, but doing so without fueling an imperialist agenda. We have let the group know that we are willing to support them, and have even gone on hunger strikes alongside them, but cannot comfortably participate if they have speakers at events who advocate Islamophobia or a war on Iran.

Establishing these conditions is not an ultimatum; it is rooted in a process of engagement—an ongoing negotiation of politics and lived experiences—as we spend hours in conversation to build trust, enact solidarities, and better understand each other. As Russell and Goldberg emphasize, alliances are not static relationships but rather a process of mutual education and transformation. "Uncomfortable alliances are not just necessary; they reflect and speak to the tremendous possibility of our political moment," they assert. "Learning how to work together is part of the process that births a new world."[7] While several anti-imperialist groups no longer work with this group of Iranian refugees, we maintain a relationship with them because we understand that the strategic alliances they make with some conservative elements comes not from seeking power within the system but instead from a sense of desperation about the violence inflicted on their loved ones that few of us have ever experienced. At the same time, solidarity is not a passive act; it is a mutual relationship that requires us to be clear and consistent in communicating our concerns about aligning with pro-imperialist forces. Montreal-based activist Martin Lukacs notes:

> When two people go walking, they talk, and solidarity at its most respectful and responsible is essentially a conversation. This is how you discover a community's vision for itself, how it would like to determine itself. . . . Solidarity is also a never-ending process to better understand each other's norms, limitations, and boundaries—whether political, cultural, psychological, or material. . . . The exchanges we have help us know when the trust is strong enough to let us push each other, push those boundaries.[8]

Alliances must be consensual and accountable, and successful alliance building requires us, first, to humble ourselves. We cannot immediately write off those who do not agree with us, especially those who are our neighbors, community members, and coworkers. As community organizers, we must refuse to see ourselves as the vanguard of the revolution who hold the moral high ground. Instead, we must understand our roles as those that can facilitate and inspire mutal learning and transformation. We all learned what we know now from someone at sometime, and we should afford that time and respect to others (that is, until our patience runs thin!). Second, we have to be prepared to meet people where they are at, but without compromising our political vision. Grassroots movements need to move beyond narrow interests and catering to lowest-common-denominator politics and single-issue alliances toward creating movements that address broader structural change. If, within our alliances, we restrain ourselves from fully expressing our systemic analysis, for instance, on prison abolition within a neighborhood meeting about increased school tuition, we are losing critical opportunities to engage with others about the interconnections in the school-to-prison pipeline.

How and when to engage in these conversations is contextual, and relies on a number of factors such as the level of preexisting trust. This leads to the third requirement: a commitment to long-term alliances that help us learn from one another rather than strategically managed alliances that only work toward winning prescribed campaign goals. While there are some alliances we would never make because they violate our basic ethical principles, alliances are generally necessary with those we may not agree with, and during the course of mutual exchange, we foster healthy debate and conversation with growing numbers of people. A lack of absolute clarity on these types of questions is to be expected. As the Zapatista saying goes, "Walking, we ask questions." In the next chapter's round-table, participants offer their own insights based on their organizing experiences.

Movement building also requires grassroots outreach in order to accrue a base of supporters. Too often outreach is reduced to posting an event on Facebook or postering a few neighborhoods. Outreach should employ an array of strategies, and can take many forms such as posters, street theater, workshops, newsletters, and educational events. Whatever form of outreach we choose, the key is that it should be frequent and with the intent of engaging with people. Movements tend to view outreach and popular education as separate. We assume that the people we outreach to are just passive receptacles of information, but outreach is most effective when it employs the popular education strategy of interaction. We need to stop and talk to people, ask them about their opinions while sharing our own, and invite them into spaces where they can expect not only to be talked at but can also provide their own thoughts. Similarly, strategies that expand prefigurative spaces, where we reduce our reliance on the state and strengthen our infrastructures of resistance by creating media, collective kitchens, infoshops, and so on, are truly revolutionary when they connect with as opposed to withdraw from people.

A final strategy for effective movement building involves the ways we choose to communicate the values and principles underlying our organizing. The intentional use of language can shift how people understand and relate to the issues we are presenting. NOII has, for example, consciously refrained from perpetuating terminology like illegal immigrants, and we have had some success in shifting popular discourse toward terms such as undocumented or nonstatus migrants. These terms are free of the shame and stigma associated with words such as illegal and alien, allowing us to have dialogue with people—directly and through media—about illegalization not as a characteristic of migrants but instead as a result of the moral illegitimacy of border controls. We also must never underestimate the power of narrative storytelling, which is at the heart of our movements. We are moved not by dry statistics but rather by the stories that touch us and compel us to act.

Movement building requires not only implementing effective strategies such as those outlined above but also discussions on what even qualifies as effective. A long-standing debate on effectiveness in evaluating campaign strategies is the question of reformism versus revolution. Within the broader Left, this debate is an ideological one: reformists charge that radicals are demanding the impossible, while radicals maintain that reformists are selling short of necessary structural change. Within the radical Left, where there is already a shared critique of the state and capitalism as the root causes of injustice and inequity, this debate is focused around strategies rather than ideology. Within this debate, reformist strategies are denounced for engaging state institutions, while revolutionary strategies are criticized for existing entirely outside and in confrontation with the state.

I would argue that this dualism pitting reformist against revolutionary strategies is often a false one, rooted more in theoretical abstractions than actual practice. Davis writes of the prison movement, "I do not think that there is a strict dividing line between reform and abolition."[9] A series of dialogues hosted by the New York Study Group in 2009 similarly concludes, "Without falling into reformism, left organizers can use reform work to lay the groundwork for more radical transformation."[10]

In NOII, as outlined in the previous chapter, direct support work with individuals frequently requires navigating state institutions like border agencies, immigration offices, the court system, and political offices in order to support those facing detention or deportation. Such organizing to meet the immediate needs of undocumented migrants and refugees changes migrants' material conditions by, for example, winning legal resident status, which then facilitates them becoming more involved in radical movements. It also works to build long-term relationships of confidence and trust in our work, and provides a means through which to share our own analysis. This contributes to migrants' further politicization and more often than not participation in more revolutionary movements. The process of direct support is therefore mutually reinforcing: by being meaningfully grounded in people's daily realities, which may involve immediate reform-oriented strategies, we have a tangible impact on the lives of oppressed communities, while we are also empowering these communities to inform and be informed by our analysis and strategy on long-term revolutionary change.

A difficult question then becomes how to balance these strategies—how to campaign around particular legislation or work with individuals to meet their basic needs within the system, while also mobilizing for the eventual abolition of oppressive systems. The momentum that has sustained NOII is the deliberate *fusion* and *cohesion* of these seemingly divergent strategies, with attentiveness to context, as well as a refusal to engage in reformist strategies that are essentially contrary to our transformative values. Ng'ethe Maina of Social Justice Leadership says that "we should not be doing campaigns that cannot be connected to a broader ideological conversation."[11] NOII would not, for example, work toward a selective regularization policy that would benefit some migrants but exclude those migrants with criminal records or those on social assistance.

We aim for campaigns with short-term goals that are not fundamentally at odds with—but rather advance and strengthen—our long-term vision of naming and transforming the roots causes of injustice. For example, we could call the Solidarity City campaign strategies, described in the previous chapter, reformist because of their engagements with bureaucratic institutions. Yet these campaigns have furthered the involvement of nonstatus migrants, women's centers, students, and labor unions within the migrant justice movement. Also, the strategies employed in these campaigns have pushed forward the systemic demand of status for all people, and been visionary in prefiguring safe spaces in which nonstatus migrants can access critical services. As a general principle, then, strategies should flow from an analysis of the current political conditions along with the movements' strengths and capacities, and be consistent with and further an overall ideological vision.

A usually confused corollary to strategy is the concept of tactics. Tactics are the tools we use to achieve our strategic goals. As Salar Mohandesi, an editor of *Viewpoint Magazine*, explains:

> A tactic, it is often said, is a specific set of maneuvers used to win a localized engagement. A strategy, on the other hand, is the way these discrete engagements are coherently strung together to realize a broader objective. The two therefore form a reciprocal relationship in practice as well as in theory. Without a strategy, tactics only produce isolated skirmishes; without tactics, a strategy is only an unfulfilled dream.[12]

A defining feature of effective social movements is the adoption of an array of bold and creative tactics to build winning campaigns. Moving beyond the regurgitation of dogma or circulation of petitions, the tactics of vibrant social movements have included flash mobs, murals, performance art, social media, culture jamming, press conferences, blockades, filmmaking, wildcat strikes, banner drops, street theater, guerrilla art, economic disruption, speaking tours, marches, and occupations. Individual tactics cannot be judged in isolation from the strategy that underwrites their utilization; rather, tactics should be judged by their effectiveness in meeting strategic goals. One way to determine whether a tactic is effective is to think about strategic points of intervention: Has the tactic been effective, for instance, in exposing or confronting a specific point within the system by either diminishing its moral legitimacy or undermining its functioning? Debates on tactics generally erroneously focus on individual tactics as being intrinsically more right (and sometimes, righteous), which detracts from more useful discussions on which tactics will be effective in channeling our power to attain our strategic objectives.

In response to property destruction at some protests, debates have coalesced around the concept of diversity of tactics and the acceptable realm of confrontational tactics that social movements should engage. Though sometimes seen as code for unqualified and unconditional support for black bloc tactics, I understand diversity of tactics to be a more nuanced principle. If the goal is to be effective, a diversity of tactics challenges us to shed our dogmatic attachment to both pacificist and black bloc tactics when correlating tactics to strategy. Mohandesi pushes us to shift the debate beyond the ritualistic confines of violence versus nonviolence principles to one, instead, of substantive strategy: "The question isn't whether to pursue a 'diversity of tactics,' but rather: what kind of strategy allows us to effectively incorporate a diverse range of tactics?"[13]

While NOII groups do not have a uniform position, many NOII members support the principle of diversity of tactics with the understanding that this means respecting a range of tactics and not intentionally ruling out any particular one from the outset, whether peaceful tactics, nonviolent civil disobedience, creative resistance, social media campaigns, blockades, lobbying, or property alteration. Maintaining communication to ensure comfort and alerting others, especially affected community members, about a chosen tactic is critical. Tactics should be chosen based on the terrain of the struggle on which they are being used and, ideally, tactics further the strategy that has been chosen. Thus the question of whether a tactic is effective or not is entirely contextual. Based on the goals and purpose of the strategy chosen to further a campaign or movement, those engaging in the action are best suited to decide on the tactics.

In conclusion, it is imperative that we build the collective power necessary for collective liberation by encouraging the participation of a broad and diverse base of people, engaging in popular education and consistent outreach, prioritizing a multiplicity of alliances across movements and communities, and thoughtfully evaluating our tactics.

On Antioppression Work

Within movement building, the strengthening of external alliances and facilitating of internal leadership both require a strong grounding in antioppression analysis and practice. Antioppression analysis attempts to examine and address the varied—often unintentional and invisible—effects of systemic marginalization and differential power dynamics between individuals, groups, and communities by providing a critical analysis of the intersecting lived realities of race, class, gender, sexuality, and ability.

Traditional class-reductionist organizing has tended to trivialize this analysis, characterizing it as "fringe" or "divisive," but as black feminist Audre Lorde maintains, "We have been taught either to ignore our differences, or to view them as causes for separation and suspicion rather than as

forces for change. . . . Community must not mean a shedding of our differences, nor the pathetic pretense that these
differences do not exist."[14] Or in the emphatic words of
Martinican poet and theorist Aimé Césaire, "I do not bury
myself in a narrow particularism. But I also do not want to
lose myself in a limitless universalism."[15] Due to the tireless
education and agitation by many before us, antioppression
work has become a core principle of social movements, key
in undoing the systemic barriers and borders put up against
and between marginalized communities.

There are, however, several persistent pitfalls of antioppression analysis. Even an intersectional approach that
acknowledges the overlapping and layered nature of power
and privilege can lead to a flattening of all oppressions—
a simple "additive effect" rather than "entirely different
conceptions of people's lived realities."[16] In the context of
antiracist organizing, for example, communities of color
do not have a common shared experience of racism. While
powerful for self-identification and denoting alliance, the
term people of color homogenizes and distorts significant differences between, say, nonnatives and natives or
citizens and undocumented migrants. Within the NOII
group in Vancouver (Indigenous Coast Salish territories),
although we describe ourselves as a group with leadership
from racialized people, we also identify ourselves as allies
to Indigenous communities and those without full legal
status. This is an acknowledgment that not only are we
differently impacted by racism but that we must be actively
responsible for challenging the processes of racialized
subjugations that impact others.

Antioppression analysis becomes rigid in its categorizations when the question becomes who is *more* oppressed, rather than engaging in a dialogue of *how* oppression, which is relational and contextual, is specifically manifesting and impacting the orientation of our movements. Oppression develops a strange quantifiable logic, a commodity that can be stocked up on. Antioppression "checklisting" can lead to a race to the bottom, where it is assumed that simply because someone fits into more categories of oppression, they must necessarily be worse off.

Working in the poorest postal code in Canada, I know that a straight white cisgendered man who is homeless faces a harsher material reality on a daily basis—with minimal to no access to food, shelter, health care, or income—than me, someone who might be able to count off more forms of oppression, but who does not have to worry about surviving through a cold night on the streets. Again, oppression is relational and contextual; we are all embedded in relations of domination and all wear privilege, albeit in different ways and to varying degrees. I have sat through countless dead-end conversations between white women and men of color arguing about "who is more oppressed." This kind of equivocal debate does nothing to grasp the underlying dynamics of race and gender, which are not embodied in the same ways and are not analogous or interchangeable forms of oppression.

A sharp lesson in antioppression work was when I was working with an incarcerated stateless refugee facing indefinite detention. Doing support work was difficult as he was extremely misogynist, taunting female activists, and making jokes about rape and violence against women. His behavior was clearly oppressive, and I raised serious safety concerns. However, this man had also been in jail for years and we had a responsibility to organize a campaign for his freedom. After many discussions, the resolution we reached within NOII-Vancouver (Indigenous Coast Salish territories) was that the men in NOII would step up to liaise with the detainee, working to both challenge his sexism and relay messages to and from the campaign outside. I remained actively involved in the campaign because I felt that I, as someone not behind bars, had a responsibility to support him, but drew my boundaries at not engaging with him in person. Instead of having different forms of oppression actively undermine each other—as so often happens— this is an example of antioppression work that recognizes it is possible to challenge privilege while still being responsible allies.

Rigidity within antioppression analysis can also lead to those with privilege abrogating their own responsibility to challenge oppression by circumscribing their roles to the safe task of perfecting antioppression language as an end in itself—one that will purge their guilt. This performance of guilt is a kind of self-absorption that centers on, and hence upholds and reproduces, oppression. Readily admitting, for example, to being racist or sexist (that is, "I am a white man, therefore I will never know what it is like to be a woman of color, and of course I am racist and sexist, but I don't know what to do") is a convenient way to quickly shut down conversation. Rather than having a more nuanced and useful dialogue about *what* and *how* specific behaviors or comments are oppressive, we get stuck in general conversations about who is the oppressed and who is the oppressor. Being cognizant of antioppression as a fluid analysis helps us move beyond unhealthy cycles of shame, guilt, and stagnation that have come to mark the terrain of "anti-o." This fluidity is most relevant within a politics of actual engagement with one another, which necessitates the difficult task of building relationships and solidarities.

Furthermore, antioppression practice is often trapped at the level of questions of representation, such as how to include and accommodate more oppressed identities into existing events or campaigns. This superficial, frequently tokenistic veneer of diversity replicates models of assimilation, and does little to reframe our activism within oppressed people's *own* analysis and experiences. Oppressed communities should be within the leadership of our movements precisely because those most impacted by systemic oppression across race, class, gender, sexuality, and ability are, not coincidentally, also those who are most impacted by the systems of border imperialism, capitalism, and empire. Race, class, gender, sexuality, and ability are not derivative *of* capitalism and colonialism; oppression is foundational *to* the structuring of capitalism and colonialism. Hence, we need to strengthen an antioppression practice that fundamentally reframes our conceptions of how social, political, and economic injustices are structured and maintained.

Concretely, this involves three steps. We begin by seeking out and offering tangible solidarity and resources to existing movements within marginalized communities.

Second, we engage and involve oppressed communities in the decision-making processes of our groups and campaigns. This supports the leadership and empowerment of these voices throughout our activism rather than simply as speakers at a few events. Third, we must frame campaigns so they align with the analyses that marginalized peoples have about the issues that impact their lives and allow them to make such articulations on their own terms. It is not uncommon to have a well-intentioned campaign on behalf of a community that carries little resonance because the campaign's messaging does not mirror a community's own understanding of the issues. Reorienting our activism toward such antioppression practices grounds it within the lived experiences and analyses of those who daily survive and resist injustice.

A final pitfall of antioppression analysis is its tendency to devolve into an essentialist politics of identity and individual complicity, which can become decontextualized, and thus cut off from the totality of social and structural relations. As Sara Mourad, a scholar on race and sexuality, writes, "Oppression is always multilayered. It is exercised by different jurisdictions, institutions, and discourses— from the secular to the religious, from the local to the transnational, from the private to the public, from the social to the economic."[17] Antioppression analysis has been particularly weak in articulating the connections between hierarchical social formations and capitalist relations of production as being mutually constructed and reinforcing. Class cannot be understood simply in an individualized framework, such as poor bashing; it must be identified as creating structural relations within capitalism, particularly of labor exploitation and divisions of labor that extend from the workplace to the home, mediated through structures of oppression. Mohanty summarizes this as the necessity to name "capitalist hegemony and culture as a foundational principle of social life. To do otherwise is to obfuscate the way power and hegemony function in the world."[18]

It is important to note that pejorative and reactionary phrases such as identity politics or oppression olympics do little to meaningfully address all these various short-comings because they ignore the materiality of oppressive hierarchies. Black Panther elder Ashanti Alston explains, "Identity politics is important to me. . . . I find my people's experience the foundation from which we will find our way to liberation and power."[19] A commitment to challeng-ing the impact of oppression is foundational to building movements where all people are equally valued. However, an *inflexible* antioppression practice is what obscures the hunger and desire for complex political and human relationships. Said states, "I've become very, very impatient with the idea of and the whole project of identity: the idea . . . that people should really focus on themselves and where they come from. . . . What's much more interesting is to try and reach out beyond identity to something else."[20]

Affirming identity-based organizing, stemming from a shared experience of oppression and a real sense of affinity, is as critical in the revolutionary process as the attempts to go beyond the hierarchies that keep us relegated to the claustrophobic positionalities of oppressor/oppressed. Instead of an antioppression practice that keeps us separated from each other based on our identities, we need to come together to address oppression with the purpose of working through and *transcending* the systemic barriers and borders that capitalism, colonialism, and oppression have thrown between us to keep us from each other. For me, antioppression analysis and practice is the dual process of firmly rooting our work in a heterogeneous understanding of how marginalization, privilege, and complicity manifests within the systems of border imperialism, while simultaneously uniting to create a transformative movement in which we are worth more than the sum of our oppressions, our labels, our baggage, and our (perceived) liabilities. This is not a call for a unity that minimizes oppression; rather, it is a call to consistently challenge oppression with the goal of achieving *genuine* trust and equity in our relations.

On Structure and Leadership

Structure and leadership are often-ignored features of social movements. Ad hoc resistance, such as planning a single event, may not need cohesive group organization. Operating on multiple levels and in multidimensional ways, however, requires ongoing conversations about divisions of labor, internal structure, and decision-making roles. These internal forms of organization influence the trajectory of how we relate to each other and the forms that political struggle will embody.

NOII groups are all organized through volunteer labor, and none of the groups are incorporated as an NGO.

There are no paid staff members, and groups rely almost entirely on donations (yes, it can be done!). This in and of itself is a considerable feat, as an increasing number of movement groups around us are becoming institutionalized in order to secure funding and establish their legitimacy as professional organizations, or are hiring staff in order to maintain mobilizing capacity. This trend has been termed the nonprofit-industrial complex, defined by INCITE! Women of Color against Violence as a system of relationships between the state, funders in the owning class, and NGO social service and social justice organizations that results in the "surveillance, control, derailment and everyday management" of movements.[21]

There are a number of ways in which the co-optation, control, and derailment of movements can play out. NGOs usually become unwilling to take radical action out of fear of losing state or foundation funding. In addition, many communities criticize NGOs for becoming mini bureaucracies that manage social movements by claiming to speak for and on behalf of communities and social issues. Author Arundhati Roy says that "NGOs form a sort of buffer between the *sarkar* [government] and public. Between empire and its subjects. They have become the arbitrators, the interpreters, the facilitators."[22] A final concern is the problematic structure of many NGOs. Reliance on a few well-trained staff activists to plan and coordinate campaigns perpetuates hierarchical divisions of labor, and can alter the participatory dynamic of grassroots organizing.

NOII's experience outside the NGO-industrial complex therefore is significant for several reasons. First, for over a decade, NOII groups have relied exclusively on the commitment and cooperation of a base of grassroots organizers as well as a network of supporters to sustain daily operations alongside movement building. Second, the politics of NOII are unconstrained by funding considerations. Third, NOII groups are structured nonhierarchically and are guided by consensus decision making. In the absence of predetermined relations privileging paid staff members over volunteer organizers, fluidity is maintained, and ensures that structure is a means to an end and not an end unto itself.

Not becoming a NGO, though, does not miraculously resolve all the challenges of group structuring. Many groups organized around principles of democratic centralism replicate the hierarchical leadership structures of both the Right and many NGOs. Such groups, typically of Leninist tendencies, rely on a strong core leadership to make critical decisions that other group members are expected to implement. While this form of leadership may be efficient, it is highly alienating as it replaces direct democracy with a centralization of power and a top-down structure.

In response to this authoritarian and elitist leadership, some groups hold that any organization and leadership is coercive and will produce oppressive power structures. Typically anarchist in tendency, they believe in structureless and leaderless forms of organization. Yet the denial of structure and leadership just creates a layer of unspoken leadership, and informal hierarchies emerge. Based on systemic power imbalances around race, gender, and education level, as well as experience and comfort in activist circles, certain voices tend to dominate over others. I remember being new to activism and joining collectives that I found to be alienating because, under the guise of "we have no leaders and everyone is equal," certain voices remained unchecked and denied accountability for their power.

Between these dichotomous positions, which have been rigorously debated within the North American Left, rests the potentiality of different forms of structure and leadership. Within NOII in Vancouver (Indigenous Coast Salish territories), for example, we have an intentional concept of *antiauthoritarian* and *group-centered* structure and leadership. Such a model recognizes that groups can have leadership without being authoritarian, and that nonhierarchical is not synonymous with structureless. Given the utility of this concept, both in theory and practice, I will elaborate on it in detail. Antiauthoritarian and group-centered structure and leadership are described individually below, although each can only be fully grasped in relation to the other.

Antiauthoritarian leadership recognizes the differential impact of systemic marginalization. Instead of seeking to equalize across diverse lived experiences, the opinions of those most impacted are prioritized as an inherent form of leadership. This form of leadership integrates an antioppression analysis, and as such, is an inversion: it strives to *encourage* rather than discourage or deny leadership. Those who have historically been denied any voice or control over issues that impact their lives are the experts in articulating the impacts of injustice, and carry the necessary awareness of how to effectively organize against power. Given systemic barriers based on race, class, gender, sexuality, and ability, marginalized people have been socialized to doubt their voices, their skills, and their capabilities. Antiauthoritarian leadership therefore takes particular care to center leadership from oppressed communities within our movements. This is not done in tokenistic or uncritical ways but as part of a long-term process of respectful and genuine engagement toward collective liberation.

While fostering leadership from oppressed communities, antiauthoritarian leadership also includes an understanding that leadership in itself need not be authoritarian, particularly if leadership roles are transparent and accountable. This is articulated within the principles of internal collective structuring of NOII-Vancouver (Indigenous Coast Salish territories):

> We recognize that we all participate in the collective differently—those of us who are more active and/or more experienced have gained the position of trust and leadership within the collective. In different moments, different collective members will "take the lead" based on their prior experience or existing relationships of trust. . . . If you find yourself being a more active member, follow the Zapatista spirit of *mandar obedeciendo* (leading by obeying) by holding yourself accountable, in an open, humble manner, to the collective.[23]

One of the ways of ensuring accountability and transparency among those in leadership positions is through active consensus. One of the most potent manifestations of horizontality that stands in contrast to centralized decision making, consensus is an inclusive method of decision making based on the active participation and consent of all group members. Rooted in many traditional Indigenous and peasant forms of self-governance, it is a testament to our ability to organize ourselves in accordance with the principles of direct democracy, and ensures that those in leadership positions are answerable to the group.

Group-centered structuring necessitates proactive steps to share skills and knowledge in order to build our collective power. This form of organization disturbs the traditional division of leader/follower; rather, it recognizes that we are all leaders in different ways and are all contributing to our communities. The NOII-Vancouver (Indigenous Coast Salish territories) principles of internal collective structuring note, "We recognize that leadership comes from daily and sustained processes and practices—such as facilitating meetings, providing emotional support, responding to requests for support from migrants, and building community. We aim to value such leadership that builds supportive and sustainable movements."[24] Some of us are public speakers, some are media producers, some create banners and art, some prepare meals. All these roles are vital, and depending on people's capacities and interests, are rotated as much as possible.

Sharing tasks within our groups decentralizes knowledge, ensures a more sustainable division of labor, encourages learning, builds confidence with new skills, and strengthens interpersonal bonds as we work on projects together. Instead of only a few people being "in the know," this approach fosters a shared sense of responsibility and ownership over the group's work. The NOII-Vancouver (Indigenous Coast Salish territories) principles of internal collective structuring further read: "We recognize that in order to effect empowerment and participatory democracy at a grassroots level, it is necessary for us to share skills and take active steps to equalize knowledge and skills amongst each other. . . . We must be able to provide the necessary room to be able to nurture these skills and learn from their successes and failures."[25]

Intentional skillshares are especially critical for those new to our groups and movements in order for them to feel fully capable of contributing to and participating in the brainstorming, logistical planning, outreach, speaking, decision making, and other leadership roles of our organizing. One of my personal priorities in NOII-Vancouver (Indigenous Coast Salish territories) is to facilitate opportunities for newer activists in the group, particularly women of color, to speak publicly about their experiences. This means turning over to the group a majority of public speaking requests that are sent to me, encouraging others to take them on, and providing support for newer members to speak by sharing useful resources and spending time practicing speeches. This is a dual practice of sharing: sharing the public space that I have gained access to as well as sharing skills so that others feel adequately prepared to step into the role of public speaking.

In this way, a group-centered approach centers a commitment to collective process: those who possess certain skills commit to imparting knowledge; those receiving these skills and knowledge commit to taking initiative in contributing to the group's collective labor and decision-making process. Black liberation activists have used the Zulu concept of "Ubuntu" (I am what I am because of who we all are) to describe this intentional sharing of roles and skills that empowers all group members to fully participate, while creating a group that has an increased overall capacity to organize in a sustainable way.

This antiauthoritarian and group-centered approach to structure and leadership is based on the notion of abundance—an abundance of space for voice, empowerment, capacity, and ownership within social movements. Centering abundance within antiauthoritarian and group-centered structure and leadership is about sharing—as opposed to competing over—space and power, and inviting and encouraging each other to step up and into our fullest potential. Instead of assuming that only some people are capable of being leaders, or dogmatically adhering to the notion that no one should be a leader, valuing abundance shifts us toward a different framework: we are all leaders, and we are all capable of becoming even more skilled as leaders. This framework requires horizontal organization, instead of hierarchical organization or no organization, in order to create and sustain a truly collective effort in which each group member is committed to the vision, analysis, and organizing of the group, because each individual's ideas, skills, leadership, and labor are reflected in and valued by the group.

Stretch

The insights I offer are not meant to be prescriptive, nor are they intended to form a definitive basis for counterhegemonic relations to the state. Strategy cannot be applied in a cookie-cutter approach; it requires collective deliberation, trial and error, and reflection. It necessitates a willingness to experiment and make mistakes, and humility to change our ways. In the words of poet Donna Kate Rushin, "Stretch or drown."[26]

The provocations here coupled with the next chapter's roundtable discussion are gleaned from the grounded experiences of organizers who are engaged in and experimenting within radical struggles, with their specific and evolving contexts and contours, over a period of ten years. Through strengthening movement infrastructure, envisioning bold strategies of confronting the state, sharpening our political analysis and education, and cultivating intergenerational networks of resistance, social movements can move from fragmentation and transience toward more intentional, militant, and coordinated forms of revolutionary struggle.

WAVES OF RESISTANCE
ROUNDTABLE

Waves of Resistance Roundtable

> Democracy is not, to begin with, a form of State. It is, in the first place, the reality of the power of the people that can never coincide with the form of a State. There will always be tension between democracy as the exercise of a shared power of thinking and acting, and the State, whose very principle is to appropriate this power.
>
> —Jacques Rancière, "Democracy Is Not, to Begin with, a Form of State"

NOII is not a centralized organization with a singular party line; there are diverse and often differing opinions across geography, lived experience, time and level of involvement in the movement, personal values, and political priorities. Throughout this book, I note that I cannot and should not be perceived as the authoritative voice on migrant justice or NOII organizing. Beyond simply making such pronouncements, I organized a roundtable that brought together fifteen voices across race, gender, class, age, sexuality, and immigration status from different NOII groups. I made particular attempts to include members from groups beyond the major urban centers as well as newer members so that fresh voices could be freely expressed in what can, admittedly, become a group constrained by the preexisting ideas and patterns of some of us older members.

I asked the fifteen roundtable participants six questions about fostering active participation and leadership from racialized communities, building effective and relevant campaigns, balancing responsive organizing with prefigurative organizing, forging alliances across diverse groups, solidarity with Indigenous communities, and future visions. Though affiliated with specific NOII groups, the organizers here speak for themselves, eloquently and passionately, about some of the lessons, challenges, and victories in which they have been involved. Despite the emphasis on NOII, their insights on alliance building, effective campaigning, and internal group dynamics are undoubtedly useful for all social movements. I am honored to be alongside such teachers, rebels, and comrades who daily plant the seeds and cultivate the soil toward freedom and liberation.

First, an introduction to the fifteen participants in the order in which they appear.

Yogi Acharya is an organizer with NOII-Toronto, and is active in other local anticapitalist and anticolonial struggles.

Sozan Savehilaghi is a Kurdish antiauthoritarian organizer who came to Canada as a refugee at the age of nine. She is engaged in migrant justice, antiracist, and anticapitalist activism, and is a collective member of NOII-Vancouver (Indigenous Coast Salish territories).

Yen Chu is a member and organizer with NOII-Toronto.

Annie Banks is a white settler woman who began her involvement with NOII-Victoria (Lekwungen and WSANEC territories). She continues to listen, learn, create, and organize around environmental justice, decolonization, and antiracism.

Robyn Maynard is a writer and radio producer involved in NOII-Montreal. She is also involved in popular education campaigns with youths of color around racial profiling and campaigns with families of people killed by the police. She works in the community health sector in advocacy as well as support for sex workers and drug users.

Jane Kirby is an organizer and writer involved in a range of antiauthoritarian, feminist, and solidarity activism. She currently organizes with NOII-Halifax.

Mac Scott is an anarchist parent who works in the law, and organizes with NOII-Toronto and the Ontario Coalition against Poverty. In his spare time he likes bad suits, beer, his collective house/family, and science fiction.

Alex Mah is a transperson of mixed-race Chinese descent. He has been organizing in Indigenous Coast Salish territories as a member of the NOII-Vancouver collective since 2005.

Nazila Bettache is an antiauthoritarian, anticapitalist, and feminist organizer based in Montreal who is involved in Indigenous solidarity, migrant justice, and antipolice work. She was part of the NOII-Montreal collective between 2005 and 2008. Her response includes contributions and input from Mary Foster, Samir Shaheen-Hussain, Dolores Chew, François Du Canal, Abby Lippman, and others.

Craig Fortier has organized for the past decade within antiauthoritarian, anticolonial, queer, and migrant justice movements including NOII-Toronto (occupied and contested Mississauga New Credit and Haudenosaunee territories). He participates in movements for migrant justice and Indigenous sovereignty as an ally.

Syed Khalid Hussan is an activist, writer, and NOII-Toronto organizer working with undocumented and migrant people as well as in defense of Indigenous sovereignty.

Ruby Smith Díaz is a Chilean Jamaican person based out of unceded Indigenous Coast Salish territories. She has been a member of NOII-Vancouver since October 2011, and is passionate about working with youths through popular education.

Harjap Grewal is an antiauthoritarian based in Vancouver

(Indigenous Coast Salish territories). Active in NOII-Vancouver and other campaigns rooted in an anticapitalist, anticolonial, and antioppression analysis, he also organizes with communities of color, in solidarity with Indigenous struggles, and within economic and environmental justice movements.

Karen Cocq is an anarchist daughter of Chilean immigrants. She has organized with NOII-Kingston, NOII-Ottawa, and NOII-Toronto. Thanks to SK, Monika Thakker, Pierre Beaulieu-Blais, and Sayyida Jaffer for contributing their ideas to this response.

Graciela Flores Mendez is an antiracist feminist, law clerk, activist, and member of NOII-Toronto. She is a Mexican migrant who "smuggled" herself and lived without status in the United States near the Mexico-US border for the majority of her life.

How is active participation from racialized communities and those with lived experiences of border imperialism fostered? How do you understand antioppression and collective leadership as it relates to NOII?

ACHARYA: There is a basic tenet of good political organizing that most people know well: leadership within any political struggle must always originate from those most impacted by its existence. In the context of Canada, where we are up against a white supremacist, capitalist, and colonial state, those most impacted by its existence tend to be poor people of color—and more specifically still, women of color who battle the added burden of patriarchy. Framed within this understanding, NOII-Toronto has long held to the principle that we need to be led by immigrant women of color.

Which brings us to two questions: What precisely does leadership look like? And how can it be fostered? The word leadership here isn't meant to imply a hierarchy of rank within organizing but instead to account for the absolute necessity of active participation and buy in from those bearing the worst excesses of the system. It means that when dealing with membership within the organization, there has been a conscious effort to recruit and retain women of color, and those with direct experience of dealing with the immigration system. It means that when representing the group to the outside world—say, in presentations and workshops, at demonstrations and rallies, or when engaging the mainstream media—first preference is given to women and trans-identified members of color.

These efforts, however, aren't always free from problematic dynamics of their own. For example, they can generate an odd sense of competition between newer members, who may feel differently favored and appreciated by older members. As a group, we have had multiple conversations about these issues and they have dealt as much with the manner in which we embody our politics as they have with the way we treat each other as human beings. Over the last few years, after dealing with and learning from incidents that happened both within and outside NOII, we also put a lot of time into brainstorming internal policies that enable us to begin to specifically address lateral racism, disablism, and sexual assault.

Another point of consideration is the question of invisible leadership or informal hierarchies. The problem isn't so much that there is a power differential within the group. This is bound to exist with people being around for varying levels of time, and having varying levels of experience with the immigration system, time availabilities, and connections to other organizing spaces within the movement. For instance, the ideas of someone who has been around longer tend to carry more weight and sway than those of a newer member. The problem, however, is with how that power is used.

To address this, we have tried a few different organizing models that attempt to more explicitly identify the informal hierarchies and create space for people to self-determine their level of participation in the organizing work. There are three things that I feel have particularly helped: dividing work into semiautonomous committees and encouraging newer members to take on coordinating roles within them, supporting newer members in taking on speaking roles on behalf of the organization, and creating more comprehensive orientations for new members and information/skill-sharing sessions.

We call ourselves an anticapitalist and anticolonial organization, and share a desire to match those politics in our everyday practice. I feel that we keep—and need to keep—learning and getting better at it with time.

SAVEHILAGHI: Reclaiming our power—as racialized people, refugees, and immigrants—by organizing around issues that affect us is a profound act of dissent. Sustaining spaces for those impacted by border imperialism so that our voices don't get swallowed whole, left behind, or relegated as a subissue in Left political movements is the first of many steps in fostering the participation of those who are impacted.

Creating antioppressive spaces to organize around is not as easy as simply adopting antioppression principles—although that is an important initial step. We must have an understanding that we are all at risk of being oppressive if we want to create a truly antioppressive space. Oppressive situations can occur within groups of people even when we ourselves are victims of oppression because we all face different and often several layers of oppression. Having the courage to recognize when we act in oppressive ways, challenging oppressive dynamics, holding each other accountable, and normalizing these discussions are just some of the ways we can work to eradicate oppression.

Connected to antioppression is the issue of leadership. NOII-Vancouver operates on consensus, but collective members come from a diversity of experiences and differing legal immigration statuses. So we honor the insight and experience of those who directly face racist border controls and state policies to ground the work that we do. People take on positions of further leadership depending on individual capacity, how connected they are to a particular campaign or struggle, and the relationships they have built with communities and movements over time based on genuine solidarity. This happens intentionally and organically at the same time. As a newer member of NOII, it has been invaluable when the experiences and histories that older members have are shared and discussed. This gives me the context to understand where NOII is now, and I appreciate how much heart and energy went into building the foundation for crucial connections.

Another example of leadership is when we support people who face detention and/or deportation. In these situations it sometimes makes more sense for a member who is from the same community, speaks the same language, and is aware of the political and social contexts impacting the individual to lead the support work on behalf of NOII. The goal in that is for the person who is impacted to feel comfortable with us and be empowered to make informed choices. It is essential that people lead their own struggle and become visible bodies that refuse to be disappeared in the state-imposed administrative maze.

Group and personal capacity is a regular topic of conversation when we organize specific projects and to avoid burnout in general. Setting aside time for skillshares—for example, regular media, facilitation, and public speaking skillshares—has been important for building people's comfort, confidence, and capacity as a means of fostering collective leadership. We possess different types and levels of skills, and have differing capacities for organizing. At the same time, it's all our responsibility to lift each other up, value all the seen and unseen work we do, and nurture an environment where not guilt but rather desire is the impetus for what and how much we take on.

What are some of the factors you take into account in deciding what campaign you will take up? Describe some of the strategies you have used and some campaign victories.

CHU: While it is important to take up campaigns that react to the specific current issues, it is also important to build sustainable grassroots campaigns that provide space to challenge borders and capitalism. The Don't Ask Don't Tell and Sanctuary City campaigns did just that. The factors that went into NOII-Toronto taking on this campaign were: the potential to mobilize across different sectors such as unions, education, social services, and health; the specificity of the demands; the history of successes in cities across the United States; and the opportunities of combining practice and theory in relation to city services, immigration status, borders, and capitalism.

The strategy of the initial Don't Ask Don't Tell campaign was to pressure the city to implement a Don't Ask Don't Tell policy where NOII-Toronto focused on the school board and police board. A couple of cases that received media coverage were used as mobilizing points to advance the campaign. One example was the case of a nonstatus woman who had been raped, but was turned over to immigration officials for deportation when she went to report it to the police. This case galvanized women's organizations across the city to work with us to demand a Don't Ask Don't Tell policy at the Police Services Board. A second example was the arrest of Kimberly and Gerald Lisano-Sossa at their school by immigration enforcement. In response, NOII-Toronto mobilized teachers and students to demand a Don't Ask Don't Tell policy at the Toronto District School Board. The declaration by the Toronto Police Service Board and Toronto District School Board attracted further support from unions, social service workers, and the community. The Education Not Deportation campaign was formed to ensure that the school board implemented the policy, and expand the campaign to other school boards as well as universities and colleges.

The Don't Ask Don't Tell campaign evolved into the Sanctuary City campaign. In this campaign our focus was on service providers. The campaign had subcommittees that focused on different sectors: health, shelters and services for women, and food banks. Each of the committees was autonomous, and worked with service users, frontline workers, and community members to answer the practical questions of how to implement a Don't Ask Don't Tell policy in these spaces and what to do when immigration enforcement came to the door. This process opened up more substantive questions of how to radicalize spaces of service provision by reclaiming spaces that the Left had created and fought for, such as women's shelters and health clinics, and ensuring that these services are provided to everyone regardless of status.

The Shelter, Sanctuary, Status campaign was pushing for women's shelters to declare themselves sanctuary zones free from immigration enforcement. The campaign held actions across the city, and as a result, the CBSA issued a directive saying it would stay away from women's shelters. This directive was later overturned. Some women's organizations met with the CBSA to discuss the policy. NOII, however, had no interest in talking with the CBSA. The policy was not our main goal; it was important for us that services publicly declared themselves sanctuary zones as a form of resistance against the state. Two of our organizers, Farrah Miranda and Fariah Chowdhury, did a lot of workshops at the shelters and talked to women who were survivors of violence—who then became involved in our actions. The campaign was able to connect people's direct experiences to the broader fight against borders and capital.

BANKS: From 2005 onward, NOII-Victoria became active in planning actions in opposition to the security certificates and imprisonment of the Secret Trial 5. I became involved as a result of a free school class for community members led by a NOII-Victoria member. NOII-Victoria was a space where students in the free school as well as community members were able to take concrete action with their newly acquired information and knowledge. I initially became involved because I couldn't believe that security certificates existed in Canada. Now I absolutely understand not only how this kind of legislation would be utilized by the Canadian government, but also the depth and intensity of Islamophobia and antimigrant sentiments and actions on the part of the Canadian government.

Participating in actions in support of the Secret Trial 5 with NOII-Victoria shifted my understandings of who can expect to receive a "fair trial" within the legal system in Canada, and the ongoing racist and colonial agenda of the Canadian government. Security certificates were such a tangible part of this broader agenda, and our primary goal was to make that visible.

In a small group in Victoria, BC, on Lekwungen, WSANEC, and Esquimalt Indigenous territories, NOII-Victoria organized actions such as opposing the presence of the CSIS at the University of Victoria's student career fair. We made cardboard prison bars, and dressed in orange jumpsuits to represent the imprisonment of the Secret Trial 5 and handed out information on security certificates. There was also a ceremony in front of the Citizenship and Immigration Canada building where hundreds of postcards were mailed to the minister of citizenship and immigration in opposition to secret trials. At this ceremony, people again dressed in prison jumpsuits to represent detainees, and supporters symbolically handcuffed themselves to the detainees in solidarity. We frequently used visuals and actively engaged the public. We handed out information to passersby and collected signatures on the postcards. These actions generated press coverage, and raised awareness among students and the general public about the reality of violent profiling and incarceration against the Secret Trial 5 and immigrants and refugees in general.

These demonstrations were also held in conjunction with those in larger cities, such as Vancouver, Montreal, Ottawa, and Toronto. For example, the ceremony in front of the Citizenship and Immigration Canada building was held in support of and in conjunction with actions taken by the families of the detainees, who were at that time making their presence known at the office of the prime minister in Ottawa. This was effective in enhancing the messages from groups in larger cities, and increasing support and solidarity in Victoria. In addition, it supported the campaign's focus on showing widespread support nationally for ending secret trials in Canada.

MAYNARD: NOII-Montreal is one of many allied grassroots migrant justice groups spanning the city that frequently collaborate on campaigns and events, while operating in a decentralized structure. The importance of groups such as Solidarity across Borders, the IWC, the Peoples' Commission, Dignidad Migrante, and Mexicanos Unidos por la Regularization cannot be understated, and because of this, our areas of focus are not strategized in a vacuum but instead always complementary to the rich and diverse array of this organizing that surrounds us.

NOII-Montreal is made up of racialized people from migrant backgrounds. Given the high levels of racial profiling and police violence in racialized immigrant communities, we have focused on bringing these realities into the larger discussions surrounding migrant rights, as these connections are often underrepresented. Members of NOII joined other allies to initiate the Forum against Police Violence and Impunity, which brought together family members of people killed by the police, migrants, youths, and drug users to discuss the commonalities and differences in the lived experiences of overpoliced communities. Crucial bonds between diverse communities were created during this forum, which led us to be active in forming a new group of directly affected individuals and allies. The group, Justice for Victims of Police Killings, works with family members and friends of people who have been killed by the police to demand justice for their loved ones along with an end to police violence and impunity.

The Forum against Police Violence and Impunity was also the beginning of NOII-Montreal's current focus on combating double punishment. Lillian Madrid, a panelist at the forum, was the mother of Fredy Villanueva, an unarmed racialized teenager who was shot and killed in 2008 by a police officer. While discussing this injustice, Lillian brought to light that her second son Dany, a permanent resident, had been served a deportation order for a crime committed in 2006, for which he had already served his prison sentence—in effect, a double punishment. As we came together with the Coalition contre la Répression et les Abus Policiers, the Collectif Opposé à la Brutalité Policière, and Montréal-Nord Républik to support the family, we realized how frequently the CBSA works with the police to target migrant communities with both racial profiling and deportation. It became clearer that many in migrant communities remain silent out of fear and shame, not wanting to be seen as "criminals" or "bad migrants," while facing discriminatory treatment at the hands of Canada's justice and immigration systems.

Breaking the silence surrounding double punishment in migrant communities has thus organically become a priority in our organizing. Popular education to bring this issue into the common vernacular has been our focus, including teach-ins and writing articles for daily newspapers and magazines. Ending double punishment was one of the demands of the Status for All march in 2012. So far our actions are modest, but it is a living project; more cases of double punishment continue to emerge and go public. Raising consciousness often feels like an uphill battle, especially given the frequent lack of societal empathy for those deemed to be "criminals" and "foreigners" who are racialized. Even so, support and awareness continues to build, and we hope that double punishment is exposed for what it is: an unjustifiable and unacceptable attack on migrant communities.

How do we effectively balance engaging with the state when involved in direct antideportation support work or responding to individual policies, while also articulating a systemic analysis that confronts and prefigures alternatives to the state?

KIRBY: We restarted what had been an inactive NOII-Halifax group as we became involved in supporting a family fighting their deportation. We thought reinitiating NOII would provide a broader platform to critique the immigration system alongside doing support work. This was especially true since a good amount of our organizing in support of the family involved building grassroots community support for their case, so we had a really good opportunity to also engage in education work.

Despite this intention, balancing support work with broader work and analysis was a challenge. Part of our support work for the family involved lobbying politicians on behalf of the family. We engaged in much more polite lobbying activities than most of us were used to. Despite being extremely cautious about the kinds of actions we were doing, we found that people were reluctant to engage with us because we politicized support work. I remember meeting with a liberal ally who was supportive of the family, but was hesitant to get involved because of the radical politics of our group and the NOII name. We then consciously distanced the support work from our broader organizing to make sure we weren't hurting the family's chances of being successful in their fight to stay. This meant, for example, not including the NOII name on the materials that we were distributing about the case. This became a contradiction since our original intention was to contextualize the family's case within a broader framework of migrant justice.

I don't think the lobbying ultimately had any direct impact whatsoever on the family eventually winning their right to stay. When you are working with people whose lives are at stake, however, you really feel the need to do whatever you can, even if it means using tactics that you don't believe in or sacrificing analysis somewhat. I do think that the approach that was most helpful was to build community support for the family, especially since things like letter writing gave people a concrete way to show their support. Community support proved really important in the successful resolution of the case, and hopefully did also build support for NOII and migrant justice work more broadly. I also think that at least some of the people who were initially unwilling to engage with us now have a little bit more respect for the work that we are trying to do.

In an ideal situation, support work helps build support for more systemic change work, and vice versa. And that is true to some extent. When in contradiction, though,

support work and the immediate needs of people fighting
the worst excesses of the immigration system are always
going to be prioritized over working toward bigger goals.
In Halifax many of us are approaching this issue as allies,
and we have found that support work has been essential to
ground us in what the issues are for directly affected communities. But this has meant that we have stayed tied up in
supporting individuals and haven't been able to seriously
advance any sustained campaigns. This is especially true
when building alternatives to the current system seems like
such a long-term and somewhat-ephemeral task, as compared to support work that is concrete and immediate.

SCOTT: NOII-Toronto does support work to fight deportations specifically when these fights work to build broader
campaigns, when it is a member who is attacked, or when a
community is mobilizing around a deportation. We also do
some policy work—for example, fighting federal immigration legislation. NOII-Toronto has also done localized
policy work such as our Don't Ask Don't Tell campaign
pushing the city to provide services to people regardless of
their immigration status. We also do work in coalitions—
for instance, the local Stop the Cuts campaign, which is
trying to reverse the austerity policies of our racist, sexist,
ableist, homophobic, antipoor mayor Rob Ford.

   We also work outside the system. This includes our
Indigenous solidarity work with the many nations in the
Ontario area fighting for recognition of their sovereignty.
We also do a lot of community organizing and educa-
tion work specific to our politics—most recently in the

low-income and migrant community of Parkdale, both around Stop the Cuts and migrant justice. NOII-Toronto has also done work to support specific community organizations such as the South Asian Women's Rights Organization.

It is important to note that the two types of work— policy work and systemic work—are often combined. While our annual May Day demonstration has demands that relate to immigration policy, it is not designed as a lobby event. It is intended to be a mobilization that uses disruptive and creative tactics. Similarly, while stopping a deportation and doing support work engages the state apparatus, we also use this work as a chance to showcase our broader politics. Deportations often mobilize communities that we may not otherwise mobilize, and this provides a wonderful organizing opportunity.

Stopping a deportation is often showcased as the work of a brilliant lawyer or skillful media work. This framing reinforces the idea that educated and privileged individuals are the actors who create change. Similarly with lobbying, winning a Don't Ask Don't Tell policy can be presented as a result of certain sympathetic trustees. In reality, however, a deportation can be stopped by mass mobilization that builds the idea of community power. A Don't Ask Don't Tell policy can be won by packing the education board meetings with community members. How we win engagements with the state, along with making it clear afterward that community mobilization was the key, is as important as making sure that we use these opportunities to advance our politics.

If we don't make efforts to protect our nonstatus community members when they are targeted by deportation or by lack of access to basic services, it will be difficult for nonstatus people to join our groups. Even if we lose in these fights, making it clear to our communities and the state that we will protect our own is extremely critical. In Europe, many groups focus on alternatives such as squatting homes for nonstatus families or direct actions such as blocking deportations at the airport. We could move in this direction. Yet I think in many nonstatus communities in Canada and the United States, policy change toward a full and accessible regularization resonates hugely, and therefore is the central demand in our organizing. This involves both approaches: making concrete changes for migrants we work with every day, while still maintaining our fight against capitalism, against imperialism, against colonialism, and against patriarchy.

NOII organizes with and within diverse social movements and communities, some of which may not share our analysis and values. What do you think determines the nature of alliances and how do you navigate alliance building?

MAH: NOII-Vancouver has negotiated many complicated dynamics of alliance building—whether it's working in a coalition, as a part of projects with specific alliances, or with directly affected communities that are resisting the immigration system or colonization. It is common that those who we build alliances with may not hold the same set of core beliefs as us, but we believe that inclusive movement building recognizes a diversity of perspectives. Our broad vision, nonetheless, remains in explicit resistance to capitalism and colonial nation-states.

The negotiation of alliances is, for example, felt in our work in solidarity with individuals struggling against deportation and detention. NOII-Vancouver upholds the vision that every individual should be entitled to freely seek a place to call home regardless of state-drawn border lines. We cannot justify refusing to support an individual in their struggles for status and against deportation because that individual does not share our beliefs. The refusal of support would only then serve to reinforce the dichotomy of good immigrant/deserving refugee versus bad immigrant/illegitimate refugee. At the same time, though, we want to demand accountability for harmful or oppressive actions.

The balance of wanting to demand accountability over someone's actions while never wanting to withdraw support has proven to be challenging in some cases. For example, a few years ago we were supporting a male refugee who was being sponsored by his female partner. In the midst of the sponsorship, his partner disclosed that she was experiencing physical violence. At her request and based on our own beliefs, we did not withdraw support, which would have placed both partners in a further precarious situation. Instead, we worked to establish a supportive circle around the woman, engaged the man in conversations about violence against women, and continued to work with the male refugee in his struggle for legal status.

Certainly this may have not been the best course of action, but we hope to continue to struggle, learn, and grow from these situations. What I am trying to say is that working in solidarity with someone does not preclude us from, but rather requires us to, challenge behaviors that are sexist, homophobic, or capitalist. This is based on the recognition of one another as changing individuals. It is through these dialogues and demands for accountability that we aim to work toward a world free of oppression, while struggling for all people to live with dignity and safety.

Another example arose during the 2007 campaign against the deportation of Laibar Singh, an elderly paralyzed refugee claimant from India. In the midst of this struggle, a racist article was published in a newspaper that implied that immigrants were eroding Canadian values. The article unearthed homophobic comments made three years prior by one of the leaders of a Sikh Gurudwara who was supporting Singh. The timing of the article placed queer people of color, and particularly queer Sikhs, in a position of having to deal with their multifaceted identities in a hostile arena. NOII-Vancouver and other queer people of color organizations released an open letter against the racism of the article (painting the actions of one individual as a broad stereotype about an entire community), while speaking against homophobia. After releasing the letter, we were accused of dividing the queer community in the fight against homophobia and muddying the waters by speaking of racism. For myself as an organizer, I believe we've got to fight against not only racism or homophobia, for example, but also continuously struggle for freedom from all forms of oppression and domination.

BETTACHE: At the core of this question lies the very nature of the political framework that informs the organizing in which we are engaged as well as our long-term goals. If the goal of our organizing is to build movements, it seems intuitive that adopting a purist politics about ideological stances, rather than a practice based in solidarity, risks ensuring that alliances can never be built. Self-righteous and alienating to potential allies, the paradigm of ideological purity ignores the various effects that the dominant systems of oppression and power have on communities and our own organizing structures.

This is not to say there aren't significant challenges when we engage in solidarity work with individuals and communities that may not share our same core principles. For example, during the campaign countering the racist and sexist attack on migrant communities brought on by the reasonable accommodation debate in 2007 in Quebec (a provincial commission was convened on the degree to which certain religious practices, such as the wearing of the niqab, should be allowed), our campaign was part of a larger coalition that included faith-based organizations whose analysis around gender, capitalism, heterosexism, and colonialism came into conflict with that of NOII-Montreal. Issues of identity and antioppression politics further complicated this dynamic. Questions around leadership and direction become tenuous as the lines blur between passive support—that is, taking the lead from those who are most directly affected (in this example, practicing Muslim women)—and active solidarity—that is, determining our terms of engagement in supporting their struggle while remaining rooted in our politics. A particular case of this tension became evident around the elaboration of a common public analysis of the situation. We felt strongly about articulating our message around the racism and sexism underlying the so-called reasonable accommodation debate, whereas some organizations insisted on a focus on "tolerance." This led to a disjointed public message and eventually fragmented our work as a coalition.

In addressing these important challenges, certain organizing principles should be kept in mind. Being open about our politics and acknowledging potential differences is crucial, while also understanding the contexts where these differences may be rooted. An example stemming out of the campaign against the national security agenda led by the Peoples' Commission in Montreal was the anti-Muslim sentiment expressed by members of an immigrant community organization who participated in several projects of the Peoples' Commission. While this racist attitude was confronted, it was done recognizing that its roots are very different from those informing the government's Islamophobia and that the organization operates out of a very different point in the power structure.

It is also important to practice a form of solidarity that is not conditional in nature, while engaging in and expressing dissent from a place of active commitment and not ideological superiority. During the Justice for Anas campaign, seeking truth and justice in the death of Mohamed Anas Bennis, a twenty-five-year-old man who was shot and killed by Montreal police in 2005, members of NOII-Montreal worked closely with Anas's family.

At the onset of the campaign, we were open about our position in denouncing the police as an inherently violent institution that could not be reformed, but still engaged in a campaign that demanded a public inquiry into the circumstances that led to Anas's death. We were honoring the agency and respecting the leadership of Anas's family and community, while maintaining an active conversation about police brutality, racial profiling, and strategies to end state violence. This was accomplished through a sustained relationship rooted in trust and respect, and building on diversity and disagreement as substrates for growth rather than alienation.

FORTIER: NOII-Toronto struggles for migrant justice as part of broader struggles for liberation (anticapitalist, queer, trans, feminist, anticolonial, and antiracist), and that has meant working with a number of communities, religious groups, and so forth that don't necessarily share our beliefs. One of my first experiences with this was the fight against the deportation of the Lizano-Sossa family in 2006. Kimberly and Gerald Lizano-Sossa were apprehended by immigration enforcement agents while sitting in class at their school, Dante Alighieri Catholic Secondary School. Since Dante Alighieri was a Catholic school, the core group we worked with to fight the family's deportation included students, clergy, teachers, and members of the church that the family attended. At the time, those of us in NOII-Toronto were predominantly racialized people, non-Catholic, non-Spanish speaking, and included those who could be visibly identified as queer.

The situation was acute as the family faced imminent deportation and it was really easy to fall into the "good immigrant family" rhetoric that we oppose. This led to a lot of internal tension within the collective as supporters of the family continually made reference to the fact that the family was a "good family" and not "criminals"—which legitimized the heterosexist and racist immigration policies of the Canadian state. Internally we struggled with whether or not this was acceptable as it meant that some of our politics (queer liberation, anticapitalist, and antiauthoritarian) were being invisibilized, and we were replicating ways in which the state determines who is a deserving migrant. Yet we saw the moment as one in which many people were mobilizing in concrete ways against immigration enforcement, particularly within the school system, even though they were wary of joining forces with a group like NOII-Toronto that had been framed by politicians and the mainstream Left as "dangerous radicals."

It was a strategy that came with a lot of internal discussion, consternation, and stress, and one that has continued to push our analysis on how best to work in solidarity with people facing deportations—especially, in this case, since it was not clear that the strategy was particularly effective. We failed in our attempt to prevent the deportation of the family, the community around the family that we had built links with eventually faded over time, and for the most part we did not succeed in having the types of broader dialogues that we had the space to engage in during that struggle. While the fight of the Lizano-Sossa family ultimately resulted in a successful campaign to win a policy at the Toronto District School Board to push immigration enforcement out of the schools, we had limited success within the Catholic school board, where the children were apprehended. Moreover, the majority of those who engaged in the subsequent campaign with the school board were from the radical, queer, and labor communities that have always been our allies.

So for me that was a really important learning experience. It showed that while it is essential to attempt to meet people where they are at, it is also critical that our group not hide our politics and the diversity of our membership. We should be cognizant of the fact that the process by which we fight deportations should match to some extent the type of antiracist, queer, anticolonial, and anticapitalist politics that we value. It also highlighted the need to explicitly make space during struggles to discuss some of these important questions in an honest way.

Can you expand on and give examples of concrete Indigenous solidarity efforts being undertaken as well as some of the alliances being built between migrants of color and Indigenous communities?

HUSSAN: There are two understandings of sovereignty. State sovereignty, which developed out of colonial and capitalist traditions of land ownership, and which concerns itself with privatization and control over people. But if we move away from state sovereignty, a different view of sovereignty and collective self-determination emerges. Self-determination is the ability to have control over one's own

life and the lives of one's communities, while state sovereignty is about making decisions over the lives of others.
State sovereignty is about owning land; self-determination
is about defending the land.

It is this community sovereignty that Indigenous
activists from Six Nations to Secwepemc harken to when
identifying themselves as sovereigntists who are caretakers
and defenders of the land. Similarly, we see frontline communities like the Algonquins of Barriere Lake assert their
sovereignty to delegitimize the authority of the Canadian
government, not to replace one capitalist system of privatization with another. Decolonization in many ways is an
inversion: land does not belong to us; rather, we belong
to it. Understanding this is the key to seeing through the
debates around sovereignty and migration.

We show that those struggling for free movement
are not in opposition to Indigenous sovereignty by the
ways we act. Often NOII-Toronto works as a solidarity
organization. Recently Kitchenuhmaykoosib Inninuwug
First Nation (KI) organizing and campaigning resulted in
255,000 square kilometers of its territory being declared
off-limits to mining. NOII-Toronto was part of a city-
based support committee. As Toronto KI Support, we were
given clear instructions and a specific mandate from the
leadership in KI, communicated to us through one community liaison. We proposed a plan, sent it to the leadership, received approval, and acted on it. Areas of activity
were clearly delineated. Little conversation took place on
migrant justice, detention, or deportation; we entered as
allies, took direction, and acted. Such direct solidarity work

serves to show other Indigenous allies that we can take direction—an essential skill for any solidarity movement. We have also focused on building an informed base of support in immigrant communities for Indigenous struggles. This allows us to mobilize people of color to support land defense in ways that other groups have not been able to and is a measurable indication of our politics.

Showing that we can take direction allows us to engage in the more difficult conversations on free movement. In 2011, we invited elder, writer, and activist Lee Maracle to speak to us about host laws here in areas now called Toronto. She explained that there are three host laws: everyone eats, every woman is entitled to a house, and everyone has access to the wealth of the land. Such an "immigration policy" recenters land as provider rather than as property. It insists that we move away from rich or poor. When countering Canadian immigration laws, we were instructed that we must posit Indigenous host laws. We have since tried to understand for ourselves what respecting these host laws would mean for migrants today and initiated conversations using this framework, most recently with organizers in Native Youth Sexual Health Network and some land defenders in Six Nations. This serves as the basis of conversation about migrant justice as opposed to colonization and settlements. These have been difficult discussions, but conversations emerge, mind-sets change, and the struggle continues.

DIAZ: Although I was born and raised on Turtle Island, I have never felt like my roots are really from here. My parents migrated from Chile and Jamaica, and I grew up with "funny-sounding accents" and vicarious memories of homelands left behind. For my parents, Canada meant safety, and being here was a dream, but that dream wasn't neccessarily determined by free choice.

I think the notion of dreaming in a time where we are told that it is foolish, futile, or not useful is one of the most revolutionary things we can do. To have our lives determined by our dreams of a free world—instead of reactions to a state-imposed reality—is one of the most powerful tools of decolonization. I dream of a community and a world where our lives can be determined by our own means. To live in a world where our actions are guided by mutual respect, and the understanding that our struggles for decolonization are different yet connected.

As a black and Latina woman, the dreams of decolonization and absolute freedom from oppression, which are expressed by many of the original peoples of this land, are not unfamiliar to me. I feel a sense of solidarity with this desire, and a sense of responsibility to this struggle. In a way, my feeling of solidarity feels fueled by my anger at knowing that because of my history of colonization, my ancestors have been displaced from "home." My anger about not being able to fight the displacement of my ancestors in my own history makes my desire to fight colonization on these territories even stronger. Colonization on these territories is happening here and now. We see it in desecrated burial sites, the exploitation of natural resources without consent, and cards to prove identity and status to a colonial government.

Over the years, different members of NOII-Vancouver seem to have also seen the value of working together in solidarity with Indigenous nations. I have only been in the collective for a few months, but already I have seen some pretty inspiring messages of these reciprocal relationships. Recently the Lhe Lin Liyin of the Grassroots Wet'suwet'en stated,

> The future generations amongst Indigenous, refugee, and settler societies have an opportunity today to make known that we all as human family require respect, compassion, and a home to live in, and our status to be complete and recognized. In a world faced with increased industrial activity, intensifying climate change, and war mongering, refugees today require a lot more understanding, respect, safety, and positive outlook on life. If the occupation of Canada will not recognize the status of refugees and migrant peoples the Indigenous peoples who are the true owners of these lands will![1]

Enough said.

For me, the notion of free migration and Indigenous sovereignty are not contradictory. People have always moved—whether for food, safety, celebration, love. What matters in most cases was that respect for the land and peoples in that area would be upheld. That we don't see our struggles as separate, but as relationships of solidarity. So let's dream on. Let's build our dreams together.

GREWAL: NOII-Vancouver has shown a consistent commitment to supporting Indigenous self-determination, and we believe that we must seriously decolonize migrant justice movements. The strength and sustainability of our work has been based on relationships of mutual aid, and engaging in direct dialogue and building relations with Indigenous communities. The dialogues are not based on abstract Eurocentric theory or radical Left analysis; rather, they arise out of the valued relations that go beyond momentary solidarity for a single campaign. This happens, for example, when we come together at community dinners and demonstrations to share our stories and histories of resistance.

NOII-Vancouver has been actively supporting the Sewepemc community for almost a decade. Simultaneously, land defenders from that community have been willing to challenge the colonial immigration system by hosting refugees that we have been supporting. These offers being extended to refugees facing deportation are a humbling and inspiring gesture of the relationship developing between Indigenous and migrant movements. Our support of the Sewepemc community has also included antideportation support, as many family members who are not legally Canadian have married into the community and have faced detention and deportation. Expressions of Indigenous and migrant solidarity have also emerged with Wet'suwet'en land defenders, who we have supported in the struggle against pipelines through their territories. "Immigration authorities" were included and named as their opponents in a traditional song they adapted to challenge pipeline companies and the Canadian government. Members of the community have also responded to calls for action to support migrants facing deportation.

During the campaign for Laibar Singh, a Punjabi refugee who took sanctuary to defy a deportation order, a Nisga'a elder visited him after seeing the story on the news. Singh could barely understand English, but we translated that he was being welcomed to Indigenous lands. Laibar said that he could see parallels with his experience as a landless Dalit and those of Indigenous people. He told us that visit was one of the most significant for him, as the solidarity extended to him was an expression of shared values.

These forms of solidarity between immigrant and Indigenous communities often exist without an expectation of reciprocity. Some of us regularly bridge between Indigenous and migrant communities—for example, by having discussions in our immigrant spaces about colonization. We evoke the historic solidarities between Indigenous communities and early Chinese migrants. I remember Indigenous leader Arthur Manuel reflecting on a map of Palestine and noting how similar it was to the reservation system. Similarly, I recall Osama, a Palestinian refugee, talking about how Canada is occupied "just like the West Bank." We had several conversations with Secwepemc antimining activist Neskie Manuel, who had found documentation of a traditional immigration policy from his community. These moments reflect what can happen when we sit together, unfiltered by colonialism, which keeps us apart.

The responsibility of immigrants and migrant justice movements is to make visible our support for Indigenous values. Even with shared experiences of racism and violence at the hands of colonizers, the struggle to defend an Indigenous way of life is not shared by all people of color. Our struggles for migrant justice cannot be limited to gaining access to nation-states or property. Migrants' relationship to the land needs to be rooted in stewardship of the land rather than colonial and capitalist ideas of landownership. Even though colonization has entrenched property ownership to such an extent that it is difficult to exist outside of it, decolonization requires us to overturn this regime. Though we may not overturn the regime tomorrow, we can decolonize our relations. Wet'suwet'en and Tsilhqot'in communities have welcomed us on to their territories after asking us what our intentions are when we arrive. These moments project an anticolonial analysis of migration, in which free movement is not governed by the state or capital relations but instead is understood as respecting Indigenous traditions and shared responsibility for the land.

What is your vision for NOII in the future?

COCQ: I have been through moments of extreme optimism about our potential, and moments of intense disillusionment about our weaknesses, missed opportunities, and wrong turns. Maybe it is because I have organized mostly in smaller towns, where it is hard to ever feel like we are building a movement because the inspiring ideas we see in bigger cities are easy to covet but hard to follow through on. But I also think that as a NOII movement in general, we can delude ourselves with our aspirations, and this leads us to make unstrategic decisions. The cost of this to our effectiveness, legitimacy, and collective power is high. So for us to have a vision, I think we need to be more realistic.

I am reluctant to use the word realistic because of its bad legacy; it is how the Right dismisses us, how older organizers patronize younger ones, and how legitimate critiques from within our movements are written off. But I want to try to use it in the spirit of strengthening us, not tearing us down. We often struggle with our own expectations. Sometimes they are too low, and we accept behavior from each other unbefitting of our politics. And sometimes our expectations go far beyond what we come together to do and what we can do. Because in our organizing, we are rarely changing the world—but that doesn't mean that we can't set our sights high for what can be done.

We should be more realistic about our place in broader struggles for social change, and more honest about our relevance and importance. When we underestimate this, we don't demand enough of ourselves in terms of effort or effectiveness, thinking it doesn't really matter. But when we focus on the sexy stuff and our egos lead us astray, we can't see from our high horses all the unglamorous work necessary to actually be effective.

Both of these problems require that we take our work more seriously to acknowledge both its potential and its limits. In a way, we take ourselves more seriously by getting over ourselves. This means being more modest about our capacity, and not deluding others or ourselves with big talk. We should be wary of the arrogance of our miscalculations;

no one can afford for us to be flippant or careless. The cost of committing to things we can't or don't do, or setting expectations we can't meet, is high. Instead, we should be tenacious in the things we can commit to: meeting the goals we set for our actions, weaving the strong relationships we want with communities to whom we should be accountable as well as with the allies we need and can learn from, building our resilience to burnout and turnover by making space and being adaptable, and learning from our mistakes with humility so that we don't repeat them.

Being realistic means being more honest about who we are, what we seek to get out of organizing, and what we can commit to doing together. Perhaps by doing this we can be more strategic so that lofty goals don't distract us, expectations don't deceive us, and we can put our energy toward conspiring effectively and successfully. Setting ourselves and others up for disappointment wastes time, burns us out, and hardens us with disillusionment. We owe it to ourselves—but more important, to those who we organize with and for—to be more real so that we can be more effective.

MENDEZ: I first heard of NOII when I had recently arrived to Canada from the United States, where I had lived without status my whole life. I had lived as a Mexican migrant close to the Mexico-US border. My daily reality was one where I was not allowed to forget that, to the general public, I was an "illegal." Though my class and lack of accent were an advantage, blatant and unapologetic anti-immigrant discourse often made me feel helpless, fearful, and enraged.

These feelings stayed with me even when I entered Canada with a student permit—the first "lawful" status I'd ever had—because it had an expiration date, and afforded me few rights and protections.

This blanket of illegality that smothered me explains the pounding of my heart when I first saw this on a poster: No One Is Illegal. This migrant rights organization, by its very name, made clear what I wanted to shout out every day of my life. It challenged the legitimacy of a country, its laws, its sense of justice, the ideology that makes the binary between citizen and alien acceptable. No. One. Is. Illegal. It bears repeating because its name professes my direct vision of NOII into the future—a future where we keep raging and challenging the state and the lies it uses to divide us. NOII as a movement is this constant affirmation that continues to awaken the consciousness and spur action.

I envision that the organization will continue to draw members who are interested in organizing around migrant justice. A main difference, however, will be that the group will be led primarily by undocumented migrants or migrants with precarious status. This means that we will have to evolve into a type of organization in which people without status feel like they can organize and trust. Questions regarding privilege, security, tactics, knowledge distribution, and structure will undoubtedly need to be asked and answered in order for this to become plausible. I don't mean to say that the experiences of nonstatus people are homogeneous and that we should organize around this *identity*. Rather, we should employ a bottom-up model of organizing, and we should make sure that those most marginalized and silenced by the *issue* of migrant justice are leading the group.

Part of the difficulty in evolving into a group led by those without status revolves around NOII's interest in being a kinship network. Some would say that they are not looking at NOII to provide community and it is not necessary to build these types of relationships. While I respect that opinion, I believe that the shift to an organization that is led by people without status will require a certain level of trust, camaraderie, respect, and sense of belonging. My strong reaction to seeing the name No One Is Illegal on that poster was partly because I had a moment of recognition of self. I saw my own conviction in the group's name, and this told me that there were other people like me who believed that borders and status had no bearing on human value. I organize with NOII because I believe in our demands, yes, but I came to my first meeting because I thought I would find the community I was looking for. In a lot of ways, I hope my current experience of NOII will be common for others in the future: I have found a way to organize around something I am passionate about, but I have also met amazing people who have offered me their friendship, their support, and a sense of home.

JOURNEYS TOWARD
DECOLONIZATION

Journeys toward Decolonization

> Our desire to be free has got to manifest itself in
> everything we are and do.
> —Assata Shakur, *Assata: An Autobiography*

Decolonization is more than a struggle against power
and control; it is also the imagining and generating of
alternative institutions and relations. Decolonization
is a dual form of resistance that is responsive to dismantling
current systems of colonial empire and systemic hierarchies, while also prefiguring societies based on equity,
mutual aid, and self-determination. Undoing the physical
and conceptual orderings of border imperialism requires
a fundamental reorientation of ourselves, our movements,
and our communities to think and act with intentionality,
creativity, militancy, humility, and above all, a deep sense of
responsibility and reciprocity. This paradigm shift is what
I would call decolonization, and I believe that creating
decolonizing conditions toward revolution, liberation, and
transformation must become our collective priority.

Decolonization is as much a process as a goal; the journey of how we get there, together, is as critical as the destination we reach. In a world where capitalism and colonialism flourish due, at least in part, to the false sense of their inevitability, decolonization is an evocation to not only dream but also to recover and carry ourselves out of erasure and victimhood. Based on my reflections and lessons from organizing over the past decade, this final chapter provides some signposts on the path to decolonizing structural colonialism, social justice movements, and social relations.

It may seem paradoxical, but what is most decolonizing about decolonization as a prefigurative practice is that it does not presume itself to be a new concept. Without romanticizing the past, we have much to learn from our ancestors and the evolution of knowledge. We are inheritors of these cultures and traditions, while inventing and informing our cultures and communities every day—despite the conditions that constrain us. Reflecting the profound title of an American Indian Movement gathering, No One Is Illegal, We Are All One River, I seek to bring existing frameworks into a holistic understanding of decolonization that holds individual autonomy alongside mutual interdependence, vulnerability as part of resiliency, and specific experiences within a universal humanity. By challenging the dehumanization intrinsic to the dominating and coercive systems of border imperialism, decolonization affirms the sacredness of all life and restores our relationship to the Earth.

Decolonizing Structural Colonialism

> Settler colonialism is being unable to fill in the
> blanks. . . . It is the logic of superiority, of primacy,
> of genocide. It is the colonization of memory and
> of events that come to be known as "History." . . .
> More than anything, settler colonialism is ongoing.
> —Maya Mikdashi, "What Is Settler Colonialism?"

Decolonizing begins with the understanding that we are
all, in some way, beneficiaries of the illegal settlement of
Indigenous lands and unjust appropriation of Indigenous
jurisdiction, both locally and globally. North America's
state and corporate wealth is based on the colonial theft
of Indigenous lands and resources, as well as the deliberate
dispossession and impoverishment of Indigenous communities within and beyond its borders. Within North
America, settler colonialism was designed to ensure the
forced displacement of Indigenous peoples from their territories, the destruction of autonomy and self-determination
within Indigenous governance, and the assimilation of
Indigenous cultures and traditions. We are inserted into
and complicit in a culture that sees "Indians" rather than
settlement as the problem.[1] This makes our participation
within anticolonial movements a necessity. Decolonization
of settler colonialism on these lands requires a commitment
to fighting colonization, and a resurgence and recenter-
ing of local Indigenous worldviews as well as memories of
another way of living.

Social movements are recognizing that Indigenous self-determination must become the foundation for all our social and environmental justice mobilizing. Indigenous self-determination is becoming increasingly intertwined within struggles against racism, poverty, police violence, empire, heteropatriarchy, and environmental degradation. Anarchists point to the antiauthoritarian tendencies within Indigenous communities, environmentalists highlight the connection to land that Indigenous communities have, antiracists include Indigenous people within dialogues on systemic racism, and women's organizations underscore the relentless violence inflicted on Indigenous women in discussions about patriarchy.

Incorporating Indigenous self-determination into these movements, however, can subordinate and compart-mentalize Indigenous struggle within the existing param-eters of leftist narratives. We cannot replicate the state's assimilation by forcing Indigenous struggles to fit within our existing narratives. As Sium, Desai, and Ritskes argue, "Decolonization is indeed oppositional to colonial ways of thinking and acting but demands an Indigenous starting point."[2] Indigenous self-determination is expressed collec-tively, and should not be subsumed within the discourse of individual human rights. Furthermore, being Indigenous is not just an identity but rather a way of life that is intricately connected to Indigenous peoples' relationships to their communities and the land. Indigenous scholars Taiaiake Alfred and Jeff Corntassel explain that "Indigenous peoples themselves have long understood their existence as peoples or nations (expressed not in these terms but in their own languages, of course) as formed around axes of land, culture, and community."[3]

Indigenous struggles cannot just be accommodated within other struggles; struggles to decolonize from settler colonialism and ongoing genocide demand our understanding and solidarity on their own terms. The Idle No More movement, for example, calls on allies to join a revolution that honors and fulfills Indigenous sovereignty, and protects the land and water for a sustainable future for all.[4] Indigenous Anishinaabe and Nehayo writer Tara Williamson explains that for her, "Idle No More is about nationhood. Not nation-state-hood, but nationhood—the ability to take care of the land, our children, and our families in the way we best know how. While the Canadian government currently plays heavily into our ability to function as self-determining nations, we know that true self-governance has to come from ourselves. . . . The best way to demand self-determination is to be self-determining."[5]

Meaningful support for Indigenous struggles should not be imposed or directed by nonnatives; nonnatives must learn to take leadership from Indigenous communities. This means taking initiative to self-educate about the specific histories of the lands on which we reside, organizing support with the clear consent and guidance of Indigenous nations or groups, being proactive in offering concrete fund-raising or campaign support as needed or requested, building long-term relationships of accountability, and never assuming or taking for granted the trust that nonnatives may earn from Indigenous peoples over time. Clear lines of communication must always be maintained, and a commitment should be made to long-term support beyond crisis, blockades, or campaigns. As described in previous chapters, for myself and others in NOII, that has meant being involved in ongoing support for grassroots Indigenous peoples who are exercising traditional governance and customs, seeking redress and reparations for state acts of genocide and assimilation such as residential boarding schools, opposing corporate development on their lands, pushing back against imposed heteropatriarchy, struggling against poverty and criminalization in urban areas, and affirming their languages, traditions, creative expressions, and spiritual practices.

We also urgently need to comprehend and stand with Indigenous communities' defense of the land. As Algerian revolutionary Frantz Fanon compellingly asserts, "For a colonized people the most essential value, because the most concrete, is first and foremost the land: the land which will bring them bread and, above all, dignity."[6] We are living in an era of unprecedented ecological catastrophe, yet states and corporations continue to plunder the Earth through resource extraction, deforestation, pollution, and reliance on an oil-dependent economy. "If there is to be any hope of a sustainable future, it is precisely economic growth that needs to be called into question," scholar Valérie Fournier writes.[7] Yet much of mainstream environmental activism has either become focused on proposing individual choices such as recycling and purchasing electric cars, or been collaborating with corporations on nuclear power technologies and carbon-trading markets that devastate the Earth. These greenwashing approaches can readily be contained within capitalism, and many ecologically destructive corporations are reaping profits by marketing "new green solutions." As Fournier further explains, "Sustainable development and ecological modernization only serve to 'sustain the unsustainable'; they not only absolve major corporations and a capitalist economy of endless growth of environmental responsibilities, but also cast them as the new heroes of sustainability."[8]

Decolonizing our views of the natural world would bring us closer to Indigenous worldviews that are also anticapitalist. Realizing that we are dependent on rapidly depleting sources of water and food, taking only what we need from the land and sharing it, understanding that humans are not superior to other species but are just one part of the natural world, respecting the inherent rights of nature including the basic right to exist, and fostering a consciousness of the Earth as a life source to be protected as opposed to private property to be exploited and traded on the market are all critical to decolonization. At recent international Indigenous gatherings, this worldview has been termed "living well" in contrast to "living more." This is a simple yet profound transformation from the belief that the market can save the environment to one that can actually suffocate industrial capitalism. Such teachings defy the capitalist and colonial system's logic of competition, commodification, and domination, and instead generate interdependency and respect among all living things.

The obligation for decolonization rests on all of us. Simpson urges nonnatives to seriously take on the struggle against colonialism within the context of collective liberation. "We don't have to uphold this system any longer. We can collectively make different choices," she writes.[9] Montreal-based Indigenous solidarity activist Nora Burke similarly says: "A decolonisation movement cannot be comprised solely of solidarity and support for Indigenous peoples' sovereignty and self-determination. If we are in support of self-determination, we too need to be self-determining. It is time to cut the state out of this relationship, and to replace it with a new relationship, one which is mutually negotiated, and premised on a core respect for autonomy and freedom."[10] Decolonization is, in essence, a subversion of border imperialism as it requires us to reimagine and reconfigure our communities based on shared ideals and visions. The Two Row Wampum agreement of peace, friendship, and respect between the Indigenous Haudenosaunee nations and first Dutch and then subsequent settlers, for example, is premised on the revolutionary notion of respectful coexistence and land stewardship.

Black Cherokee activist Zainab Amadahy uses a relationship framework to describe the process of decolonization: "Understanding the world through a Relationship Framework . . . we don't see ourselves, our communities, or our species as inherently superior to any other, but rather see our roles and responsibilities to each other as inherent to enjoying our life experiences."[11] Author Stephanie Irlbacher-Fox similarly describes why meaningful relationships are central to the process of dismantling colonialism. She writes, "Relationship is fundamental to meaningful co-existence, and an antecedent to motivating change within settler society over the long term. Co-existence through co-resistance is the responsibility of settlers. . . . Relationship creates accountability and responsibility for sustained supportive action."[12] Decolonization encourages us to think of this interconnectedness, not separation or isolation, as we strengthen alliances and enact solidarities to dismantle colonial structures and ideologies. Smith cautions us "not to individualize Indigenous struggles but to see that genocide and colonization are part of a larger global framework of domination." While decolonization necessitates specific attention on the differential impacts of colonialism, decolonization cannot happen in a vacuum where people are segregated from or pitted against each other; rather decolonization, as Smith suggests, "happens in a framework of global liberation" and encourages an expansive rather than exclusive politics.[13]

Decolonizing Social Movements

> What we want is democracy and inclusion of all—
> not in a nation, a state or an identity that always
> presupposes exclusion—but in a life in common.
> —Carlos Fernandez, Meredith Gill, Imre
> Szeman, and Jessica Whyte, "Erasing the Line,
> or, the Politics of the Border"

Decolonizing migrant justice movements from border imperialism, and the internalization of its logic, requires us to shed those ideas that perpetuate divisions between the worthy, deserving, and desirable migrant and the disposable, undeserving, and undesirable migrant. As discussed throughout this book, migrant justice movements must insist on the humanity of migrants beyond what they represent to capital relations and the dictates of empire. Prevalent stereotypes of undesirable migrants include those who have criminal records or those who are poor or unemployed, racialized, religious but non-Christian, single mothers or members of nonnuclear families, non-English speakers, differently abled, and/or genderqueer.

These notions of undesirability are a reflection of broader systemic societal hierarchies that render some lives less assimilable, less human, and hence less worthy of a life of dignity and justice. In thinking through how to reject the discourses of worthiness versus disposability inherent to border imperialism *and* all other forms of injustice, our social movements can learn vital lessons from prison abolition, anti-imperialist, gender liberation, and disability justice movements. Here I focus on the ways in which these four movements deconstruct and decolonize our understandings of the distinction between worthy versus disposable lives.

Similar to the mechanisms of illegalization within border imperialism, the prison-industrial complex criminalizes and incarcerates racialized bodies in order to control them, while corporations reap profits from prison contracts and prison labor. Prison abolition movements, as activist and scholar Julia Sudbury argues, "demand a radical restructuring of the way in which we deal with the social conditions that generate 'crime.'"[14] Beyond merely advocating for prison reform, such movements highlight the socioeconomic roots of crime, interrogate the deliberate targeting of poor and racialized communities by the criminal justice system, and reveal that prisons are more about protecting social hierarchies and capitalist interests than addressing safety. For instance, statistics reveal that police and prisons actually underprotect and overpolice racialized women, youths, queers, and transpeople.

While confronting state control, prison abolition movements are also increasingly incorporating community accountability processes to provide safety for survivors of sexual violence. This is a decolonizing prefiguration toward violence-free communities, achieved by strategizing together on how we can keep each other safe. When we divide ourselves between those who are law abiding and those who are not, between those who are victims and those who should be locked up, we reproduce the state narrative on deviance—that homeless people, sex workers, drug users, gang-involved youths, Indigenous communities, black people, men of color, and women who defend themselves are all dangerous. With the prison-industrial complex engulfing entire communities, the sentiment expressed by socialist Eugene Debs decades ago rings true with greater fervor today: "While there is a lower class, I am in it, and while there is a criminal element I am of it, and while there is a soul in prison, I am not free."[15] Aligning with prison abolition movements holds those who exist as villains in the eyes of the state and much of our society within the center of our movements.

At the global level, anti-imperialism goes beyond just expressing opposition to Western militarization.

Because the justifications for imperialist engagements are often based on a racist belief of civilizational superiority, anti-imperialist movements challenge cultural imperialism and its imposition of Eurocentricism as the marker of progressive values. Cultural imperialism has essentialized communities of color as innately barbaric and reactionary toward women, children, and queers, who are constructed in infantilizing ways devoid of any choice or agency—forced to veil, subjected to honor killings, forever closeted, coerced into arranged marriages. In writing about the architecture of feminisms in the service of imperialism, feminist author Leila Ahmed charges, "Whether in the hands of patriarchal men or feminists, the ideas of western feminism essentially functioned to morally justify the attack on native societies and to support the notion of the comprehensive superiority of Europe."[16] Extending this to discourses of sexuality in the service of empire, theorist Jasbir Puar coined the phrase "homonationalism" to describe how queer rights are framed as national gifts bestowed by Western states.[17]

In the post-9/11 context of heightened Islamophobia, cultural imperialism is evident in debates about gender and Islam that force a singular feminism—secular, sexually expressive, and liberal autonomist—on women and queers of color, who experience heteropatriarchy within complex layers of subjugation and survival. To be clear, I am not aligning myself with those who use discourses of cultural essentialism as rigid tropes to police sexual boundaries or those who minimize the universal epidemic of gender violence. Rather, I wish to highlight how anti-imperialist movements emphasize that cultural formations and vocabularies *do* matter, and that they are being interpreted, practiced, and contested in a multiplicity of ways by those who actually live with them.

Muslim feminists Dana Olwan and Sophia Azeb probe, "Why, for example, do Muslims feel compelled to answer the question of whether Islam is compatible with feminism by repeatedly defining and defending Islam and showcasing its gender equal principles to non-Muslims? Why don't we alter the frames of the question, asking, instead, what feminism actually means and whether feminism, as both a political movement and analytical tool, is amenable to Islam and religious identity and practice?"[18] Anti-imperialist movements reject the white man's (and woman's) burden—or what author Teju Cole characterizes as the "White Saviour Industrial Complex"—represented by state interventions and certain progressive movements, to rescue women, children, and queers from their so-called backward traditions. By challenging the ideologies of superiority *and* uniformity underlying cultural imperialism, anti-imperialist movements diversify and hence decolonize our understandings of how coercion is experienced.

While anti-imperialist movements have disputed certain aspects of feminism, there are many noteworthy contributions to decolonization from gender liberation movements. Gender liberation encompasses a range of struggles against heteropatriarchy and assimilation into its normative hegemony. I wish to spotlight two such struggles: the challenge to rigid gender binaries and the challenge to what is valued as labor.

Gender liberation struggles—particularly those that understand queer, gender nonconforming, and transgender as political identities—defy the policing and surveillance of gender and sexual boundaries. Rather than simply seeking equal rights for women, as some strands of feminism do, gender liberation strives to abolish the gender binary from which the violence of heteropatriarchy and cis-sexism— and the resulting unequal conditions of women, transfolks, and genderqueer people—stems. As HAVOQ declares, "We see a connection between the policing of people's genders and sexualities with the policing of borders. . . . We reject the regulation of ourselves and our relationships through socially-created borders, such as those used to define traditional families, acceptable sex practices, ideal bodies and gender presentations, and love."[19] Gender thus becomes a space for contestation against border imperialism, a border-bending site that refuses to be a unified subject with zones of exclusion, and instead constitutes itself as fluid and inclusive. The transgressions of patriarchal, heterosexual, and cis-sexist binaries as well as the centrality of the concept of self-determination in expressing gender identity are decolonizing orientations.

The challenge to what is valued as labor takes up women's reproductive labor and care work, which is devalued and invisiblized within capitalism. Capitalism not only creates the conditions for precarious labor, it also defines what can even be characterized as labor. Single mothers become marginalized as "unemployed" and "uncontributing" when they are in fact, as scholar Silvia Frederici observes, reproducing labor power as a key source of capitalist accumulation: "The wage relation hides the unpaid, slave-like nature of so much of the work upon which capital accumulation is premised."[20] Feminist Ann Ferguson describes the flip side of this phenomenon, arguing that it has been easier to shift the traditional male-breadwinner–female-caregiver model toward female breadwinner than it has been to shift it toward male caregiver.[21] This reveals how, regardless of the numbers of women in the paid workforce, patriarchal relations and an anticommunitarian social ordering of labor are central to the structuring of capitalism. Since single mothers, poor women, women of color, and transfolks are relegated to the lowest ranks of those deemed disposable, gender liberation is at the core of disarming the social and economic hierarchies within border imperialism.

Disability justice movements similarly challenge the assumption that valuable labor is that which can be commodified and sold on the market. Disability justice goes beyond ensuring better access for those facing physical and mental barriers, and even beyond challenging the confining standards of so-called normal abilities. Because ableism dictates the norms of productivity, disability justice forces a contestation of how we live under colonialism and what labor we value under capitalism.

A queer and physically disabled woman of color, Mia Mingus outlines how ableism underpins the notion of undesirability central to hierarchies of social control:

> Ableism set the stage for queer and trans people
> to be institutionalized as mentally disabled; for

communities of color to be understood as less
capable, smart and intelligent, therefore "naturally"
fit for slave labor; for women's bodies to be used
to produce children, when, where and how men
needed them; for people with disabilities to be
seen as "disposable" in a capitalist and exploitative
culture because we are not seen as "productive"; for
immigrants to be thought of as a "disease" that we
must "cure" because it is "weakening" our country.[22]

Because capitalism has linked human worth to an individual's ability to produce and have their labor extracted
for profit, disability justice subverts capitalism and border
imperialism by celebrating the contributions of all those
differently abled and aging bodies that we are conditioned
to believe are unproductive, burdensome, and worthless.

Though each movement is discussed separately,
incorporating an interconnected and intersectional analysis
of prison abolition, anti-imperialism, gender liberation,
and disability justice moves us away from discourses that
reinforce expendability for those who refuse to or cannot
assimilate into systems of domination, and instead, brings
us closer to a vision of decolonization.

What I suggest here is *more* than an antioppression
analysis seeking to diversify our movements through
the politics of inclusion or representation, and I suggest
something *different* from equal opportunity and access
within state structures or in the performance of wage labor.
What these interrelated analyses help us realize is that striving to be more visible and desirable within an oppressive

system—one that is built on our social discipline and compels our obedience—will never set us free. What will free us is the collective and public recognition of all bodies, all abilities, all genders, all experiences, and all expressions as inherently valuable, and by virtue of their very existence, as distinctly *human*. Since border imperialism and its constituent processes of capitalism and colonialism have psychologically dispossessed as well as structurally divided us, decolonization is an assertion of our intrinsic self-determining beauty and humanity.

Decolonizing Social Relations

> Life is no longer becoming, but simply being. . . .
> We will not surrender the rhythm of life to the
> timing of gears. . . To make a noise that will not
> go away. To burn all that is not true. To rip up the
> paving stones and discover, beneath them, the
> earth. To begin to grow roots again.
> —Anonymous, "The Witch's Child"

One of the contradictions of border imperialism and capitalism is that while we are increasingly dependent on intricate production processes for our basic clothing and food, we are increasingly isolated from one another. Each of us plays such an atomized role in the global economy—like cogs in a wheel—that our social relations come to mimic that atomization. This psychological and social isolation, first, encourages our addiction to consumer culture, which in turn feeds endless capitalist production, and second, perpetuates our fears of one another, which justifies ever-expanding state surveillance and criminalization within border imperialism.

Given that colonialism and capitalism require and perpetuate isolation, decolonization calls on us to affirm community. Resilient movements and communities can rarely be sustained simply based on shared analysis about the system's flaws. The motivation for strong movements and communities is genuine, empathetic, healthy, and loving social relations forged in the process of struggle, as we overgrow the logic of the dominant system. In this section, I explore healing justice and emotional justice as foundations for decolonizing social relations, which Copwatch LA and Native Youth Movement member Joaquin Cienfuegos notes is connected to the decolonization of our entire social conditioning: "We have to learn how to be human again; this battle is one where we not only decolonize ourselves and our minds, but decolonize our condition."[23]

Within activist circles, well-being is often described as "self-care." I have several criticisms of the discourse and practice of self-care. Self-care is highly individualized, and ignores the reality that it is frequently impossible to suspend familial, community, or movement obligations in order to care for one's self. This is not simply a matter of choice; rather, the ability to practice self-care is constrained by child and elder care obligations, lack of financial access, and ongoing responsibilities. The focus on "self" is particularly problematic within movements that prioritize

solidarity work. We do not always have the option of step-
ping away when others are relying on us to help overturn
a deportation order the next day or arrange a press conference about an urgent blockade. As healing practioner
Yashna Maya Padamsee suggests, "Self care, as it is framed
now, leaves us in danger of being isolated in our struggle
and our healing. Isolation of yet another person, another
injustice, is a notch in the belt of Oppression. A liberatory
care practice is one in which we move beyond self care into
caring for each other."[24]

Healing justice is a liberatory care framework that
shifts the discourse from self-care to community care,
and centers a "political and philosophical convergence of
healing inside of liberation."[25] Healing justice is a holistic
concept and intentional project that addresses personal,
collective, and systemic trauma. It aims to transform
the individualistic, privatized, and capitalist conditions
of healing that appropriate and then deny low-income
communities access to food, medicines, support systems,
and traditional healing methods due to a lack of financial
resources, and often, the privilege of time. Healing justice
is a value system of creating and sustaining communities of
care that honors both our individual care needs as well as
our responsibilities to each other and the Earth. It decon-
structs the rigid borders that separate the self from the
broader community by recognizing that we are interdepen-
dent; self-care requires community care and community
care requires self-care.

Given that systems of exploitation and oppression
aim to annihilate and break us, prefiguring the conditions

to feel healthy, whole, and purposeful are vital. But it is impossible for a community to heal independently of the well-being of each individual, and conversely, it is impossible for an individual to be healthy in isolation from the trauma within their community and on the land. In an interview, nonstatus Algerian activist Massaouda Kellou proclaimed, "Injustice is my illness. When it's gone, I'll be healthy."[26] Decolonizing communities therefore incorporate a reciprocal vision of healing: cultivating an ethic of care for individuals, and simultaneously, individuals need to be responsible in caring for others and the Earth. Healing practitioner Dori Midnight envisions community care as a tenderness toward all living things, drawing attention to how "we can gently and fiercely take care of the little baby bodies, the disabled bodies, the aging and dying bodies, the green bodies, the blue bodies of water, the four legged bodies, each other's bodies and the one body you were born into, this time around."[27]

Emotional justice is one expression of community care; it is the praxis of understanding and fully experiencing one another with empathy, and sustaining kinship beyond the bounds of capitalism and border imperialism. In the words of educator Yolo Akili, "Emotional justice requires that we find the feeling behind the theories. It calls on us to not just speak to why something is problematic, but to speak to the emotional texture of how it impacts us; how it hurts, or how it brings us joy or nourishment."[28] Emotional justice fosters the spiritual, physical, and mental well-being needed to create community, to bring our best selves, and to reach for and experience liberation.

Emotional justice involves, for example, sharing in the moments of everyday life through eating together and checking in with one another when we experience stress, grief, or illness. Creating bonds of love, trust, respect, compassion, and mutual aid between self-expressing individuals, in turn, empowers self-determining and decolonizing communities by grounding social relations within political organizing along with extending the borders of what is considered legitimate political work. Emotional justice centers our whole selves, and allows us to unfold our messy experiences and broken bodies. We have to keep reminding each other that despite what colonialism and capitalism try to ingrain in us, we are not disposable, nor worth only what we produce or how "well" we function.

Emotional justice, community building, and deconstructing the borders between one another is extremely hard. As Akili points out, "Emotional justice is very difficult for many activists, because historically most activist spaces have privileged the intellect and logic over feeling and intuition. This is directly connected to sexism and misogyny, because feeling and intuition are culturally and psychologically linked to the construct of woman."[29] Emotional justice challenges us to bring voice to those unnamed hurts and complicated edges that stem from our deepest cracks, the interpersonal dynamics that traverse often-contradictory layers of power and marginalization, and the frustration that cannot easily be qualified or quantified into a boxed category of oppression. Filipino American emcee Kiwi Illafonte courageously shares his own experiences:

Overlapping layers of silence and privilege make
truly connecting with one another more work
than we may have the energy for. . . . Some people's
contusions are too blemished to simply jump into
a space and function productively. Others have to
navigate both the power they have and their lack
of, which I imagine can be pretty damn confus-
ing. And we neither have the understanding or
compassion to individually nor collectively struggle
through these dynamics in a healthy way. So we
fight. And we resent. And we talk shit. And we
cut off. And we ignore. And we fear. And we feel
shame. And we hurt. And we recycle and regurgi-
tate all that trauma onto each other, and onto the
generations after us.[30]

As difficult as working through these dynamics of
community is, especially beyond our comfortable friendship circles, it is crucial, and must be valued as a form
of labor. It behooves us to build (and share the labor of
building) movements where we are emancipated rather
than alienated, where we are more resilient and have more
capacity to be present for movement projects because
we feel supported as we move through our own traumas,
and where we encourage honesty among each other and
challenge each others' harmful behaviors, but learn to do
so without hurling daggers at ourselves or one another.
This requires intentional practice—a deliberate learning of
how to manifest and align ourselves with our vision for the
world.

A discussion on decolonizing social relations is incomplete without a mention of revolutionary love. Philosopher Alain Badiou argues that love is a political subjectivity: "It's necessary to invent a politics that is not identical with power. Real politics is to engage to resolve problems within a collective with enthusiasm. It's not simply to delegate problems to the professionals. Love is like politics in that it's not a professional affair. There are no professionals in love, and none in real politics."[31] As a generative and relational force, love compels individual and collective transformations; love expands our capacity to engage in emotional and healing justice work by unmasking vulnerabilities while acknowledging our need for one another. Love, as a practice, disrupts the hyperindependence and sovereignty of self that capitalism conditions us into. "The thing I like about love as a concept for the possibility of the social, is that love always means non-sovereignty," theorist Lauren Berlant explains. "Love is always about violating your own attachment to your intentionality, without being anti-intentional."[32]

I have witnessed how communities of color, and even more so queer women of color, transfolks of color, and/or people of color with disabilities, have persistently articulated as well as practiced a politics of revolutionary love. This includes resource redistribution, affinity groups during and between actions, community kitchens, family care support, emotional laboring, and participating in bartering and mutual aid networks. This is not a coincidence. Those who experience an avalanche of oppressions, and cannot rely on the state or market for relief or redemption, know how much we need and depend on one another in order to survive. Indigenous lesbian poet Paula Gunn Allen remarks,

> We survive war and conquest; we survive colo-
> nization, acculturation, assimilation; we survive
> beating, rape, starvation, mutilation, sterilization,
> abandonment, neglect, death of our children, our
> loved ones, destruction of our land, our homes,
> our past, and our future. We survive, and we do
> more than just survive. We bond, we care, we fight,
> we teach, we nurse, we bear, we feed, we learn, we
> laugh, we love.[33]

Communities that value emotional justice and healing justice by nurturing loving and regenerative forms of
social relations are transformative. This can be understood
as a queering of our communities, where we rejoice in the
unlimited trajectories of love, self-expression, and kinship.
Such communities are subversive to the logic of alienation
within capitalism, colonialism, and border imperialism,
and move us toward decolonization by fulfilling our yearn-
ings for a culture that is not synonymous with capital or
consumption and by enacting our desires for connection to
one another and the Earth.

Within and Through

and you, who laugh without shame
live every moment intended and
sing when the moon does not rise
you who do not shirk from the sweet rot of dreams
who revolt and refuse to be small,
and choose this unfinished labyrinth
over the neat architecture of genocide
you are my nation.
—Cynthia Dewi Oka, "Kindred"

Making sense of my own life, marked by countless state borders and marred by innumerable systemic barriers, has been a process of decolonization. Lacking full legal status as a result of border imperialism coupled with daily humiliations as a woman of color has meant decades of feeling expendable, powerless, ashamed, fragmented, inadequate, tentative, and quite literally crazy. My journey to a place of self-actualization and self-affirmation, as well as responsible allyship where I am complicit in other systems of oppression such as settler colonialism locally and Western militarism globally, has been a direct result of my involvement in the overlapping processes of political struggle against injustice and building community among allies and comrades.

For me, as for many others, social movement organizing has been healing and empowering precisely because *within it* and *through it* I have found a means to redeem and liberate myself from all the injustices, categories, and assumptions laid on me. Author Mia McKenzie's words reverberate through me, "The things we learn to do to survive at all costs are not the things that will help us get free. Getting free is a whole different journey altogether."[34] This is not to suggest that social movements are never oppressive or problematic but for me, the hardships and heartbreak pale in comparison to a life of hiding, silence, passivity, and defeat, or the constant attempts to measure up within capitalism and colonialism by increasing my production and consumption levels.

We must embody and enact decolonization in order to claim it. Decolonization is a generative and prefigurative process whereby we create the conditions in which we want to live and the social relations we wish to have—for ourselves *and* everyone else. It is an act of faith to overcome fear in order to organize against authoritarian governance, oppressive hierarchies, and capitalist economies, while also shedding our internalized prejudices and suspicious ways of relating to one another. In order to rid ourselves of border imperialism along with the barriers we erect within ourselves against one another, our movements have to supplant the colonial and bordered logic of the state itself. Almost a century ago, anarchist Gustav Landauer wrote: "The State is a condition, a certain relationship between human beings, a mode of behaviour; we destroy it by contracting other relationships."[35]

Striving toward decolonization requires us to challenge a dehumanizing social organization that robs us from one another and normalizes a lack of responsibility and care for one another and the Earth. This does not suggest a simple call for unity across our differences—particularly those rooted in systemic colonial privilege—but rather evokes a necessary struggle from our specific histories and locations, while refounding alliance, community, and kinship with one other. Decolonization calls on us to learn about and challenge each other in our complicities and contradictions within asymmetric relations of power and oppression, as we unlearn colonial strategies that foster competition and division among each other. Perhaps more than anything else, decolonization invites us to actively become good ancestors to future generations.

Decolonization presents expansive and universal visions of self-determination over our own bodies, lives, cultures, lands, and labor; where we strive for noncoercive communities committed to Indigenous, racial, migrant, gender, economic, disability, reproductive, and environmental justice; where we can live free from cages, militaries, borders, reserves, segregation, toxic industries, corporations, sweatshops, and instead thrive with unquenchable purpose, fullness, connection, joy, and nourishment.

As outlined in this chapter and throughout this book, fulfilling this anticolonial, anticapitalist, and antioppressive vision necessitates a decolonizing praxis, including strategic and revolutionary organizing to confront power, an ethic of self-reflection, and intentionally respectful and just relations with each other and the land. Movements that orient themselves toward decolonization—through structural analysis and action as well as by rectifying our relations with one another and in particular with Indigenous communities and lands—are transformative, healing, and revolutionary. Ultimately, such decolonizing movements are sustainable *and* sustain us precisely because they provide meaning and purpose to those in the struggle. Celebrated historian Howard Zinn reminds us, "The reward for participating in a movement for social justice is not the prospect of future victory. It is the exhilaration of standing together with other people, taking risks together, enjoying small triumphs and enduring disheartening setbacks together."[36]

For me, NOII has been one such decolonizing movement. Particularly in Vancouver (Indigenous Coast Salish territories), NOII organizes strategically and effectively while prioritizing meaningful and accountable alliances and solidarities across diverse communities. In addition to being constantly awe inspired by a number of monumental victories as a result of NOII's mobilizing, my personal connection and commitment to NOII exists because it is a community of comrades grounded in love and interdependency where I have been nurtured as well as challenged in all aspects of my life, and where I have been gifted with a multiplicity of intergenerational teachings. It is not a space that I engage with from a place of guilt or where my spirit is drained from activism. In fact, the opposite is true. Because this space has facilitated a community and movement that sustains me and cultivates my growth at every level, I am compelled to engage more actively and responsibly in the service of its vision—and resistance aimed at—undoing border imperialism.

Epilogue

My heart thumping, I hurtled into the bush in the dark street. With shaky fingers, I dialed Mac's number. "Mac, the cops showed up, and started beating us, and I ran." I heard a sharp intake of breath on the other end of the line. I could hear the question in the silence. Why did I run? Every legal workshop I've ever been in always teaches one fundamental rule: when approached by the police, answer the most basic of questions, ask if you are detained and request a lawyer. Don't run, don't fight.

I always fight or run. As a child in Dubai, hanging out with Baloch boys who had been born without immigration documents, a cop siren meant only one thing: run. Anything could trigger police beatings, ID checks, deportations. As a young man in Karachi, caught in the middle of sectarian riots or yet another military dictatorship, rights were for the rich—those who could drive away—the rest of us fought or ran. In Chicago, working for five dollars an hour, for twelve hours a day, without immigration papers, scrubbing floors and drinking in parks with migrants from Mexico, Guatemala, and El Salvador, there was an unstated understanding that when Immigration and Customs Enforcement or the police came, we ran.

Locked in by borders, pushed out by wars, entrenched in poverty and living in homes where the land, air, and water get murkier by the day, for too many of us, standing still and speaking politely is not an option. I write this because our actions are just as much visceral as they are analytical, theoretical, or intellectual. Political organizing is also a response in rage, a response in emotion, a response in bodies, rooted in our collective experiences.

My grandparents shuddered if the year 1947 was ever mentioned. The year of freedom, the year of partition, the year of being wrenched apart. My father was born in a refugee camp. My mother was a migrant in a city where xenophobia was on the rise. Forces beyond their control decided where they lived, when they lived, how they lived. Beaten down by the world outside, my grandfather brutally beat up his seven sons and three daughters. Together they carried the brutality that they could not and did not name—a tradition that my father carried on to my body and those of my four sisters.

I was born in Libya. My family was forced to leave when I was five. My mother recalls clutching a tin of dried milk as she made her way on to the airplane. Since then I have been coerced into leaving three other countries, each time for different reasons. There have been too many boxes, suitcases, tickets, and loves lost. I now live in Toronto, and for the last five years the same dark cloud of whether I stay or go looms over my head. Six people who were charged with conspiracy alongside me during anti-G20 protests in

2010 have gone to jail for up to a year, partly to ensure that I did not get deported.

These stories of my grandparents, my parents, my siblings, and my friends are not new stories. I do not write them to assert an exception. These are everyday stories, stories of forty-five million migrants around the world. Stories of the millions more who are children of displaced and colonized peoples.

And yet too few people without full immigration status have been able to speak out about that which ails us and that which can liberate us. When migrant workers and undocumented people speak out against injustice, the repercussions are immense, the support uncertain. That I chose, despite my precarious legal status, to be so public is partially because I do not have a child who I must worry about or parents who I have allegiance to. That I can walk unmasked, speak on the microphone, and appear in front of cameras is because the language of the ivory tower comes too easily to me. That I went public is because I have enormous community support from people who put me up in their homes, feed me, find me lawyers, mobilize political support on my behalf, and even go to jail so that I would not be convicted. I am not alone.

Around the world glimmers of other ways of living, not clear still, are lighting up streets and alleys, neighborhoods and academies, the world over. The simmers and the ashes of these fires rest in communities of the dispossessed. Be it the riots that began in anger over the murder of Alexandros Grigoropoulos in Greece or the self-immolation of Mohamed Bouazizi in Tunisia, uprisings are, as they always have been, rooted in the lives and bodies of those who do not have the option of speaking politely, and just stopped running.

The Undocumented and Unafraid actions emerging out of the United States, the Sans Papiers movement in France, or the migrants' assemblies in Greece are all moments where people are turning from running to fighting. The resistance long simmering under the surface is breaking through the imaginary line into the public sphere.

The same call echoes: what we need and aspire for is total transformation. What we seek is freedom. Freedom to move, return, and stay. We must reach a world without rich or poor, where work is about creation not bosses, where wars are not fought, where social oppressions do not breed, where the Earth is not suffering. We must reach worlds where people live freely with respect and dignity, without fear and without injustice.

We could do this by fighting to expand our legal rights, but we don't have to. We may be able to do so by repeatedly electing a lesser evil into power and hounding them, but we don't have to. Maybe we could do it by getting offices, using a river of ink to write grants to hire staff, to leech off the beast as we try and destroy it, but we don't have to. We could do it by putting our bodies on the barricades. We could do it by having running battles in the streets, occupying, squatting, until enough people join us, but we don't have to. We could do it by forming little groups to seep into the political parties to transform them from the inside, but we don't have to.

We could achieve freedom in all these ways, or none of them. But whatever way we choose, it must be in the hundreds, thousands, millions. We must create a polyphony, a tune of many voices that is truth for all of us. Our answers must be for all our questions.

Migrant justice movements particularly on Turtle Island, like other movements of people, have and continue to struggle to create and maintain leadership from communities directly under attack, people directly fighting back. A future that continues to be led by students and professionals, those who speak in a glossary of activist terms played on repeat, will not be led anywhere, nor arrive anywhere. Every time an undocumented mother walks into a school to enroll her child, it is an act of resistance and defiance. Each time a migrant worker chooses to take the twelve-hour shift over the nine-hour shift to scrape together a little more for her ailing parents, it is an act that must be honored. Simply staring down the bared face of violence and continuing to breathe is incredible resistance. Linking our political organizing to this chain of freedom is critical and one of our most urgent concerns.

The roads to all the worlds we want to live in are not going to emerge from a single map, a single shift in cartography. They will be found in alleys and on little trails, found in the little struggles that we create, fight, and win. And at each step, we must mark our victories and our losses. Learn, celebrate, mourn, and share. We must light torches. Groping in the dark, only knowing what the next two steps are, is not the way to fight. We must grow visionaries;

cultivate our desires into plans. Plans that last for years, even decades. Plans that do not just cumulate in one cyclic end but rather ones that encompass many spikes and turns. Plans that adjust to sudden changes in terrain and survive overwhelming paradigm shifts.

We must be relevant. We must show victories. We must prove ourselves worthy of trust to people who have been misled too many times before. We must show that what we bring is both a vision for the future and a way to make things a little better in the present. Be it the actions of the (de)Occupy movement that gave people hope, or the organizing to stop the deportation of Alvaro Orozco, or the much-broader mobilization to stop the deportation of Laibar Singh, communities of people join resistance movements that act on issues that matter and do so in ways that will win.

We must understand that people act in a myriad of places—schools, shelters, food banks, health centers, housing projects, art galleries. Imagined spaces as much as material ones, gathering around particular music, shared stories, diverse identities. Our fights must be rooted in experiences, in stories, and in anecdotes. People remember these more than sterile numbers or facts. Myths are powerful magic and can turn enemies into friends. In a world where too many still tell stories that some are illegal and that to be free we must control the movement of others, the work of making new myths is essential. We have to write them, sing them, paint them. Repeat them as they become imbued with the power of everyone who utters them.

To make these new myths, to liberate these gathering places from the mind-sets that keep some documented and others not, will require alliances. Some alliances are about meeting people where they are at and moving together, one step forward. Others are about comradeship. Some alliances are about focusing on what unites us. Others are about the very clear specifics of what separates us. Alliances are not merely exchanges but also about coming together to create new possibilities. We need alliances where short-term gains do not compromise long-term ends.

We have to ensure that victories won are not slowly eroded; that our roots don't crumble underneath as we sit mesmerized by the fragrance of flowers on the trees. We must act with humility. We walk on paths chipped at for centuries before us. We live in a world where what we know sits like one pebble on the shore of an ocean of what we don't know. We must act with respect. Respect for the lands, air, water, and all living beings. Respect to the Indigenous people whose lands we live on. We must move with joy. Joy snatched back from the most trying of times. We must have compassion, for ourselves and others. We must have honor. Naming wrongs and accepting errors. Asking for forgiveness and giving up egos toward account-ability. We must act every day. We must act.

—Syed Khalid Hussan

Notes

Preface

1. Brenda Norrell, "Native Americans Lock Down Occupy Border Patrol Headquarters Tucson, " *Narcosphere*, May 23, 2010, http://narcosphere.narconews.com/notebook/brenda-norrell/2010/05/native-americans-lock-down-occupy-border-patrol-headquarters-tucson (accessed January 9, 2013).

Introduction

1. Cherríe Moraga, "It's the Poverty," *Loving in the War Years: Lo que nunca pasó por sus labios* (Boston: South End, 1983), 63.

2. Amartya Sen, "Population: Delusion and Reality," *New York Review of Books* 41, no. 15 (1994): 62–71.

3. Ami Sedghi and Simon Rogers, "UNHCR 2011 Refugee Statistics: Full Data," *Guardian*, June 20, 2011, http://www.guardian.co.uk/news/datablog/2011/jun/20/refugee-statistics-unhcr-data (accessed October 31, 2012).

4. Dawn Paley, "Violence Doesn't Spill over Borders, Militarized Borders Create Violence," *Unembedded*, May 22, 2012, http://dawnpaley.tumblr.com/post/23543672055/violence-doesnt-spill-over-borders-militarized (accessed October 31, 2012).

5. Michael Hardt and Antonio Negri, *Empire* (Boston: Harvard University Press, 2001), 12.

6. Alex Soto, "Border Patrol Occupiers Trespassing Charge Dropped: Call for Action for June 29, 2011," *Oodham Solidarity*, June 2011, http://oodhamsolidarity.blogspot.ca/2011/06/news-releasedate-thursday-june-23-2011.html (accessed September 8, 2012).

7. Jessica Yee, "Akwesasne Under Siege," *Rabble.ca*, June 5, 2009, http://rabble.ca/columnists/2009/06/akwesasne-under-siege (accessed September 8, 2012).

8. McKenzie Wark, "Globalisation from Below: Migration, Sovereignty, Communication," in *Sarai Reader 2002: The Cities of Everyday Life* (Delhi: Sarai, CSDS, and the Society for Old and New Media, 2002), 342–49.

9. Tania Willard, "Las Paredes Vueltas de Lado son Puentes," *People's History of Kanda Poster Project*, http://noii-van.resist.ca/wp-content/uploads/2007/11/tania-for-web.gif (accessed October 31, 2012).

10. Edward Said, *Culture and Imperialism* (New York: Vintage Books, 1993), 7.

11. Darnell Moore, "Reflection of a Black Queer Suicide Survivor: Part 2 of 2," September 27, 2011, http://yoloakili.com/2011/09/reflections-of-a-black-queer-suicide-survivor-part-2-of-2/ (accessed September 8, 2012).

12. Kiran Desai, *The Inheritance of Loss* (New Delhi: Penguin Books, 2006), 149.

13. Robin D. G. Kelley, *Freedom Dreams: The Black Radical Imagination* (Boston: Beacon Press, 2002), 12.

14. Aman Sium, Chandni Desai, and Eric Ritskes, "Towards the 'Tangible Unknown': Decolonization and the Indigenous

Future," *Decolonization: Indigeneity, Education, and Society* 1, no. 1 (2012): v.

15. Judith Butler, *Undoing Gender* (New York: Routledge, 2004), 19.

16. No One Is Illegal, "Important NOII Announcement about Future Communications," April 12, 2012, http://noii-van.resist.ca/?p=4805 (accessed October 31, 2012).

17. Ibid.

18. Nicholas Keung, "Out to Change 'Regressive' Immigration System," *Toronto Star*, October 1, 2008, http://www.thestar.com/federal%20election/article/509331--out-to-change-regressive-immigration-system (accessed September 8, 2012).

19. Jason Kenney, "NDP Backs Radical and Lawless 'No One Is Illegal,'" press release, March 26, 2012, http://www.jasonkenney.ca/news/ndp-backs-radical-and-lawless-%E2%80%9Cno-one-is-illegal%E2%80%9D/ (accessed October 31, 2012).

20. Gary Kinsman, "Mapping Social Relations of Struggle: Activism, Ethnography, Social Organization," in *Sociology for Changing the World: Social Movements/Social Research*, ed. Caelie Frampton, Gary Kinsman, Andrew Thompson, and Kate Tilleczek (Black Point, Nova Scotia: Fernwood, 2006), 134.

21. Leanne Simpson, *Dancing on Our Turtle's Back: Stories of Nishnaabeg Re-Creation, Resurgence, and a New Emergence* (Winnipeg: Arbeiter Ring Publishing, 2011), 33–34.

22. Aurora Levins Morales, "My Name Is This Story," in *Telling to Live: Latina Feminist Testimonios*, ed. Latina Feminist Group (Durham, NC: Duke University Press, 2001), 100.

Chile Con Carne

1. This is an excerpt from the one-woman show *Chile Con Carne*, published by Blizzard Press, which premiered to rave reviews and full houses in Vancouver in 1995. *Chile Con Carne* takes place in Vancouver in 1976 and is about an eight-year-old Chilean refugee called Manuelita.

The Bracelet

1. Thank you to Naava Smolash for the translation of this text from the French original.

What Is Border Imperialism?

1. Quoted in Refugee Action Coalition Sydney, "Aboriginal Passports Issued to Indefinitely Detained Tamils, Denied Australian Residency on 'Security' Grounds," May 13, 2012, http://www.refugeeaction.org.au/?p=1755 (accessed June 14, 2012).

2. Alessandra Moctezuma and Mike Davis, "Policing the Third Border," *Colorlines*, Fall 1999, http://nypolisci.org/files/poli15/Readings/Policing%20the%20Third%20Border.pdf (accessed July 14, 2012).

3. Naoki Sakai, *Translation and Subjectivity: On "Japan" and Cultural Nationalism* (Minneapolis: University of Minnesota Press, 1997), 154–55.

4. Frassanito Network, "Movements of Migration: Editorial," 2004, http://www.noborder.org/files/movements_of_migration.pdf (accessed July 23, 2012).

5. International Organization for Migration, "Launching of the IOM World Migration Report 2011 Seminar," August 17, 2012, http://www.iom.ch/cms/en/sites/iom/home/

news-and-views/speeches/speech-listing/launching-of-the-iom-world-migra.html (accessed August 28, 2012).

6. UN Refugee Agency, "UNHCR Report Finds 80 Percent of World's Refugees in Developing Countries," June 20, 2011, http://www.unhcr.org/4dfb66ef9.html (accessed June 30, 2012); UN Refugee Agency, "Internally Displaced People: Figures," 2011–12, http://www.unhcr.org/pages/49c3646c23.html (accessed July 5, 2012).

7. UN Refugee Agency, "Young and Innocent," http://www.unhcr.org/pages/49c3646c1e8.html (accessed July 8, 2012).

8. UN Relief and Works Agency for Palestine Refugees in the Near East, "Who Are Palestine Refugees?" http://www.unrwa.org/etemplate.php?id=86 (accessed July 6, 2012).

9. UN Refugee Agency, "UNHCR Global Trends 2011," http://www.unhcr.org/4fd6f87f9.html (accessed July 6, 2012).

10. Gilbert Burnham, Riyadh Lafta, Shannon Doocy, and Les Roberts, "Mortality after the 2003 Invasion of Iraq: A Cross-Sectional Cluster Sample Survey," *Lancet*, October 11, 2006, http://brusselstribunal.org/pdf/lancet111006.pdf (accessed October 3, 2012).

11. Edward Said, *Culture and Imperialism* (London: Vintage, 1994), 8.

12. Derek Gregory, "Counterinsurgency and the Humanitarian Present," *Geographical Imaginations*, July 30, 2012, http://geographicalimaginations.com/2012/07/30/counterin-surgency-and-the-humanitarian-present/ (accessed September 3, 2012); Office of Refugee Resettlement, "Fiscal Year 2009 Refugee Arrivals," July 18, 2012, http://www.acf.hhs.gov/pro-grams/orr/resource/fiscal-year-2009-refugee-arrivals (accessed July 31, 2012).

13. UN Refugee Agency, "UNHCR Statistical Handbook 2010," http://www.unhcr.org/4ef9c8d10.html (accessed July 7, 2012).

14. Ibid.

15. Laura Carlsen, "NAFTA Is Starving Mexico," *Foreign Policy in Focus*, October 20, 2011, http://www.fpif.org/articles/nafta_is_starving_mexico (accessed September 21, 2012); David Bacon, *The Children of NAFTA* (Los Angeles: University of California Press, 2004).

16. William Robinson, "Globalization and the Struggle for Immigrant Rights in the United States," *ZNet*, March 2007, http://www.zmag.org/znet/viewArticle/1864 (accessed July 6, 2012).

17. Quoted in Carolina Morena, "Border Crossing Deaths More Common as Illegal Immigration Declines," *Huffington Post*, August 17, 2012, http://www.huffingtonpost.com/2012/08/17/border-crossing-deaths-illegal-immigration_n_1783912.html (accessed October 12, 2012).

18. American Civil Liberties Union, "U.S.-Mexico Border Crossing Deaths Are a Humanitarian Crisis," September 30, 2009, http://www.aclu.org/immigrants-rights/us-mexico-border-crossing-deaths-are-humanitarian-crisis-according-report-aclu-and (accessed July 6, 2012).

19. Mary Pat Brady, "The Homoerotics of Immigration Control," *Scholar and Feminist* 6, no. 3 (2008), http://sfonline.barnard.edu/immigration/print_brady.htm (accessed July 3, 2012).

20. Incite Women of Color against Violence, "Immigration Policing and Border Violence," http://www.incite-national.org/index.php?s=109 (accessed July 6, 2012).

21. McKenzie Wark, preface to *In Fear of Security: Australia's Invasion Anxiety*, by Anthony Burke (Annandale: Pluto Press, 2001), xix.

22. Reece Jones, "Something There Is That Doesn't Love a Wall," *New York Times*, Opinion section, August 27, 2012, http://www.nytimes.com/2012/08/28/opinion/Border-Fences-in-United-States-Israel-and-India.html?_r=1&ref=global (accessed August 30, 2012).

23. Glen Coulthard, "Place against Empire: Understanding Indigenous Radicalism," *Media Co-op*, Events section, http://halifax.mediacoop.ca/events/9500 (accessed July 31, 2012).

24. Neskie Manuel and Emma Feltes, "World Bank Darling Promotes Privatization of Reserves," *Vancouver Media Coop*, October 28, 2010, http://vancouver.mediacoop.ca/story/world-bank-darling-promotes-privatization-reserves/4998 (accessed December 29, 2012).

25. Mike Konczal, "Against Law, For Order," *Jacobin*, April 2012, http://jacobinmag.com/2012/04/against-law-for-order/ (accessed September 28, 2012).

26. Stephen Eldon Kerr, "CIDA Under Fire for Partnering with Mining Company," *Alternatives International Journal*, March 30, 2012, http://www.alterinter.org/spip.php?article3786 (accessed July 3, 2012); Mining Watch Canada, http://www.miningwatch.ca (accessed July 3, 2012).

27. Yinka Dene Alliance, "Submission to United Nations Committee on the Elimination of Racial Discrimination," February 2012, http://yinkadene.ca/images/uploads/Yinka_Dene_Alliance_CERD_submission_Final_copy.pdf (accessed July 3, 2012).

28. Jennifer Nez Denetdale, "Indigenous Feminisms,"

First Peoples New Directions in Indigenous Studies, March 11, 2010, http://www.firstpeoplesnewdirections.org/blog/?p=511 (accessed July 4, 2012).

29. UN Habitat, "Slum Dwellers to Double by 2030: Millennium Development Goal Could Fall Short," April 2007, http://www.unhabitat.org/downloads/docs/4631_46759_GC%2021%20Slum%20dwellers%20to%20double.pdf (accessed July 2, 2012).

30. Manuel Pombo, in Leslie Crawford, "Migrants Perish at Sea as Africans Risk All to Reach Europe via the Canaries," *Financial Times*, March 18, 2006, http://www.ft.com/intl/cms/s/0/34c50014-b62d-11da-9cbb-0000779e2340.html#axzz2CUWXD6qd (accessed July 2, 2012).

31. International Red Cross and Red Crescent Movement, "Deadly Passage," 2006, http://www.redcross.int/EN/mag/magazine2006_2/12-14.html (accessed September 2, 2012).

32. Étienne Balibar, "The Borders of Europe," trans. J. Swenson, in *Cosmopolitics: Thinking and Feeling beyond the Nation*, ed. Pheng Cheah and Bruce Robbins (London: University of Minnesota Press, 1998), 217–18.

33. UNITED for Intercultural Action, "List of 16,264 Documented Refugee Deaths through Fortress Europe," June 13, 2012, http://www.unitedagainstracism.org/pdfs/listofdeaths.pdf (accessed September 29, 2012).

34. Joanna Zelman, "50 Million Environmental Refugees by 2020, Experts Predict," *Huffington Post*, February 22, 2011, http://www.huffingtonpost.com/2011/02/22/environmental-refugees-50_n_826488.html (accessed July 7, 2012).

35. Duncan Clark, "Which Nations Are Most Responsible for Climate Change," *Guardian*, April 21, 2011, http://www.

guardian.co.uk/environment/2011/apr/21/countries-responsi-ble-climate-change (accessed July 6, 2012).

36. Rachel Morris, "What Happens When Your Country Drowns," *Mother Jones*, November–December 2009, http://www.motherjones.com/environment/2009/11/tuvalu-climate-refugees (accessed July 2, 2012).

37. Clark, "Which Nations Are Most Responsible for Climate Change?"

38. Quoted in Adrian Harewood, "Xenoracism and the Hypocrisy of Managed Migration: An Interview with Liz Fekete of the Institute of Race Relations," *Canadian Dimension*, February 27, 2006, http://canadiandimension.com/articles/1865 (accessed July 6, 2012).

39. Peter Nyers, "Abject Cosmopolitanism: The Politics of Protection in the Antideportation Movement," *Third World Quarterly* 24, no. 6 (2003): 1070.

40. US Immigration and Customs Enforcement, "ICE Total Removals," August 25, 2012, http://www.ice.gov/doclib/about/offices/ero/pdf/ero-removals1.pdf (accessed October 3, 2012).

41. Anna Pratt, *Securing Borders* (Vancouver: UBC Press, 2005), 1.

42. Quoted in Nelli Kambouri, "Judith Butler: Ungrievable Lives," *Reimagining Democracy*, http://www.re-public.gr/en/?p=317 (accessed September 2, 2012); see also Judith Butler, *Precarious Life: The Powers of Mourning and Violence* (New York: Verso, 2004).

43. Katrina Schlunke, "Sovereign Hospitalities," *Borderlands Journal* 1, no. 2 (2002): http://www.borderlands.net.au/vol1no2_2002/schlunke_hospitalities.html (accessed July 2, 2012).

44. Global Detention Project, "About the Global Detention Project," http://www.globaldetentionproject.org/about/about-the-project.html (accessed July 2, 2012).

45. Michel Foucault, *Society Must Be Defended* (London: Penguin, 2004), 45.

46. Quoted in No One Is Illegal–Vancouver, "Hunger Striking Refugee Detained for Six Years," December 8, 2011, http://noii-van.resist.ca/?p=4579 (accessed July 31, 2012).

47. Jacob Fenton, Catherine Rentz, Stokely Baksh, and Lisa Hill, "Map: Immigration Detention Facilities, 1981–2011," *Investigative Reporting Workshop*, October 17, 2011, http://investigativereportingworkshop.org/investigations/immigration-detention/htmlmulti/immigration-detention-map/ (accessed July 5, 2012).

48. "Special Issues of Women Prisoners," *Columbia Human Rights Law Review*, 2011, http://www3.law.columbia.edu/hrlr/jlm/chapter-41.pdf (accessed July 5, 2012).

49. "Australia Probes Self-Harm by Asylum Seekers," *BBC News*, June 29, 2011, http://www.bbc.co.uk/news/world-asia-pacific-14337404 (accessed October 2, 2012).

50. Phil Mercer, "High Suicide Rate at Australian Detention Centers Worries Officials," *Voice of America*, July 28, 2011, http://www.voanews.com/content/high-suicide-rate-in-australian-detention-centers-worries-officials-126390043/167812.html (accessed November 2, 2012).

51. Global Detention Project, "Canada Detention Profile," July 2012, http://www.globaldetentionproject.org/countries/americas/canada/introduction.html (accessed November 1, 2012).

52. Catrina Stewart, "Israelis Build the World's Biggest

Detention Centre," *Telegraph*, March 10, 2012, http://www.independent.co.uk/news/world/middle-east/israelis-build-the-worlds-biggest-detention-centre-7547401.html (accessed October 2, 2012).

53. Ali Abunimah, "Africans as 'Flood,' Palestinians as 'Demographic Threat': Ruth Marcus' Vulgar Racism in *Washington Post*," *Electronic Intifada*, July 25, 2012, http://electronicintifada.net/blogs/ali-abunimah/africans-flood-palestinians-demographic-threat-ruth-marcus-vulgar-racism (accessed November 17, 2012).

54. Quoted in Chris Kirkham, "Private Prisons Profit from Immigration Crackdown, Federal and Local Law Enforcement Partnerships," *Huffington Post*, June 12, 2012, http://www.huffingtonpost.com/2012/06/07/private-prisons-immigration-federal-law-enforcement_n_1569219.html (accessed November 17, 2012).

55. Detention Watch Network, "The Influence of the Private Prison Industry in Immigration Detention," http://www.detentionwatchnetwork.org/privateprisons (accessed July 5, 2012).

56. Laura Sullivan, "Prison Economics Help Drive Arizona Immigration Law," National Public Radio, October 28, 2010, http://www.npr.org/2010/10/28/130833741/prison-economics-help-drive-ariz-immigration-law (accessed November 1, 2012).

57. Naomi Klein, *The Shock Doctrine* (New York: Metropolitan Books, 2007), 299.

58. "Israel Shows Off Its Homeland Security Technologies to International Visitors," *Times of Israel*, May 20, 2012, http://www.timesofisrael.com/israel-shows-off-its-homeland-security-technologies-to-international-visitors/ (accessed July 6, 2012).

59. Jimmy Johnson, "A Palestine-Mexico Border," *North American Congress on Latin America*, June 29, 2012, http://nacla.org/blog/2012/6/29/palestine-mexico-border (accessed July 2, 2012).

60. Chandra Talpade Mohanty, "Imperial Democracies, Militarised Zones, Feminist Engagements," *Economic and Political Weekly* 46, no. 13 (March 2011): 76–84.

61. Amnesty International USA, "Women in Prison: A Fact Sheet," http://www.prisonpolicy.org/scans/women_prison.pdf (accessed July 7, 2012); Jodie M. Lawston, "Women and Prison," *Sociologists for Women in Society Factsheet*, Spring 2012, http://www.socwomen.org/web/images/stories/resources/fact_sheets/fact_1-2012-prison.pdf (accessed July 6, 2012).

62. National Association for the Advancement of Colored People, "Equal Justice Legal Defense Report," 1998; Natalie Sokoloff, "Women Prisoners at the Dawn of the 20th Century," *Women in Criminal Justice* 16, nos. 1–2 (2005): 127–37.

63. University of New South Wales Australian Prisons Project, "Women in Prison Western Australia, 1970–2010," http://www.app.unsw.edu.au/women-prison-western-australia-1970-2010 (accessed July 4, 2012).

64. "Aboriginal Women Imprisoned in Soaring Numbers," CBC, September 27, 2012, http://www.cbc.ca/news/canada/story/2012/09/27/aboriginal-women-prison-report.html (accessed September 30, 2012).

65. Angela Davis, "Masked Racism: Reflections on the Prison Industrial Complex," *Colorlines*, September 10, 1998, http://colorlines.com/archives/1998/09/masked_racism_reflections_on_the_prison_industrial_complex.html (accessed November 17, 2012).

66. Michel Foucault, *The Foucault Reader*, ed. Paul Rabinow (London: Penguin, 1984), 230.

67. Angela Y. Davis, *Abolition Democracy: Beyond Empire, Prisons, and Torture* (New York: Seven Stories Press, 2005), 40.

68. Sharon Martinas and Challenging White Supremacy Workshop, "Definition of White Supremacy," http://www.cwsworkshop.org/resources/WhiteSupremacy.html (accessed November 10, 2012).

69. Elizabeth Povinelli, *The Cunning of Recognition* (Durham, NC: Duke University Press, 2002), 16.

70. Yasmin Jiwani, "Trapped in the Carceral Net: Race, Gender, and the 'War on Terror,'" *Global Media Journal* 4, no. 2 (2011): 13–31.

71. Juan Cole, "Top Ten Differences between White Terrorists and Others," *Informed Comment*, August 9, 2012, http://www.juancole.com/2012/08/top-ten-differences-between-white-terrorists-and-others.html (accessed November 16, 2012).

72. Sherene Razack, *Casting Out: The Eviction of Muslims from Western Law and Politics* (Toronto: University of Toronto Press, 2007).

73. Gayatri Chakravorty Spivak, *A Critique of Postcolonial Reason: Toward a History of the Vanishing Present* (Cambridge, MA: Harvard University Press, 1999), 287.

74. Razack, *Casting Out*.

75. Mimi Thi Nguyen, "Clothing the Terrifying Muslim: Q&A with Junaid Rana," *Threadbared*, May 7, 2012, http://iheartthreadbared.wordpress.com/2011/05/07/clothing-the-terrifying-muslim-qa-with-junaid-rana/ (accessed November 16, 2012).

76. Bonita Lawrence, "Gender, Race, and the Regulation of Native Identity in Canada and the United States: An Overview," *Hypatia* 18, no. 2 (Spring 2003): 3–31.

77. Gargi Bhattacharyya, *Dangerous Brown Men: Exploiting Sex, Violence, and Feminism in the War on Terror* (London: Zed Books, 2008), 121.

78. Justin Akers Chacón, Introduction to *No One Is Illegal: Fighting Racism and State Violence on the US-Mexico Border*, ed. Justin Akers Chacón and Mike Davis (Chicago: Haymarket Books, 2006), 90.

79. International Labor Organization, "86 Million Migrant Workers Active in Global Economy," May 21, 2004, http://www.ilo.org/global/about-the-ilo/newsroom/news/WCMS_005197/lang--en/index.htm (accessed November 16, 2012).

80. Mehran Kamrava and Zahra Babar, *Migrant Labor in the Persian Gulf* (New York: Columbia University Press, 2012).

81. Jean Shaoul, "The Plight of the UAE's Migrant Workers: The Flipside of a Booming Economy," *World Socialist Web Site*, November 9, 2007, http://www.wsws.org/articles/2007/nov2007/duba-n09.shtml (accessed July 4, 2012).

82. Johann Hari, "The Dark Side of Dubai," *Independent*, April 7, 2009, http://www.independent.co.uk/voices/commentators/johann-hari/the-dark-side-of-dubai-1664368.html (accessed July 6, 2012).

83. North-South Policy Institute, "Migrant Workers in Canada: A Review of the Canadian Seasonal Agricultural Workers Program," 2006, http://www.nsi-ins.ca/content/download/MigrantWorkers_Eng_Web.pdf (accessed July 6, 2012).

84. Sandro Contenta and Laurie Monsebraaten, "How We're Creating an Illegal Workforce," *Toronto Star*, November 1, 2009,

http://www.thestar.com/news/investigations/article/719355-
-how-we-re-creating-an-illegal-workforce (accessed July 7,
2012); Julia Preston, "11.2 Million Illegal Immigrants in U.S. in
2010," *New York Times*, February 1, 2011, http://www.nytimes.
com/2011/02/02/us/02immig.html (accessed July 7, 2012).

85. Nandita Sharma, "On Being Not Canadian: The Social
Organization of Migrant Workers in Canada," *Canadian Review
of Sociology and Anthropology* 38, no. 4 (November 2001), 418,
436.

86. David McNally, *Another World Is Possible: Globalization
and Anti-Capitalism* (Winnipeg: Arbeiter Ring Publishing,
2006), 137.

87. Harold Troper, "Commentary," in *Controlling
Immigration: A Global Perspective*, ed. Wayne Cornelius
(Stanford, CA: Stanford University Press, 2004), 137.

88. Carlos Fernandez, Meredith Gill, Imre Szeman, and
Jessica Whyte, "Erasing the Line, or, the Politics of the Border,"
Ephemera 6, no. 4 (2006): 467.

89. Cecilia Diocson, "Organizing and Mobilizing
Filipino Migrant Women in Canada," Asia-Pacific Research
Network, June 18, 2003, http://www.aprnet.org/index.
php?option=com_content&view=article&id=163:or
ganizing-and-mobilizing-filipino-migrant-women-in-
canada&catid=97:impact-of-globalization-on-women-
labor&Itemid= (accessed July 4, 2012).

90. Himani Bannerji, *Thinking Through: Essays on Feminism,
Marxism, and Anti-Racism* (Toronto, Toronto Women's Press,
1995), 24.

91. Quoted in Southern Poverty Law Center, "SPLC Exposes
Exploitation of Immigrant Workers," August 16, 2006, http://

www.splcenter.org/get-informed/news/splc-exposes-exploitation-of-immigrant-workers (accessed July 4, 2012).

92. Nandita Sharma, "Travel Agency: A Critique of Anti-Trafficking Campaigns," *Refuge* 21, no. 3 (May 2003): 62.

93. Gargi Bhattacharyya, John Gabriel, and Stephen Small, *Race and Power: Global Racism in the Twenty-First Century* (New York: Routledge, 2002), 34.

94. Gloria Anzaldúa, *Borderlands La Frontera: The New Mestiza* (San Francisco: Aunt Lute Books, 1999), 101.

95. Étienne Balibar, "Es Gibt Keinen Staat in Europa: Racism and Politics in Europe Today," *New Left Review* 186 (March–April 1991): 5–19.

96. Henk Van Houtum, Olivier Thomas Kramsch, and Wolfgang Zierhofer, *B/Ordering Space* (Aldershot, UK: Ashgate Publishing Ltd., 2005), 3.

97. No One Is Illegal–Vancouver, "Our Vision," http://noii-van.resist.ca/?page_id=17 (accessed November 17, 2012).

98. Wadjularbinna, "A Gungalidda Grassroots Perspective on Refugees and the Recent Events in the US," *borderlands e-journal* 1, no. 1 (2002), http://www.borderlands.net.au/vol1no1_2002/wadjularbinna.html (accessed November 17, 2012).

Cartography of NOII

1. No One Is Illegal–Vancouver, "Victory for Ali Reza Monemi," January 11, 2005, http://noii-van.resist.ca/?p=409 (accessed October 31, 2012).

2. Solidarity across Borders, "Surprise Direct Action Report," July 12, 2006, https://masses.tao.ca/pipermail/act-mtl/2006-July/002724.html (accessed October 31, 2012).

3. No One Is Illegal, "Important NOII Announcement about

Future Communications," April 12, 2012, http://noii-van.resist.ca/?p=4805 (accessed October 31, 2012).

4. Quoted in David Ball, "Mexican Journalist Karla Ramírez Wins Battle against Deportation," *Vancouver Observer*, April 9, 2012, http://www.vancouverobserver.com/politics/2012/04/09/mexican-journalist-karla-ram%C3%ADrez-wins-battle-against-deportation-others-face (accessed October 31, 2012).

5. Chris Ramsaroop, "Canada: Justice for Migrant Workers: Why We Will March," *Bullet*, May 1, 2008, http://www.socialist-project.ca/bullet/bullet103.html (accessed October 31, 2012).

6. Quoted in Robyn Maynard, "Dignity and Solidarity: Community Support Work and Movement Building," *Briarpatch*, November 1, 2010, http://briarpatchmagazine.com/articles/view/dignity-and-solidarity (accessed September 30, 2012).

7. No One Is Illegal–Montreal, "10 Days of Picket: Justice for Montreal's Non-Status Algerians," September 22, 2003, http://update.ocap.ca/node/646 (accessed September 30, 2012).

8. Quoted in Michelle Lowry and Peter Nyers, "No One Is Illegal: The Fight for Refugee and Migrant Rights in Canada," *Refuge: Canada's Periodical on Refugees* 21, no. 3 (2003): 66–72.

9. No One Is Illegal, "Principles for Regularization," http://noii-van.resist.ca/?page_id=89 (accessed September 30, 2012).

10. Steve Cohen, *No One Is Illegal: Immigration Control and Asylum* (London: Trentham Books, 2003), 263.

11. Faria Kamal and Mohan Mishra, "Regularisation from the Ground Up: The Don't Ask Don't Tell Campaign," May 6, 2007, http://noii-van.resist.ca/?p=149 (accessed September 30, 2012).

12. Lisa M. Seghetti, Stephen R. Vina, and Karma Ester, "Enforcing Immigration Law: The Role of State and Local Law Enforcement," *Immigration Law Publisher*, August 14, 2006,

http://www.ilw.com/immigrationdaily/news/2006,0912-crs.pdf
(accessed September 12, 2012).

13. No One Is Illegal–Toronto, "Toronto Schools a Little
More Welcoming for Undocumented Students," November 11,
2010, http://toronto.nooneisillegal.org/node/497 (accessed
September 25, 2012).

14. Farrah Miranda, "Resisting Deportation of Women
Fleeing Violence," *Rabble*, December 6, 2010, http://rabble.ca/
news/2010/12/resisting-deportation-women-fleeing-violence
(accessed September 30, 2012).

15. Ibid.

16. Quoted in Thomas Nail, "Building Sanctuary City:
NOII-Toronto on Non-Status Migrant Justice Organizing,"
Upping the Anti, 11 (2010), http://uppingtheanti.org/journal/
article/11-noii-sanctuary-city/ (accessed September 30, 2012).

17. Razack, *Casting Out*, 9.

18. No One Is Illegal–Vancouver, "What Are Security
Certificates," http://noii-van.resist.ca/?page_id=90 (accessed
September 12, 2012).

19. Quoted in Justin Podur, "Security Certificates and the
Case of Adil Charkaoui," *Killing Train*, March 1, 2009, http://
www.killingtrain.com/node/694 (accessed August 12, 2012).

20. Mary Foster, "Organizing in Solidarity with Threats to
'National Security': The Campaign against Immigration Security
Certificates," in *Organize!: Building from the Local for Global
Justice*, ed. Aziz Choudry, Jill Hanley, and Eric Shragge (Oakland,
CA: PM Press, 2012), 258.

21. Sophie Harkat, "Fighting for Mohamed Harkat," *Rabble*,
January 11, 2011, http://rabble.ca/news/2011/01/fighting-
mohamed-harkat (accessed September 30, 2012).

22. Luke Vervaet, "The Violence of Incarceration: A Response from Mainland Europe," *Race and Class* 51, no. 4 (2010): 31.

23. Matthew Behrens, "Get on Board: Freedom Caravan and Camp Hope," *Homes Not Bombs*, 2006, http://www.homesnot-bombs.ca/caravan.htm (accessed September 20, 2012).

24. Andrea Smith, "Indigeneity, Settler Colonialism, White Supremacy," in *Racial Formation in the Twenty-First Century*, ed. Daniel Martinez HoSang, Oneka LaBennett, and Laura Pulido (Berkeley: University of California Press, 2012), 68.

25. Ibid.

26. Andrea Smith, "Heteropatriarchy and the Three Pillars of White Supremacy: Rethinking Women of Color Organizing," in *The Color of Violence: The Incite! Anthology,* ed. INCITE! Women of Color Against Violence (Boston: South End Press, 2006).

27. Bonita Lawrence and Enakshi Dua, "Decolonising Anti-Racism," *Social Justice* 32, no. 4 (2005): 120–43.

28. Ibid., 136.

29. Nandita Sharma and Cynthia Wright, "Decolonizing Resistance, Challenging Colonial States," *Social Justice* 35, no. 3 (2009): 120–38.

30. Beenash Jafri, "Privilege vs. Complicity: People of Colour and Settler Colonialism," Federation for the Humanities and Social Sciences, March 21, 2012, http://ideas-idees.ca/fr/blog/privilege-vs-complicity-people-colour-and-settler-colonialismx (accessed September 10, 2012).

31. Ibid.

32. Smith, "Indigeneity, Settler Colonialism, White Supremacy," 77.

33. Mostafa Henaway, Nandita Sharma, Jaggi Singh, Harsha Walia, and Rafeef Ziadah, "Organizing for Migrant Justice and Self-Determination," October 22, 2007, http://www.leftturn.org/organizing-migrant-justice-and-self-determination (accessed September 23, 2012).

34. Craig S. Fortier, "Decolonizing Borders: No One Is Illegal Movements in Canada and the Negotiation of Counter-National and Anti-Colonial Struggles from within the Nation State," York University, September 2010, http://www.yorku.ca/raps1/events/pdf/Craig_Fortier.pdf (accessed October 12, 2012).

35. bell hooks, *Feminist Theory: From Margin to Center* (London: Pluto Press, 2000), 67.

36. Various, "Declaration of Non-Indigenous Support for Defenders of the Land," November 2008, http://www.defendersoftheland.org/supporters (accessed September 11, 2011).

37. No One Is Illegal–Toronto, "May Day 2011 March for Status for All," video (Melissa Elliott at 03:54), http://www.youtube.com/watch?v=RKR1atTluCw (accessed September 13, 2012).

38. Quoted in No One Is Illegal–Ottawa, "No One Is Illegal Ottawa Says Let Them Stay," August 3, 2010, http://noii-ottawa.blogspot.ca/2010/08/no-one-is-illegal-noii-ottawa-says-let.html (accessed September 13, 2012).

39. Lee Maracle, "Lee Maracle Speaking at May Day Assembly 2011," video, https://www.youtube.com/watch?v=FNK3KDfMrRc&list=PL966D86F55E443E2A&index=1 (accessed September 13, 2012).

40. Vijay Prashad, *The Karma of Brown Folk* (Minneapolis: University of Minnesota Press, 2000), 102.

41. Olivia Chow, "Crooked Consultants, Temporary

Foreign Workers," November 19, 2009, http://www.oliviachow.ca/2009/11/olivia-chow-moves-concurrence-motion-on-immigration-consultants-and-temporary-foreign-workers/ (accessed July 12, 2012).

42. Canadian Council for Refugees, "Migrant Workers: Canada's Disposable Workforce," http://ccrweb.ca/en/migrant-workers (accessed September 12, 2012).

43. No One Is Illegal–Vancouver, "Labour Resolutions to Uphold Dignity of (Im)migrant Workers," June 13, 2007, http://noii-van.resist.ca/?p=440 (accessed July 21, 2012).

44. No One Is Illegal–Toronto, "May Day 2011 March for Status for All," video (Parambir Gill at 09:10), http://www.youtube.com/watch?v=RKR1atTluCw (accessed September 13, 2012).

45. Quoted in Kriss Sol, "Roundtable on G8 Resistance: Perspectives for the Next Phase of Global Anti-Capitalist Uprisings," *Upping the Anti* 6 (2008), http://uppingtheanti.org/journal/article/06-roundtable-on-g8-resistance/ (accessed July 21, 2012).

46. Take the Capital, "No One Is Illegal! (June 27, OTTAWA): Character and Tone of March," June 12, 2002, http://www.ainfos.ca/02/jun/ainfos00212.html (accessed June 4, 2012).

47. David Harvey, "The 'New' Imperialism: Accumulation by Dispossession," in *The New Imperial Challenge*, ed. Leo Panitch and Colin Leyes (London: Merlin Press, 2003), 83.

48. No One Is Illegal, "No One Is Illegal Solidarity with the Anti-G20 Resistance," July 3, 2010, http://noii-van.resist.ca/?p=2108 (accessed July 12, 2012).

49. Clare O'Connor and Kalin Stacey, "Defunding the Public

Interest," *Briarpatch*, September 1, 2012, http://briarpatchmaga-zine.com/articles/view/defunding-the-public-interest (accessed September 22, 2012).

50. Angela Y. Davis, *Abolition Democracy: Beyond Prison, Torture, and Democracy* (New York: Seven Stories Press, 2005), 20–21.

51. Mahmoud Jaballah, Mohammad Mahjoub, and Hassan Almrei, "An Open Letter from Hunger Striking Detainees at Canada's Guantanamo Bay," *Seven Oaks*, January 16, 2007, http://www.sevenoaksmag.com/features/openletter.html (accessed June 30, 2012).

52. No One Is Illegal–Montreal, "Anti-Canada Day Solidarity Statement with Akwesasne," July 1, 2009, http://nooneisillegal-montreal.blogspot.ca/2009/07/anti-canada.html (accessed July 10, 2012).

53. No One Is Illegal–Vancouver, "Take Back Our City! Join the 'No One Is Illegal, Canada Is Illegal' Contingent," February 5, 2010, http://noii-van.resist.ca/?p=1810 (accessed July 12, 2012).

54. No One Is Illegal–Toronto, "Toronto Schools A Little More Welcoming for Undocumented Students," November 11, 2010, http://toronto.nooneisillegal.org/node/497 (accessed September 25, 2012).

55. Various, "Immigrants in support of Idle No More," December 2012, https://www.facebook.com/events/459526197437894/?ref=ts&fref=ts (accessed March 2, 2013).

To Prevent a Deportation

1. A Canadian Radio, Television, and Telecommunications Commission (CRTC) complaint was filed against CBC TV, CBC Radio, CKNW, CTV, and Global TV on the grounds that

despite numerous clarifications including by legal experts, broadcasters failed to provide accurate, comprehensive, fair, full, and unbiased coverage when they reported falsely that Laibar Singh "came to Canada illegally" or that he "was illegal" in Canada prior to taking sanctuary in July 2007.

Overgrowing Hegemony

1. Chris Dixon, "Building 'Another Politics': The Contemporary Anti-Authoritarian Current in the US and Canada," *Anarchist Studies* 20, no. 1 (2012): 33.

2. Quoted in Notes from Nowhere Collective, ed., *We Are Everywhere: The Irresistible Rise of Global Anti-Capitalism* (London: Verso, 2003), 499.

3. Ai-Jen Poo and Harmony Goldberg, "Organizing with Love," *Organizing Upgrade*, February 1, 2010, http://www.organizingupgrade.com/index.php/modules-menu/community-organizing/item/77-ai-jen-poo-organizing-with-love (accessed September 9, 2012,

4. Eric Mann, "The 7 Components of Transformative Organizing Theory," *Labor Community Strategy Center*, 2010, http://www.thestrategycenter.org/node/5143 (accessed October 30, 2012).

5. Horizontal Alliance of Very (or Vaguely or Voraciously) Organized Queers, "Undoing Borders: A Queer Manifesto," http://undoingbordersblog.files.wordpress.com/2011/09/undoing-borders-letter-size-.pdf (accessed September 9, 2012).

6. Joshua Kahn Russell and Harmony Goldberg, "New Radical Alliances for a New Era," *ZNet*, May 9, 2012, http://www.zcommunications.org/new-radical-alliances-for-a-new-era-by-joshua-kahn-russell (accessed September 9, 2012).

7. Ibid.

8. Norman Matchewan and Martin Lukacs, "Widj-e-nia-mo-dwin: Walking together for Indigenous rights," *Canadian Centre for Policy Alternatives*, Spring 2012, http://www.policyalterna-tives.ca/publications/ourschools-ourselves/our-schoolsour-selves-spring-2012WT (accessed November 10, 2012).

9. Angela Y. Davis and Dylan Rodriguez, "The Challenge of Prison Abolition: A Conversation," http://www.histo-ryisaweapon.com/defcon1/davisinterview.html (accessed September 9, 2012).

10. New York Study Group, "Radical Approaches to Reform Struggles," *Organizing Upgrade*, September 1, 2010, http://www.organizingupgrade.com/index.php/modules-menu/community-organizing/item/64-radical-approaches-to-reform-struggles (accessed September 9, 2012).

11. Ng'ethe Maina, "It's Time to Experiment," *Organizing Upgrade*, April 7, 2010, http://www.organizingupgrade.com/index.php/modules-menu/community-organizing/item/72-ng%E2%80%99etha-maina-its-time-to-experiment (accessed September 9, 2012).

12. Salar Mohandesi, "On the Black Bloc," *Viewpoint Magazine*, February 12, 2012, http://viewpointmag.com/2012/02/12/on-the-black-bloc/ (accessed September 10, 2012).

13. Ibid.

14. Audre Lorde, "The Master's Tools Will Never Dismantle the Master's House," *Sister Outsider* (Berkeley: Crossing Press, 1984), 110.

15. Quoted in James D. Le Sueur, *Uncivil War: Intellectuals and Identity Politics during the Decolonization of Algeria*

(Philadelphia: University of Pennsylvania Press, 2001), 28.

16. Junie Désil, Kirat Kaur, and Gary Kinsman, "Anti-Oppression Politics in Anti-Capitalist Movements," *Upping the Anti* 1 (March 2005), http://uppingtheanti.org/journal/article/01-anti-oppression-politics-in-anti-capitalist-movements/ (accessed October 31, 2012).

17. Sara Mourad, "Politics at the Tip of the Clitoris: Why, in Fact, Do They Hate Us?" *Jadaliyya*, May 3, 2012, http://www.jadaliyya.com/pages/index/5355/politics-at-the-tip-of-the-clitoris_why-in-fact-do (accessed September 12, 2012).

18. Chandra Talpade Mohanty, *Feminism without Borders: Decolonizing Theory, Practicing Solidarity* (Durham, NC: Duke University Press, 2003), 183.

19. Ashanti Alston, "Beyond Nationalism But Not without It," *Colors of Resistance*, 2002, http://www.coloursofresistance.org/572/beyond-nationalism-but-not-without-it/ (accessed September 30, 2012).

20. Quoted in "Edward Said Talks to Jacqueline Rose," *Edward Said and the Work of the Critic: Speaking Truth to Power*, ed. Paul A. Bové (Durham, NC: Duke University Press, 2000), 25.

21. INCITE! Women of Color against Violence, "Beyond the Non-Profit Industrial Complex," http://www.incite-national.org/index.php?s=100 (accessed October 31, 2012).

22. Arundhati Roy, *Public Power in the Age of Empire* (New York: Seven Stories Press, 2004), 43.

23. No One Is Illegal-Vancouver, "No One Is Illegal Vancouver Internal Organizing Principles" (unpublished internal document, 2007).

24. Ibid.

25. Ibid.

26. Donna Kate Rushin, "The Bridge Poem," in *This Bridge Called My Back: Writings by Radical Women of Color*, ed. Cherríe Moraga and Gloria Anzaldúa (Berkeley: Third Woman Press, 2002), xxii.

Waves of Resistance Roundtable

1. No One Is Illegal, "Across Canada, Refugee Activists Occupy Tory and Immigration Offices," April 6, 2012, http://noii-van.resist.ca/?p=4796 (accessed October 31, 2012).

Journeys toward Decolonization

1. Adam Barker, "Being Colonial: Colonial Mentalities in Canadian Settler Society and Political Theory" (master's thesis, University of Victoria, 2006), http://web.uvic.ca/igov/research/pdfs/Adam%20Barker%20-%20Thesis.pdf (accessed September 13, 2012).

2. Aman Sium, Chandni Desai, and Eric Ritskes, "Towards the 'Tangible Unknown': Decolonization and the Indigenous Future," *Decolonization: Indigeneity, Education, and Society* 1, no. 1 (2012): i.

3. Taiaiake Alfred and Jeff Corntassel, "Being Indigenous: Resurgences against Contemporary Colonialism," *Government and Opposition* 40, no. 4 (September 2005): 597–614.

4. Idle No More, "Press Release: Idle No More," *Idle No More*, January 2, 2013, http://idlenomore.ca/about-us/press-releases/item/58-press-release-idle-no-more (accessed January 15, 2013).

5. Tara Williamson, "Idle No More Provides Us with Opportunity to Examine Nationhood," *Divided No More*, January 15, 2013, http://dividednomore.ca/2013/01/15/

idlenomore-provides-us-with-opportunity-to-examine-nation-hood/ (accessed March 1, 2013).

6. Frantz Fanon, *Wretched of the Earth*, trans. Constance Farrington (New York: Grove Press, 1965), 44.

7. Valérie Fournier, "Escaping from the Economy: The Politics of Degrowth," *International Journal of Sociology and Social Policy* 28, 11–12 (March 2008): 530.

8. Ibid.

9. Leanne Simpson, "Attawapiskat, Revisited," *Briarpatch*, May 1, 2012, http://briarpatchmagazine.com/articles/view/attawapiskat-revisited (accessed September 12, 2012).

10. Nora Butler Burke, "Building a 'Canadian' Decolonization Movement: Fighting the Occupation at 'Home,'" *Colours of Resistance*, August 2004, http://www.coloursofresis-tance.org/360/building-a-canadian-decolonization-movement-fighting-the-occupation-at-home/ (accessed September 12, 2012).

11. Zainab Amadahy, "Community, 'Relationship Framework,' and Implications for Activism," *Rabble*, July 13, 2010, http://rabble.ca/news/2010/07/community-%E2%80%98relationship-framework%E2%80%99-and-implications-activism (accessed September 12, 2012).

12. Stephanie Irlbacher-Fox, "Idle No More: Settler Responsibility for Relationship," *Decolonization Journal*, December 27, 2012, http://decolonization.wordpress.com/2012/12/27/idlenomore-settler-responsibility-for-relation-ship/ (accessed December 29, 2012).

13. Sharmeen Khan, David Hugill, and Tyler McCreary, "Building Unlikely Alliances: An Interview with Andrea Smith," *Upping the Anti* 10 (May 2010), http://uppingtheanti.org/

journal/article/10-building-unlikely-alliances-an-interview-with-andrea-smith/ (accessed September 12, 2012).

14. Julia Sudbury, "A World without Prisons: Resisting Militarism, Globalized Punishment, and Empire," *Social Justice* 31, no. 1–2 (2004): 9–30.

15. Eugene V. Debs, "Statement to the Court upon Being Convicted of Violating the Sedition Act," *Eugene V. Debs Internet Archive*, http://www.marxists.org/archive/debs/works/1918/court.htm (accessed September 14, 2012).

16. Leila Ahmed, *Women and Gender in Islam: Historical Roots of a Modern Debate* (New Haven, CT: Yale University Press, 1992), 154.

17. Jasbir K. Puar, T*errorist Assemblages: Homonationalism in Queer Times* (Durham, NC: Duke University Press, 2007).

18. Dana Olwan and Sophia Azeb, "Reframing the Discussion: Concluding Thoughts on the Forum on Muslim Feminisms," *Feminist Wire*, August 5, 2012, http://thefemi-nistwire.com/2012/08/reframing-the-discussion-concluding-thoughts-on-the-forum-on-muslim-feminisms/ (accessed September 14, 2012).

19. Horizontal Alliance of Very (or Vaguely or Voraciously) Organized Queers, "Undoing Borders: A Queer Manifesto."

20. Silvia Federici, "Precarious Labor: A Feminist Viewpoint," *Variant* 37 (Spring–Summer 2010): 23–25, http://www.variant.org.uk/pdfs/issue37_38/V37preclab.pdf (accessed September 14, 2012).

21. Ann Ferguson, "Labor, Love, Community, and Democracy," *ZNet*, July 19, 2009, http://www.zcommunications.org/labor-love-community-and-democracy-by-ann-ferguson (accessed October 31, 2012).

22. Mia Mingus, "Moving toward the Ugly: A Politic beyond Desirability," *Leaving Evidence*, August 22, 2011, http://leavingevidence.wordpress.com/2011/08/22/moving-toward-the-ugly-a-politic-beyond-desirability/ (accessed September 14, 2012).

23. Joaquin Cienfuegos, "Beyond Survival," *Joaquin Cienfuegos*, June 16, 2012, http://joaquincienfuegos.blogspot.ca/2012/06/beyond-survival.html (accessed September 14, 2012).

24. Yashna Maya Padamsee, "Communities of Care, Organizations for Liberation," *Naya Maya*, June 19, 2011, http://nayamaya.wordpress.com/2011/06/19/communities-of-care-organizations-for-liberation/ (accessed September 16, 2012).

25. Cara Page, "Reflections from Detroit: Transforming Wellness and Wholeness," *Incite! Blog*, August 5, 2010, http://inciteblog.wordpress.com/2010/08/05/reflections-from-detroit-transforming-wellness-wholeness/ (accessed September 16, 2012).

26. Craig Segal, "Status Struggle Winds Down," *Montreal Mirror*, July 17, 2003, http://noii-van.resist.ca/?p=386 (accessed September 15, 2012).

27. Dori Midnight, "More Healing, More of the Time," *Midnight Apothecary*, October 17, 2012, http://midnightapothecary.blogspot.ca/2012/10/more-healing-more-of-time.html (accessed October 31, 2012).

28. Yolo Akili, "The Immediate Need for Emotional Justice," *Crunk Feminist Collective*, November 16, 2011, http://crunkfeministcollective.wordpress.com/2011/11/16/the-immediate-need-for-emotional-justice/ (accessed September 16, 2012).

29. Ibid.

30. Kiwi Illafonte, "Random Thoughts on Building

Community," *Kiwi Illafonte*, http://kiwizzo.tumblr.com/
post/13504383269/random-thoughts-on-building-community
(accessed September 16, 2012).

31. Stuart Jefferies, "Alain Badiou: A Life in Writing,"
Guardian, May 18, 2012, http://www.guardian.co.uk/cul-
ture/2012/may/18/alain-badiou-life-in-writing (accessed
September 16, 2012).

32. Heather Davis and Paige Sarlin, "No One Is Sovereign
in Love: A Conversation between Lauren Berlant and Michael
Hardt," *Nomorepotlucks*, http://nomorepotlucks.org/site/no-
one-is-sovereign-in-love-a-conversation-between-lauren-berlant-
and-michael-hardt (accessed September 16, 2012).

33. Paula Gunn Allen, The *Sacred Hoop: Recovering the
Feminine in American Indian Traditions* (Boston: Beacon Press,
1992), 190.

34. Mia McKenzie, "The Summer We Got Free," *Mia
McKenzie*, http://miamckenzie.net/the-summer-we-got-free/
(accessed March 6, 2013).

35. Quoted in Colin Ward, *Anarchy in Action* (London:
Freedom Press, 1973), 23.

36. Howard Zinn, *You Can't Be Neutral on a Moving Train:
A Personal History of Our Times* (Boston: Beacon Press, 1994),
83.

Credits for Anarchist Interventions

Harsha Walia

Harsha is a South Asian activist, writer, and popular educator who has been active in migrant justice, antiracist, feminist, Indigenous solidarity, Palestinian liberation, anti-imperialist, and anticapitalist movements and communities for over a decade. She has most recently been organizing through NOII, South Asian Network for Secularism and Democracy, Women's Memorial March Committee for Missing and Murdered Women, Downtown Eastside Is Not for Developers Coalition, and the Olympic Resistance Network. She is the cocreator of a short film, and her writings have appeared in thirty academic journals, anthologies, magazines, and mainstream newspapers as well as on alternative websites. Harsha immigrated from India and currently resides in Vancouver, on the traditional lands of the Indigenous Coast Salish people, and works in the Downtown Eastside, which is the poorest postal code in Canada. She graduated from law school, but her passion and focus has been in radical community-based grassroots movements that refuse complicity with authority and injustice. This book is a reflection of the collective wisdom and experience she has been gifted from ancestors, teachers, family, and comrades who have influenced her, and who she is honored to be alongside with in militant resistance and life-affirming struggle. Harsha can be found on Twitter @ HarshaWalia.

Andrea Smith

Andrea is an assistant professor of Media and Cultural Studies at the University of California at Riverside. She is the award-winning author and editor of several books, including *Native Americans and the Christian Right: The Gendered Politics of Unlikely Alliances*, *Conquest: Sexual Violence and American Indian Genocide*, *The Revolution Will Not Be Funded: Beyond the Nonprofit Industrial Complex*, and *Color of Violence: The INCITE! Anthology*. Andrea currently serves as the US coordinator for the Ecumenical Association of Third World Theologians, and is cofounder of INCITE! Women of Color against Violence. She recently completed a report for the United Nations on Indigenous peoples and boarding schools.

Jessica Danforth

Jessica is a self-described multiracial Indigenous hip-hop feminist reproductive justice freedom fighter. She is the founder and executive director of the Native Youth Sexual Health Network, an organization by and for Indigenous youths within the full spectrum of sexual and reproductive health, rights, and justice in the United States and Canada.

Carmen Aguirre

Carmen is an award-winning Vancouver-based theater artist who has written and cowritten twenty plays, including *The Refugee Hotel*, *The Trigger*, and *Blue Box*. Her first book, *Something Fierce: Memoirs of a Revolutionary Daughter*, won the CBC's Canada Reads 2012 competition and is a number one national best seller.

Adil Charkaoui

Adil was arrested on a security certificate in 2003. He was released from jail on February 18, 2005, with a long list of draconian conditions, including having to wear a GPS bracelet. Adil was never found guilty of any crime or even criminally charged. He took the security certificate legislation to the Supreme Court of Canada, which declared the law unconstitutional in February 2007. The security certificate against him was thrown out in 2009.

Tara Atluri

Tara holds a doctorate of philosophy. She is currently affiliated with the project Oecumene: Citizenship after Orientalism.

Leah Lakshmi Piepzna-Samarasinha

Leah is a queer mixed Sri Lankan writer, teacher, and cultural worker. She cofounded Mangos with Chili and Toronto's Asian Arts Freedom School, is the author of *Love Cake* and *Consensual Genocide*, and coeditor of *The Revolution Starts at Home: Confronting Intimate Violence in Activist Communities*, and won the 2012 Lambda Award in queer poetry.

Lily Yuriko Shinde

Lily is a sixty-four-year-old Japanese Canadian lesbian who is a political activist living in Vancouver.

Toghestiy, Mel Bazil, and Freda Huson

Toghestiy, Mel, and Freda are cofounders of the Lhe Lin Liyin and Grassroots Wet'suwet'en. Freda, a spokesperson of the Unist'ot'en, and Toghestiy, a Likhts'amisyu hereditary chief, have built and are currently living in a log cabin that is in the direct pathway of approximately ten proposed pipeline projects, including Enbridge Northern Gateway and the Pacific Trails Pipeline.

Rafeef Ziadah

Rafeef is a Palestinian refugee, human rights activist, and spoken word artist. She is active in the Palestinian boycott, divestment, and sanctions movement, and is completing her PhD in political science at York University in Toronto.

Karla Lottini

Karla is a Mexican writer and journalist.

Aylwin Lo

Aylwin is a volunteer with Justice for Migrant Workers, and has been a laborer-teacher with Frontier College and an Into the Fields intern with Student Action with Farmworkers.

Cecily Nicholson

Cecily belongs to the Press Release and NOII collectives. She is a curatorial resident at the VIVO Crista Dahl Media archive. *Triage* (2011) is her first book.

Nassim Elbardouh

Nassim is active with NOII-Vancouver (Indigenous Coast Salish territories).

Mostafa Henaway

Mostafa is a Montreal-based community organizer with Tadamon and the IWC, an education and campaign center for immigrant workers.

Syed Khalid Hussan

Syed is a writer and community organizer in Toronto working with undocumented and migrant peoples and in defense of Indigenous sovereignty. He works to bridge environmental justice, antiwar movements, and movements for economic equity across southern Ontario and Canada, and has been involved in NOII-Toronto, the Toronto Community Mobilization Network, the Stop the Cuts Network, the Justice for Mahjoub Network, KI Support, and others.

Institute for Anarchist Studies

The IAS, a nonprofit foundation established in 1996, aims to support the development of anarchism by creating spaces for independent, politically engaged scholarship that explores social domination and reconstructive visions of a free society. All IAS projects strive to encourage public intellectuals and collective self-reflection within revolutionary and/or movement contexts. To this end, the IAS awards grants twice a year to radical writers and translators worldwide, and has funded nearly a hundred projects over the years by authors from numerous countries, including Argentina, Lebanon, Canada, Chile, Ireland, Nigeria, Germany, South Africa, and the United States. It also publishes the journal *Perspectives on Anarchist Theory* and the Lexicon pamphlet series, organizes anarchist theory tracks and other events, offers the Mutual Aid Speakers List, and collaborates on this book series, among other projects. The IAS is part of a larger movement seeking to create a nonhierarchical society. It is internally democratic and works in solidarity with people around the globe who share its values. The IAS is completely supported by donations from anarchists and other antiauthoritarians—like you—and/or their projects, with any contributions exclusively funding grants and

IAS operating expenses; for more information or to contribute to the work of the IAS, see http://www.anarchist-studies.org/.

AK Press

AK Press is a worker-run collective that publishes and distributes radical books, visual and audio media, and other material. We're small: a dozen people who work long hours for short money, because we believe in what we do. We're anarchists, which is reflected both in the books we provide and the way we organize our business. Decisions at AK Press are made collectively, from what we publish, to what we distribute and how we structure our labor. All the work, from sweeping floors to answering phones, is shared. When the telemarketers call and ask, "who's in charge?" the answer is: everyone. Our goal isn't profit (although we do have to pay the rent). Our goal is supplying radical words and images to as many people as possible. The books and other media we distribute are published by independent presses, not the corporate giants. We make them widely available to help you make positive (or hell, revolutionary) changes in the world. For more information on AK Press, or to place an order, see http://www.akpress.org/.

Justseeds Artists' Cooperative

Justseeds Artists' Cooperative is a decentralized community of twenty-two artists who have banded together to both sell their work, and collaborate with and support each other and social movements. Our website is not just a place to shop but also a destination to find out about current events in radical art and culture. We regularly collaborate on exhibitions and group projects as well as produce graphics and culture for social justice movements. We believe in the power of personal expression in concert with collective action to transform society. For more information on Justseeds Artists' Cooperative or to order work, see http://www.justseeds.org/.

Anarchist Intervention Series

Anarchism and Its Aspirations, by Cindy Milstein (2010)

Oppose and Propose! Lessons from the Movement for a New Society, by Andrew Cornell (2011)

Decolonizing Anarchism: An Antiauthoritarian History of Indian's Liberation Struggle, by Maia Ramnath (2011)

Imperiled Life: Revolution against Climate Catastrophe, by Javier Sethness-Castro (2012)

Anarchists Against the Wall: Direct Action and Solidarity with the Palestinian Popular Struggle, edited by Uri Gordon and Ohal Grietzer (2013)

Undoing Border Imperialism, by Harsha Walia (2013)

Self and Determination, by Joshua Stephens (forthcoming)

Support **AK Press!**

AK Press is one of the world's largest and most productive anarchist publishing houses. We're entirely worker-run & democratically managed. We operate without a corporate structure—no boss, no managers, no bullshit. We publish close to twenty books every year, and distribute thousands of other titles published by other like-minded independent presses and projects from around the globe.

The Friends of AK program is a way that you can directly contribute to the continued existence of AK Press, and ensure that we're able to keep publishing great books just like this one! Friends pay $25 a month directly into our publishing account ($30 for Canada, $35 for international), and receive a copy of every book AK Press publishes for the duration of their membership! Friends also receive a discount on anything they order from our website or buy at a table: 50% on AK titles, and 20% on everything else. We've also added a new Friends of AK ebook program: $15 a month gets you an electronic copy of every book we publish for the duration of your membership. Combine it with a print subscription, too!

There's great stuff in the works—so sign up now to become a Friend of AK Press, and let the presses roll!

Won't you be our friend? Email friendsofak@akpress.org for more info, or visit the Friends of AK Press website: www.akpress.org/programs/friendsofak